Ansett
THE COLLAPSE

Ansett
THE COLLAPSE

GEOFF EASDOWN & PETER WILMS

Lothian
BOOKS

Acknowledgement is made to the owners of copyright for permission to reproduce material. Every effort has been made to contact all copyright holders. The publishers would appreciate notification of any omissions for inclusion in future editions

Thomas C. Lothian Pty Ltd
132 Albert Road, South Melbourne, Victoria 3205
www.lothian.com.au

First published 2002
Reprinted 2002

National Library of Australia
Cataloguing-in-Publication data:

Easdown, Geoff.
  Ansett. The Collapse

  ISBN 0 7344 0444 1

  1. Ansett Australia. 2. Airlines – Australia. 3. Business
  failures – Australia. I. Wilms, Peter. II. Title.

387.710994

Cover photograph by Joe Armao, reproduced courtesy of the *Age*.
Photographs on pages 7, 11, 17–74, 88–98, 110, 117, 178, 186, 201 and 225 reproduced courtesy of the Ansett Corporate Affairs Library.
Photographs on pages 61, 64, 137, 147, 149, 159, 162, 172, 208, 216, 233, 243–244, 299, 250–251, 254 and 255 reproduced courtesy of the Herald and Weekly Times.
Photographs on pages 104, 120 and 123 reproduced courtesy of Newspix.
Cover and text design by David Constable
Typesetting by John van Loon
Printed in Australia by Griffin Press

CONTENTS

PREFACE

ANSETT AIRLINES CAME to an ignominious end on 4 March 2002 after sixty-six years of operation. Bad debts and mismanagement claimed the carrier that, throughout its lifetime, had flown as a symbol of free enterprise against the whims of politicians intent on nationalising air services. Ansett provided jobs for three generations of Australians. Fathers, mothers, sons, daughters and grandchildren variously worked for the airline. They formed what became the proud Ansett 'family'. At one point—rare as it is today—Ansett Airlines could boast more than 2500 employees who had served the company for at least a quarter of a century. Typical of the continued family links is the grand-daughter of the airline's founder Sir Reginald Ansett, Sarah Richards. She worked for the airline for eight years and was the voice of the 15 000-plus staff who were displaced when the nation's number two airline 'crashed'.

Ansett's demise was no ordinary company failure. While it may have had the hallmarks of a normal insolvency, the company's peculiar and special place in Australian folklore guarantees that Ansett will be remembered long after other failed groups have been forgotten: for what it was, from its pioneering beginnings to its ignominious end; for the people who helped shape its destiny; and for the tens of thousands of employees who became part of the Ansett 'family'. Ansett also occupied a unique place in the pantheon of Australian corporate history. Ironically, its failure and the administration that tried to save it probably gained more media coverage than the airline enjoyed during its lifetime.

Material gathered for this book relied on a number of sources. We, the authors, spoke with many people involved with Ansett—not only in its death throes but earlier, when it was considered a great airline. Interviews were conducted with senior members of the Australian Government, including Deputy Prime Minister John Anderson, with leading figures in the union movement, including ACTU secretary Greg Combet who played a pivotal role in Ansett's attempted revival, with former Ansett executives and with long-standing members of the airline's 'family'. Mark Korda and Mark Mentha, the administrators who sifted through the ruins, offered invaluable help.

The book explores Ansett from its earliest days, providing a chronology of events that helped shape its future and its ultimate failure. It was not written as a history and nor does it set out to blame any single party— a multitude of factors caused the carrier to collapse; any apportionment of blame must be left to the reader. Ansett touched the lives of too many people for there to be a single view about why events happened. As a company Ansett was a precocious child and a caring parent to travellers, frequent flyers, Golden Wings members and employees. Each will have their own memories and want to make their own judgment. The book seeks to relive the spirit of a business and the people it employed.

This book also details the roles played by the two Marks—Mentha and Korda—the company 'doctors' who did their best to resuscitate the airline and keep it flying. Unfortunately, the disease turned out to be fatal, their prescription for a cure inadequate. They will be remembered for their effort.

Various attempts were made to elicit comment from the Tesna partners and to allow Lindsay Fox and Solomon Lew to offer, in their own words, an explanation of why they did not proceed with their bid to revive the airline. Mr Fox's daughter Katrina replied that her father 'was not available at this time'. Mr Lew responded neither to telephone calls left with his staff nor to e-mail messages sent by one of the authors. That was their prerogative.

The authors are grateful to many people—to the many members of the Ansett 'family' who gave of their time and memories, the Federal Government of Australia, people who knew and worked with Sir Reginald Ansett, former CEOs, the unions, ordinary employees and the administrators and their team of partners, managers, support staff and advisers.

Special thanks must go to John Anderson, Australia's Deputy Prime Minister and Minister for Transport; Greg Combet, secretary of the Australian Council of Trade Unions; Captain Trevor Jensen, a senior Ansett executive and holder of the all-important Air Operator's Certificate; Leon Zwier, of the legal firm Arnold Bloch Liebler, and legal counsel to the administrators; and, of course, to the administrators themselves—Mark Mentha and Mark Korda, who carried on their attempts to save Ansett as their own accounting firm, of which they were senior partners, was imploding around them.

Many people who contributed to the substance of this book chose for various professional reasons not to be named, but thank them we do; they know who they are.

To everyone who had any part in the preparation of this book the authors are grateful, acknowledging the time and valuable contributions they made in helping to build up a picture of Ansett, thus ensuring that its memory, if nothing else, will survive.

INTRODUCTION

IF ANSETT CAPTAIN Jon Swift had a sense of history he would have noticed the rare coincidence between the first and last passenger flights flown by Australia's beleaguered airline that Tuesday morning. Down the back of flight AN 4051 were six passengers, three from the office of

Cockpit of last flight, First Officer Greg Toole and Captain Jon Smith (pictured).

the airline's official administrator, an aviation lawyer and two public relations men from the consultancy that orchestrated the media coverage of the six-month financial crisis that had engulfed the nation's 66-year-old second airline.

After flight AN 4051 had disembarked Andersen Consulting staffers Gary Rothville and Louise Curcuruto, Andersen legal partner, Dominic Emmett, aviation lawyer Tony Pyne, and Nic Jarvis and Peter Wilms from Jarvis Communications, Ansett would never fly again.

Had Captain Swift cast his mind to a Monday, just after noon, sixty-six years earlier when a Fokker Universal took off from Hamilton in Western Victoria, he would have recalled that the very first Ansett flight, which landed at Essendon Airport, also carried six passengers, as well as the pilot Vern Cerche and Managing Director Reg Ansett, all packed into the small aircraft.

Fast forward to 4 March 2002, when VH-HYI eased back from Gate 31 at Kingsford Smith Airport. 'Don't forget to put the cat out,' quipped Captain Swift, opening the storm window and farewelling the ramp manager for the last time. Grief had given way to humour as the A320 Airbus pushed back and began the slow taxi to the takeoff point. In Melbourne, seventy minutes later, Captain Swift joined the rest of the 15 000-strong Ansett 'family' soon to join the unemployment queue.

It was around 7.30 a.m. on Tuesday, 5 March 2002. The last flight from Perth to Sydney had arrived a short time earlier, its complement of passengers greeted by the glow of television lights, the thrust of radio microphones and the pens and notebooks of reporters, all seeking an angle about the final journey across the continent. While this happened, Captain Swift and his co-pilot, First Officer Greg Toole, waited to take their place at the controls of AN 4051.

Ansett Airlines had always struggled in what was a complex, competitive and take-no-prisoners environment. But even in its last years Ansett was judged one of the world's finest airlines. The man deemed to be its best chief executive, Rod Eddington, had once described it as 'a great airline but a lousy business'. His aphorism would have relevance to everyone who touched Ansett—whether it was Reg himself, the extraordinarily profligate Peter Abeles, the intellectually attuned Eddington or, finally, the two Marks, Korda and Mentha, administrators from the accounting firm Andersen.

The Marks had been brought in to salvage the wreck set adrift by Air New Zealand, which got itself too deep in debt when it bought outright control of the carrier in June 2000. Fate, and fallout from the unexpected 11 September terrorist crisis in the United States, signalled the end for the airline.

Thousands of people suffered because of the demise of Ansett, 15 000 of whom were loyal to a fault. Ansett folk saw themselves as a big 'family'. There was, in the words of one flight attendant 'a very family-type feeling'. As this book goes to press, all that is left are memories ...

The Sydney airport porter who spent twenty-eight years with the airline, remembers the good times, such as every Christmas when all staff got a Christmas pudding and those who had to work were waited on by the bosses.

The senior maintenance executive who was hired by Reg Ansett himself at the age of fourteen and stayed till he retired in 1994, remembers hanging around the Hamilton aerodrome in western Victoria, birthplace of the Ansett business, in awe of what was going on. His first job was to clean up vomit and wash the planes. And he remembers going out with the boss at weekends trying to drum up business. In his words, 'every day was different, it was wonderful, absolutely unbelievable'.

And the flight attendant who was in the air during the Vietnam war remembers transporting troops to their home states when they returned from overseas. She also remembers bringing people out of Darwin after Cyclone Tracy devastated that city in 1974. She has fond memories of the company to which she devoted much of her working life.

For each of the few mentioned there are thousands of other people, ordinary Australians, whose lives Ansett touched and whose recollections of what the airline did for them will remain as a constant reminder of what might have been. This was an airline with a heart, a heart that has now stopped beating.

Captain Swift might have wondered how the airline, of which he had been made chief pilot just a month earlier, had come to such a sorry pass. His airline, the one of which he was so proud and to which he had devoted nearly thirty years of his life, would no longer be part of the Australian aviation scene. The 52-year-old father of two returned to Brisbane to consider his future, probably with an overseas airline, leaving the local industry to the younger pilots, like First Officer Greg Toole.

For the small group on board, it was a sad experience. They had worked so hard in the preceding six months, committed to seeing Ansett back in the skies. They had put in an average of twelve to fifteen hours a day on this major company restructuring. It had been a gruelling yet exhilarating period, working alongside the administrators, attempting to make possible what constantly threatened to be impossible. Like Jon Swift, they contemplated what might have been—what could have been a mighty success, a mighty reality. They sat amidst the detritus of the last evening's celebrations on board the last commercial flight from Perth to Sydney. Streamers, bon-bons, party blowouts, half-eaten sandwiches, coffee cups and empty water bottles were scattered around the aircraft. Sad, coffee-stained copies of *Panorama*, the Ansett in-flight magazine, lay on seats, discarded for the last time.

Passengers and crew outside aircraft after last flight (left to right): Tony Pyne, Captain Jon Swift, Peter Wilms, Gary Rothville, First Officer Greg Toole, Louise Curcuruto, Nic Jarvis and Dominic Emmett.

As he approached Melbourne Jon Swift announced that he intended to do a couple of circuits of the central activities district. He wanted to say goodbye to a city he had come to love, the home of his airline. All aboard appreciated the gesture, this final act of defiance. Jon Swift did not want Ansett flight AN 4051 to be just another flight; he wanted to say goodbye to Melbourne and allow Melbourne to say goodbye to Ansett, an Australian icon.

The night before, the Ansett Golden Wings lounges around the country, silenced since the original grounding, reverberated to the sounds of the biggest collective wake in Australia's corporate history. The crowds that came hoped—hoped against hope—that the administrators and their team could keep alive their dream. It wasn't to be. The Ansett story had ended. Still they celebrated, yarned about the past, expressed concern for the future, fought back bitter tears, laughed over the good times.

Reg Ansett would have admired their determination. He would have regarded them as worthy descendants of his own well-chronicled struggles with power and influence. Disappointed he would be at the outcome, but satisfied with the battle that preceded it.

Captain Jon Swift taxied flight AN 4051 to a spot on the tarmac where he was greeted by the news media. He and Greg Toole had a champagne breakfast on board. Descending from the plane to hand in their papers, they looked back and saluted their aircraft.

It was, like Ansett, now a giant awaiting burial. As were all the other silent-winged monsters that sat on the tarmac, their job done.

Ansett may be as dead as the planes that lie in state at Melbourne airport and in the desert graveyards of the United States of America. But its spirit and the memories of the good times live on.

1
ANSETT—ON A WING AND A PRAYER

THE TINY AIRCRAFT that clambered into the skies over the Victorian town of Hamilton on a Monday lunchtime just thirty years into the twentieth century launched a craggy-faced young man into the airline business. Reginald Myles Ansett had two months earlier begged from grazier friends 1000 pounds to buy a third-hand Fokker Universal from a cash-strapped showman in Sydney. As his long-time friend and employee Colin MacDonald later remembered, 'For the first three months we ran the plane up and down from Hamilton to Melbourne every day. We had no spares, no spare engine. Nothing.'[1] Reg Ansett, whose enterprise and business acumen would see his memory inscribed in the record of twentieth-century Australian folklore, bought the Fokker in a telephone deal and later hassled his friends to back him with what would have been well over $1 million at today's values.

Ansett was just twenty-eight years old and his lean build and long, sharp features would have wrongly typecast him as a simple farm lad. But that face emanated a piercing stare that mirrored determination. Anyone meeting him for the first time in the mid-1930s either took an immediate liking to him or despised his impertinence at wanting to make a pile and retire early. The Victorian Government soon learned there was more to the man who faced them in a parliamentary office over a newly enacted government ban on allowing road transport to compete with the railways in the bush. Ansett had stormed out of a meeting in 1935 with a government official shouting 'I'll go over your head' and expounding personal views in language unsuited to conduct expected of visitors to the Victorian Parliament. And over the official's head he went, later picking up a telephone and sealing the deal on the Dutch-built Fokker in Sydney.

Not surprisingly Ansett ran his infant airline on a wing and a prayer. But his seat-of-the-pants approach can be compared to the challenge that insolvency experts Mark Mentha and Mark Korda faced when they relaunched Ansett as a going concern in late September 2001, two weeks after an earlier administration led by PriceWaterhouseCoopers accountant Peter Hedge had ordered the airline grounded.

'We have taken over a business with no books, no bank accounts, and no executive management,' Mark Mentha lamented, sixty-six years after Reg and his first pilot made their inaugural commercial passenger flight from Hamilton to Melbourne. To their credit, Mentha and Korda (the 'two Marks') were to salvage vital pieces of the mainline carrier and bring the business to the threshold of recovery. But their efforts, along with the

Ansett Roadways

hopes and aspirations of thousands of Ansett workers, were frustrated at the eleventh hour, leaving in their wake a barrage of bitter claim and counter-claim as the deal to rescue and revive the airline faltered then fell apart.

When Reg Ansett was just twenty-two and took his first tilt at the transport industry armed with a second-hand Studebaker taxi, he had ten shillings left—barely enough money to buy petrol. His one-man taxi service between the central Victorian centres of Ballarat and Maryborough involved

'We have taken over a business with no books, no bank accounts, and no executive management.'

eighteen-hour days and failed after a year. Moving south-west to the then-rich wool-growing town of Hamilton, Reg challenged bigger and better established operators and began a daily road service to Melbourne. The experiences of these tough, lean years set a pattern for his business life and behaviour. He quickly learned never to bow to threats from anyone—individuals *or* governments. The next year, Reg Ansett pitted his wits against the intellect and eloquence of Robert Gordon Menzies, then

Ansett Motors

Attorney-General of Victoria and due to become Prime Minister of Australia within a decade. Already a King's Counsel in 1933, and of well-acclaimed legal brilliance, Menzies had introduced into the Victorian Parliament the Bill aimed at stopping road services competing with the passenger services of the Victorian Railways.

Folklore has it that a desperate Reg Ansett bought the Fokker and took to the air to overcome regulations that were laid down by Menzies. But Arthur Schutt, who would watch the Ansett cars pass the farm where he worked, offered a very different story. Schutt, later the founder of a successful general aviation business himself, recalled in a 1981 interview:

> Reggie was going to start his own airline anyway. He loved flying but he wasn't going to give up his road service just because of a few government regulations. When that transport regulation act went through in 1933, Reg just took out a fruit vendor's licence. From then on, he would sell his passengers an orange for, say, two pounds 10 shillings, and give them a free ride from Hamilton to Melbourne. The passengers chewed oranges all the way to Melbourne, and no one could touch Reggie.[2]

Reg's drivers took to the back roads, resorting to all kinds of subterfuge to dodge police patrols under orders from the state's chief law officer to shut down the rebel from Hamilton. Colin MacDonald, who joined Reg Ansett in those days and later became general manager of Ansett Transport Industries, remembered years later:

> We couldn't take passengers beyond Ballarat, so we got up to all sorts of lurks. We would learn the police were waiting in Bacchus Marsh, so we would send out a scout car, loaded with bags on the roof—all dummies. No offence was committed because the passengers were cousins of the driver and nobody was paying a fare. Our other car would skid down another road, through Geelong and back into Melbourne. It was a case of cat and mouse.[3]

Ansett's wealthy woolgrower customers wanted to travel in comfort, certainly not on a government train and to any set timetable. The road-versus-rail row was Reg Ansett's first—but certainly not his last—encounter with Menzies and the bureaucrats of big government. Twenty years on, Reg Ansett and Robert Menzies would stare each other down in the nation's highest courts over government claims to fix the price of air fares and the right to issue licences for new air routes. These fights, too, were ones that Ansett would win.

Reg Ansett had a humble background. He was born on Friday, 13 February 1909 in the whistle-stop town of Inglewood, on the main Bendigo–Mildura rail line. His father had a bicycle store, but the family moved to Melbourne when he joined the Army after war was declared in 1914. Reg's mother started knitting to make ends meet, a piecemeal task that grew into a business at Camberwell and which later expanded with a dye works and mill at Seymour. The young Reg attended Swinburne Technical School, trained as a sewing and knitting machine mechanic and entered the workforce at fourteen. Three years later, he was earning twice the basic wage, working night and day assembling industrial equipment.

Like most Australians in the 1930s, Reg was gripped with the excitement of the new era of air travel and wanted to fly. He had caught the flying bug from the exploits of pioneer Charles Kingsford Smith. At twenty-one he learned to fly, paying for his lessons by selling insurance policies as

Reg in 1937

'I got the idea of an aviation business when I was driving. All my best ideas came when I was behind the wheel of a car.'

a door-to-door salesman. However, the Great Depression provided a temporary setback, stifling his first attempts to become a commercial pilot.

Reg headed north to Darwin with the quaint notion of earning his fortune growing peanuts. But the only job he got was as an axeman, roughing it in the outback with a party of government surveyors for twelve months until the winds of the Great Depression blew cold on the bush and all government survey work stopped. Out of a job, Ansett set off down the west coast to Perth, with plans to search for new riches in South Africa. A farewell visit to his family in Victoria caused him to change his plan to cross the Indian Ocean and fate intervened in the form of that first Studebaker taxi.

He paid fifty pounds for the car and became the owner and sole employee of a Maryborough-to-Ballarat licensed passenger run. The business lasted less than a year. Worry and fatigue outstripped his earnings and Reg moved to Hamilton, traded in the Studebaker and bought a new vehicle on the treadmill of time payment. Reg drove up to 240 miles (390 kilometres) a day and sweated over mechanical repairs at night, reducing his sleep time to two hours. It was an existence that could not last, so he took on his mate Colin MacDonald as another driver.

For the first two months the bills were spiked and nobody got paid. But wealthy farmers rode in comfort each day to Ballarat in a brand new Chrysler that Reginald bought when he hired MacDonald as his driver assistant. Wiser now from his earlier experience, Ansett made sure his

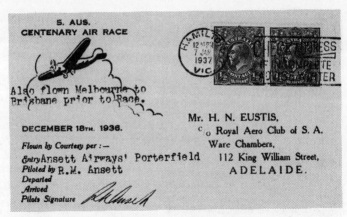

Postcard from the 1935 Brisbane–Adelaide air race won by Ansett.

new venture was debt-free within two months. He would, over the following twenty-two months, build a new garage in Hamilton and expand the now bus–car operation to 150 staff. Still not satisfied, he dreamed of building an operation that would expand into aviation and take on the might of the government railways. Years later he would tell an interviewer: 'I got the idea of an aviation business when I was driving. All my best ideas came when I was behind the wheel of a car. My wife always used to say that I was never much company in a car.'[4] Ansett had bought a small De Havilland Gipsy Moth aircraft which he used to commute between bush depots. With his brother Jack he also acquired a two-seater, single-engine Porterfield and won the 500-pounds first prize in the 1935 Brisbane–Adelaide air race.

Ansett spent his cash prize from the Brisbane–Adelaide race on an eight-seat British-built Airspeed Envoy, which he used to start an air service between both state capitals. With money being tight and civil aviation still in its infancy, Reg Ansett improvised to keep his business alive. He ran a flying school at Hamilton. At weekends, he took the Porterfield and his Fokker barnstorming, charging brave bush souls fifteen shillings for a straight level flight and double that to loop the loop. One of his engineers was taught to parachute and would jump from a wing. The initiatives were typical of his manner and early entrepreneurial style to sell the very idea of air travel to the public. It was helped in no short measure by his own image as a pioneer aviator who sought to convey the message that flying was safe.

Porterfield VH-UVH—Reg's race-winning aircraft

Reg receiving trophy

Aware that the government intended to take a much tougher anti-competition line to support the railways and could stop him from renewing his road licences, Reg bought the Dutch-built Fokker Universal from Harry Purvis, then a pilot for the Kingsford Smith Air Service. Purvis, who had bought the aircraft in Britain for 300 pounds, had shipped it to Sydney and barnstormed it at weekends, charging five shillings a flight. He decided to snip the young man from Hamilton for 1000 pounds in selling him the

Ansett Airways' Airspeed Envoy

aircraft. When Reg accepted the price, he mailed Purvis a cheque. Purvis returned it, pointing out that Reg had forgotten to add the few shillings extra of interstate duty. Purvis was sent back a new cheque with an accompanying letter, saying: 'you are the toughest businessman I have dealt with'.[5]

Having bought the Gipsy Moth, Reginald boarded it and headed to Sydney. Colin MacDonald later recalled that Reg and Jack Ansett made that trip in December 1935 by following the railway line and using a road map to navigate. 'Reg had done a deal over the phone to buy a new plane, a beautiful single-engine aircraft,' he recalled. 'He paid 1000 pounds for the

> **'For the first three months we ran the plane up and down from Hamilton to Melbourne every day. We had no spares, no spare engine. Nothing.'**

plane and had to put up another 250 for the engine. He didn't have the extra 250, so he had to give a promissory note. For the first three months we ran the plane up and down from Hamilton to Melbourne every day. We had no spares, no spare engine. Nothing.' The circumstances would have struck a chord with the two Marks when their turn came to take charge of the company.

Fokker Universal VH-UTO began its first commercial flight—from

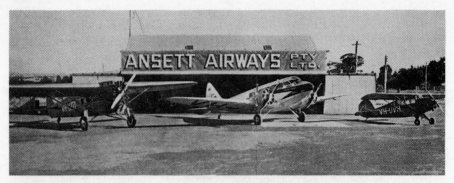

Ansett Airways' first fleet: the Fokker Universal VH-UTO, the Airspeed Envoy and the Parterfield.

Hamilton to Essendon—on 17 February 1936. Two hundred locals turned out to watch the plane leave the runway at 12.30 p.m. that Monday. So big was the occasion that Hamilton radio 3HA challenged the technical dilemmas of the era and staged a live outside broadcast. 'Hamilton makes aviation history' proclaimed the *Hamilton Spectator* the next day in a bold front-page headline that would be of great amusement to readers today. The paper went on to report:

> Amid great public interest the new daily air service to Melbourne and return was inaugurated by Ansett Airways Pty Ltd yesterday. Precisely at 12.30 p.m. the graceful metal bird took to the air and in a very few minutes was winging swiftly away with its full complement of six passengers plus the pilot, Mr. Vern Cerche, and the Managing Director of Ansett Airways, Mr. R.M. Ansett. To prove by personal experience that the schedule of 1¾ hours from Hamilton to Melbourne could be maintained comfortably, Mr Ansett accompanied the machine on its first journey and expressed complete satisfaction with the success of the timetable, the operation of the machine and the careful man-oeuvring by the pilot.

The newspaper reported that the aircraft landed at Essendon Aerodrome at 2.15 p.m., and the same schedule was maintained for the return journey. 'At one minute before 4.30 p.m. a speck on the horizon loomed larger and larger, stabbing the sky in split seconds, hovering over the heads of the spectators to become the awaited aeroplane, and landed

Boarding the Fokker Universal for the first flight from Hamilton to Essendon on 17 February 1936.

perfectly to taxi to the hangar.' The *Hamilton Spectator* added that Mr Reginald Ansett was warmly congratulated by leading citizens as he stepped from the cabin. 'He had been to Melbourne and back in four hours of glorious flying weather and over beautiful flying country.'

The pilot named in the flight manifest for that now-historic flight was Vern Cerche. He had been with Ansett only a few weeks, having been hired by Reg Ansett on the spot at Sydney's Kingsford Smith Airport to ferry the aircraft to Hamilton. The passengers paid a fare of two pounds, sat on wicker chairs and went without such luxuries as hostess service. The various stages to Essendon and back to Hamilton had carried a total of just seven passengers. They were listed as Keith Barr, Ted Heine, Mrs Rosalie Pearson, Miss E.T. Lascelles, Miss A. Shields, Mr J.R. Simpson, and Mr K.M. Wilson. Their white-knuckled, no-frills introduction to the new age of air travel was far more basic than today's standard of even the most basic flight. Not only was there no food and no drink; passengers could not move around and there was no lavatory for the inevitable call of nature. The aircraft flew at 3000 feet and reached a top speed of eighty knots, and the journey was bumpy and uncomfortable. Mrs Pearson recalled forty years later that she let Reg Ansett down by not smiling her best for the newspaper photographer who greeted the party at Essendon. 'The bumps on the way had got the better of my feelings,' she said.

Vern Cerche and his boss, Reg Ansett.

Ted Heine, seventy-seven and a veteran air traveller, well remembered that day when he attended the airline's fortieth birthday celebrations in 1976. Still resident in Hamilton and still on the job in a car business, he never lost the flying bug. Mr Heine continued to catch the commuter service to Melbourne to pick up new cars for his customers. He recalled that he made his first trip firmly believing that Reg Ansett's air travel business would be short-lived. 'I could not see him making a go of it, but I was determined to be on the first flight,' he said.

What Reg Ansett began that day would, in the span of sixty years, make his a household name and touch in some way the lives of most Australians. Ansett Transport Industries expanded to a fleet of more than 150 aircraft, diversified into passenger road and freight movement, bought hotels and lured travellers with five-star accommodation that included a lavish resort on a Great Barrier Reef island. A measure of how vast the Ansett group became can be gauged by the 47 related companies listed on the Corporations Register that came under the charge of the two administrators when then owner Air New Zealand cut the group adrift on 12 September 2001 and left it to go belly-up and into administration. Yet it remains a testament to Reg Ansett's memory that he established his airline in the midst of the Great Depression, when most of the country was broke and very few people could afford to spend their hard-earned cash on air travel.

When Ansett floated his company on the Melbourne Stock Exchange on 14 April 1937, he flew the Porterfield around the bush, landing on the big station properties of well-heeled squatters and selling shares in his fledgling transport group. He had little trouble raising the issued capital of 8303 pounds among friends and contacts but it was an altogether different story trying to sell an additional 110 000 ordinary shares to the public at one pound each. Ansett fell foul of his underwriter and offended the broking establishment by brashly advertising his shares in Melbourne's daily newspapers.

On moving his operation to Essendon, he bought three ten-seat Lockheed Electras—one of which, VH-UZO, remains on the Australian Aircraft Register as the only original Ansett aircraft in existence. In its first year, Ansett Airways flew 1 433 573 kilometres and carried 12 624 passengers, opening new routes to Broken Hill, Sydney–Adelaide, and fuel stops at Mildura and at Narrandera, in the New South Wales Riverina.

> **'I could not see him making a go of it, but I was determined to be on the first flight.'**

The year 1938 was a bad one for Ansett Airways. The company lost 20 000 pounds and Reg Ansett sacrificed some of his holdings to pay off debts. The crisis continued, exacerbated by commitments on the new ten-seat Lockheed aircraft. Abandoned by the Melbourne financial establishment, the price of Ansett stock plunged from one pound to eight shillings. The Lockheeds, valued at 60 000 pounds, remained unclaimed on the wharf; there was no money to collect them. Reg's one-time friend and company chairman Ernest O'Sullivan urged shareholders to forgo their losses and accept a nine-shillings-a-share bid from the Holyman shipping company. (Holyman was owned and operated by Ansett's much bigger rival, Australian National Airways (ANA), that wanted Ansett off the interstate routes.) In typical fashion, Reg stood his ground and stared down a meeting of shareholders, forcing O'Sullivan's resignation and winning the support of his shareholders. But further disaster followed when a hangar at Essendon Airport caught alight, destroying the Fokker, an Electra and some training planes used by the Ansett flying school.

The death of the business appeared imminent, with the company deep in debt, and shares plunged to less than a tenth of their value. Years afterwards Reg Ansett confided to friends that he was saved from bank-ruptcy in 1938 by a 33 000-pounds lifeline from the Commonwealth Government. His nemesis, Robert Menzies, Prime Minister of Australia in 1939, went on to establish the Federal Department of Civil Aviation, which began to subsidise airline operators flying certain air routes.

Ansett became a key supplier to the needs of the Australian war effort at the outbreak of the Second World War in September 1939 and to the United States military in the Pacific later. It built hangars and repair facil-ities at Essendon, servicing government contracts for the RAAF and US Army Air Force. Ansett was manufacturing aircraft parts that could not be supplied from overseas sources and damaged planes were finding their way to Ansett's Essendon workshops. By 1942 the loss-making company was reporting a steady eight-per-cent profit. Reg Ansett had not only become an integral part of Australia's war effort but, in the process, had earned himself an enviable reputation as both a leading wartime industri-alist and an entrepreneur in his own right. Good luck and guile had kept Ansett Airways alive. The chrysalis of an Australian icon was emerging.

By 1942, with the Japanese on Australia's doorstep, Ansett Airways ceased all regular services with the exception of the original leg between Melbourne and Hamilton. Its aircraft were contracted to the US Army, flying troops between Melbourne and Townsville and on to Cairns and Darwin. The two remaining Lockheeds were conscripted for the evacua-tion of Darwin and Broome following the Japanese bombings. Employee numbers rose to a peak of 2000 in 1944.

Long-time Ansett confidant Ross Alexander told how his friend and boss came into his own during the war years. His Essendon workshops were operating around the clock but according to Alexander many of the workers were SP bookies looking to avoid the call-up by joining an essen-tial industry. Towards the end of the war Reg Ansett bought Pioneer Coaches and, with no planes to fly, turned his attention to road transport.

Alexander recalled: 'Cars were almost impossible to get and petrol was rationed. So, too, were buses. But the environment was right for holiday packages and eventually we got access to some chassis—left-hand-drive American Super Clippers that had to be converted to right-hand drive.

Early travel by Pioneer coach.

We built our own coaches using the name Ansair, which was to become one of the nation's most successful motor bodybuilders.'

With the end of the war in August 1945, Reg Ansett flew to Manila and bought three US surplus Douglas C47s and resumed commercial flying. With his pre-war routes handed to rival Australian National Airlines (ANA), he was back in the courts and once again fighting Canberra. Eventually, Ansett was able to access routes that linked Melbourne to Adelaide via Mount Gambier, and Melbourne to Canberra via Wagga Wagga. He was refused rights to sell tickets on direct inter-capital flights.

His problems were compounded by the Chifley Labor Government's decision to nationalise and merge the nation's three carriers, Ansett, ANA and the then Commonwealth-owned Trans Australia Airlines (TAA). Once again Reg Ansett was fighting Canberra for his very survival in a battle that ultimately was decided by the full bench of the High Court.

The Government-owned TAA made its first flight with a DC-3 from Laverton to Sydney on 9 September 1946. Regular flights were introduced the following month. Ansett countered by introducing holiday airfares to Hobart and road tour packages of the island state. With the introduction of TAA, Ansett and its free-enterprise rival ANA lost all government business, including travel and mail, to the government airline.

Government-enforced restrictions were also imposed for the first time on the purchase of new aircraft. Ansett had a new war to wage. Not only did the private enterprise carrier face loss of lucrative government business, but TAA was given free access to government-owned facilities at airports for which Ansett was charged.

Despite all of these obstacles, Ansett was a profitable company and going places. Now with a share capital of one million pounds, Ansett Airways became, on 31 May 1946, a division of the new Ansett Transport Industries Ltd. Having survived a difficult Depression-era birth, Ansett was growing, as a result of post-war boom prosperity, into a promising adult.

2
FIGHTING THE FEDS

The Finest Service in the Air

When Ansett Airways state that they have the "finest service in the air" that's just what they mean. Every Ansett air hostess is a friend—kind, alert, understanding. Ansett air hostesses are chosen for competence, character and charm and are thoroughly trained in the execution of their specialised work . . . you will appreciate their unfailing courtesy. Reading or writing matter, drinks, matches, delicious meals are yours for the asking, so that your flight will be a pleasant and memorable event.

Ansett Douglas Airliners, with Hostess service, fly daily between Adelaide, Mt. Gambier, Wagga, Canberra, Sydney, Hobart and Melbourne. There is also a daily Ansett service to and from Hamilton.

AIRWAYS PTY. LTD.

BOOKINGS

SYDNEY BX1161. MELBOURNE MU6014. ADELAIDE C2514. HOBART 6221

THE SECOND WORLD War had not ended when the Curtin Labor Government embraced a plan for post-war Australia in which Canberra would take over the banking system and merge the major airlines into a single government-run carrier. Prime Minister John Curtin was convinced that post-war prosperity could only be assured by a continuation of wartime controls and government economic activity with private enterprise. Seriously ill and far from recovered from his heart attack the previous November, Curtin called a conference of the nation's manufacturers on 5 February 1945, at which he stressed the benefits he perceived would accrue from greater government involvement in the economy. His biographer, David Day, wrote that Curtin's idea was not well received: 'It seemed to his conservative critics that Curtin and his colleagues were trying to achieve by stealth what they had failed to achieve at the 1944 referendum'.[1] Australians had been asked to vote for a constitutional change that would hand the government new powers over issues that ranged from employment and monopolies to uniform railway gauges and health, and to have powers to make laws for Aborigines. A government-owned single-airline system was high in the order of planning.

Reflecting on the Ansett story at the time of the airline's fiftieth anniversary in February 1986, the aviation writer for the *Australian* newspaper, Stanley Brogden, wrote that, shortly before Curtin's death on 6 July 1945, he instructed his deputy, Frank Forde, to ensure that air transport was nationalised.[2] Forde need not have worried about fulfilling the dying wish of a leader whose office he would hold down for six days until the Labor Caucus found a permanent replacement in J.B. (Ben) Chifley. Prime Minister Ben Chifley and his Minister for Civil Aviation, Arthur Drakeford, were old railwaymen. They held to the tenet that God intended all transport systems to be state-owned, especially those competing with the trains for patronage. Brogden argued that these old-style Labor politicians loathed the foreign shipping interests that held a significant stake in Ansett's big airline rival, ANA.

Sir Robert Menzies explains what happened next in his 1967 memoir *Afternoon Light*.[3] Noting that the Chifley Government had decided in 1945 to nationalise the civil air services, Sir Robert argues that Australia's air services had been pioneered by private enterprise with notable success. 'I remind my readers that the Labor scheme was, first to create a National Airlines Commission with power to conduct air services on behalf of the

Government, and then, by a series of statutory devices, give it a monopoly, thus eliminating the private services.' Challenged in the High Court, the Airlines Bill was subsequently quashed. The Court found that the government could establish and run an airline, but a government monopoly in interstate air services would violate Section 92 of the Australian Constitution, which guarantees the freedom of interstate trade, commerce and intercourse. The government might have had the legal right to use tax-payers' funds to establish and operate an airline, but it could not equip itself with powers to acquire private enterprise companies compulsorily and to force them out of business. Chifley's objective was flawed and his government's subsequent attempt to nationalise the banking system met a similar fate before the same Bench of learned justices.

Realising that any deal would have to be done by stealth and in secret, the Chifley Government decided on a different ploy. Reg Ansett and the Holyman family who controlled ANA received tempting offers to sell. The new government-owned TAA was still five months away from making its first flight when the Airlines Commissioner, Arthur Coles, approached both carriers in April 1946 to fold their fleets into government ownership. Readers of Melbourne's *Sun News-Pictorial* on 23 December 1947 learned that, having first been blocked by the High Court, the government was later prepared to pay three million pounds for ANA—a sum three times the carrier's nominal capital value. They read that Ansett Airways refused the offer because the government rejected a claim for 20 000 pounds goodwill. Ansett's asking price was not disclosed but it would seem more than a mere coincidence that a strategically timed leak that was embarrassing to the government surfaced at a time when Canberra had sought to control the price of airline travel and to hike the cost of airfares up by twenty per cent against the expressed wishes of Ansett.

Ansett Airways had defied a Department of Civil Aviation instruction to match fares on routes where its planes competed with TAA and ANA aircraft. Reg Ansett told reporters: 'For barefaced audacity, the government instruction must surely be without equal in any democratic country. One can only wonder where this Canberra despotism is going to end.' He told the same press conference that the government separately blocked his attempt to buy US war surplus aircraft in India to convert for use on interstate passenger services. Ansett argued that he could have bought the planes for 3000 pounds each while the government was prepared to allow TAA to order Convair aircraft worth US$2 million each at a time when Australia confronted a so-called US dollar famine.

The airline chief counter-punched, threatening to return to the High Court where he would seek an injunction supported by the constitutional argument that, yet again, the government was seeking to interfere with the right to freedom of interstate trade.

The Ansett and Canberra stand-off lasted for almost a month and ended with an awkward backdown by the government and Civil Aviation Minister Arthur Drakeford. At one point Ansett Airways was told that its planes would be banned from using Commonwealth-owned airports. The airline chief counter-punched, threatening to return to the High Court where he would seek an injunction supported by the constitutional argument that, yet again, the government was seeking to interfere with the right to freedom of interstate trade. Acknowledging that he had lost the row, Drakeford later said: 'I do not wish to be placed in the position of appearing to deny the public the right to travel at the lowest economic fare.' Reg Ansett had the last word, saying: 'We are delighted that the Minister should concur with the principle we were fighting for.'

Soon afterwards Reg Ansett set out a plan to expand his already growing group of companies. Airline losses up till that point were being subsidised by his profitable road travel subsidiary Pioneer Coaches and a fast-growing hotel chain, which was meeting demands for low-cost holiday travel. It was a time when cars were scarce and any sort of car—new or old, and irrespective of mileage travelled—was a 'new' car. Petrol stocks were still subject to wartime rationing. The airline came out the following February, 1947, with a new share issue that almost doubled the issued capital of the Ansett group of companies. The plan was to raise 300 000 pounds by issuing 200 000 shares valued at one pound each, and issuing a further 100 000 one-pound preference shares to existing shareholders. The total issued capital of the company, by then known as Ansett Transport Industries (ATI), would amount to 660 000 pounds, comprising 460 000 ordinary shares and 200 000 preferences. The market was told the funds were needed to finance expansion of Pioneer Coaches and to expand further the growing chain of Ansett tourist hotels.

Pioneer Coaches was operating a fleet of eighty new coaches within a year. Wartime aircraft repairs had converted to peacetime motor body-building. The Ansair factory at Essendon was turning out two completed coaches a week and planned to use the new capital to create fifty stream-lined US-style road clippers.

The first Ansett hotel was at Leufra, near Eaglehawk Neck in south-west Tasmania. Between 1948 and the following year, ATI became the largest hotel operator in Australia, with more than twenty-five properties down the eastern seaboard, in the Northern Territory and New Guinea. Ross Alexander recalled: 'The big problem was that the hotel standards [in Australia] were like something out of Dante. We knew from this that it was essential to own our own hotels.' A Great Barrier Reef island destination, Hayman Island, was acquired and would become the dream resort of southern holiday-makers. But many came to regard it as too lavish for ordinary Australians. Alexander later said: 'It wasn't cheap to fly there and it was expensive to stay. Reg took a big risk buying that island.'[4]

> **'The big problem was that the hotel standards [in Australia] were like something out of Dante. We knew from this that it was essential to own our own hotels.'**

In the late 1940s the air travel market was dominated by TAA, which was given lucrative mail contracts and a monopoly on all public service travel. People travelled with Ansett to save money, sitting four abreast in DC-3s and taking longer to reach their destination because of stopovers that were laid down in route orders issued by the Department of Civil

Aviation. TAA and ANA flew passengers in DC-4s and other more modern aircraft. The trickle of business to Ansett meant the difference between profit and loss for its bigger ANA rival. ANA's share of domestic operations had dropped from 80 per cent in 1946 to 42 per cent by 1949, and the New South Wales-based Butler Air Transport and Ansett were then sharing 10 per cent between them. The market's remaining 10 per cent was split between four intrastate operators, with Butler having acquired Queensland Airlines (QAL) in 1947 and East-West Airlines having been formed the previous year.

In September 1948 TAA imported a Convair 240, the first pressurised commercial airliner to enter service in Australia. The government airline also bought Viscount 700 planes, the first prop jet aircraft to operate here and which remained in TAA service until the early 1970s.

When the Menzies Liberal–Country Party Government took office in 1949 TAA was retained but a new policy was drawn up that would become the cornerstone of Australian civil aviation policy for the next fifty years, until the industry was deregulated in 1990. Commonly known as the Two Airlines policy, it was based on an agreement signed jointly by the government and ANA and later confirmed by the *Civil Aviation Agreement Act* on 18 November 1952. The Two Airlines policy ensured that the then privately owned major carrier ANA and the government-owned TAA shared equally in airmail contracts and other government business, and would operate on equal terms on all trunk routes. As a result, real competition between the major carriers all but ceased in what effectively became a market protected by government. Both airlines for years would operate services that cost the same and that took off and landed within minutes of each other.[5]

After 1954–55, ANA's fortunes dived. The airline's market share dropped to about thirty-one per cent while TAA still enjoyed forty-two per cent patronage. Coupled with the cheaper fares offered by Ansett and Butler Air, ANA's finances had become precarious. ANA resisted the push to introduce pressurised aircraft and could not buy a place on the Viscount assembly line. The carrier had to settle for expensive-to-operate piston-driven DC-6s and began incurring huge losses. The climax came on 18 January 1957 when the airline's books were opened after the death in Hawaii of Sir Ivan Holyman, the airline's chairman and managing director. The ANA board immediately sought a new deal from Canberra to merge their operation with TAA. But Prime Minister Menzies, who came to office eight years earlier espousing the principles of free enterprise, would have nothing to do with the plan. The same was true for TAA, which feared the likely consequences of being at the beck and call of governments while trying to run a business.

With his group's finances already stretched to the limit, he would have to raise more than three million pounds to acquire his larger competitor.

Various newspaper accounts of these events tell how rumours abounded that Pan American would enter the market. Nothing happened … until Reg Ansett came from nowhere some two months later and announced he would make a takeover bid for ANA. With his group's finances already stretched to the limit, he would have to raise more than three million pounds to acquire his larger competitor. A David versus Goliath it might have been, but Reg Ansett got support from unlikely quarters. The backing came as a result of a chance encounter in Melbourne's fashionable Collins Street with Fred Haig, chief of aviation fuels at Vacuum Oil Australia. After hearing Ansett's plans, Haig persuaded his management to put up 500 000 pounds cash and the same in fuel credits. A phone call to Haig's opposite number at Shell, Frank Wright, brought a matching offer.

Reg Ansett would offer the ANA board one million pounds as a down payment, a second payment of 1 250 000 pounds in 1958 and the remaining 1 050 000 pounds two years later. As Brogden recalled: 'At the time it was the most unlikely and impossible takeover in Australian commercial

Vintage Ansett

Ansett Airways management staff 1948 (below)

Ansett Airways advertisement (above)

A Pioneer stream-lined coach

Buying new planes

history. People had to see it in print to believe it.' The resulting merger made ATI larger than TAA, adding six DC-6s, eight DC-4s, 20 DC-3s, two helicopters and three Bristol freighters to the Ansett fleet of one Convair Metropolitan, two Convair 340s, four DC-4s and two flying boats. Reg Ansett was also about to take delivery of seven additional Convair Metropolitan airliners, four of which were due to arrive within weeks. He had committed the company to spend a further one million pounds each on three Lockheed Electra turbo-prop aircraft that would be delivered the following year.

Ansett then embarked on a campaign of airline takeovers. Part of the inheritance from the ANA deal was a major stake in the then Sydney-based carrier, Butler Air Transport, headed by C.A. Butler. Butler was the first man to design and build an all-metal aircraft in Australia and to fly a single-seat aircraft from England to Australia, and had only shortly before been involved in a bitter struggle for control of his company with ANA, headed then by Sir Ivan Holyman.

ANA was disturbed because Butler had imported new Viscount aircraft and was using them on both country and city air routes in competition with ANA and Ansett. But once Reg Ansett gained control of ANA, he decided to bid for the remainder of Butler Air and thus touched off one of the most bitter and spectacular takeover battles in Australian company history. Butler declared that he would fight to the last against Ansett, accusing his rival of considering his ego rather than aviation history.

The New South Wales Minister for Transport, G.A. Enticknap, came out on Butler's side, saying he would do everything in his power to prevent Butler from being swallowed 'by a huge monopoly seeking complete control of air services in NSW'. He assured Butler that the NSW Government would protect Butler Air's licences. Butler's staff sided with their employer and decided at a stop-work meeting to appeal to Prime Minister Menzies to block Ansett. The chairman of the Butler employee–shareholders committee released a statement claiming that the staff was firmly behind Mr Butler, who 'deserves the tangible support of every Australian who appreciated achievement and the traditional Australian standards of fair play'.[5]

As the corporate brawl dragged out, Butler offered to sever all connections with the company, provided Reg Ansett and his interests did so,
too. Ansett replied, in his characteristically blunt way, 'I have no intention
of getting out.' His objective was to put Butler Air on a solid basis of development.

Despite Ansett's holding in Butler Air, a sliding scale of voting power
prevented Ansett from initially gaining control. Reg Ansett began buying
more shares on the open market, then cunningly split them into parcels of
a hundred to gain maximum voting power and, in an unprecedented
move, parcelled them out to employees
as nominees. Thus began *the* corporate
fight of the 1950s. Seeking to oust the
Butler board, Ansett flew his 630
'shareholders' to a company meeting
held at Mascot airport. Nine special
flights of Ansett aircraft ferried 386
'shareholders' from Melbourne alone.
It was the biggest privately organised
airlift seen in Australia.

Nine special flights of Ansett aircraft ferried 386 'shareholders' from Melbourne alone. It was the biggest privately organised airlift seen in Australia.

The Butler forces had also split their
shareholding among nominee shareholders, and almost 1000 shareholders
attended the stormy meeting that was held in one of Butler's hangars. The
Ansett forces, many of whom had never seen the shares for which they
were nominees, were briefed by section leaders to vote exactly as Reg
Ansett did.

Around this time Ansett retained Sir Garfield Barwick, then a Queen's
Counsel practising at the Sydney Bar, to apply to the Equity Court seeking to stop Butler Air from voting with employee shares issued during the
takeover struggle. Before the battle was over, Reg Ansett had to go to
court for a ruling that his nominations had won. He gained control of the
Butler board and soon afterwards Arthur Butler retired from the company he had founded.

The bitterness remained. Thirty years on, Arthur Butler, by then aged
seventy, was asked whether he felt sympathy for Reg Ansett when a simi-

Ansett–ANA poster

Ansett–ANA hostess

Ansett–ANA turbo prop Electra.

lar takeover attempt was made for ATI. Butler replied: 'No, I don't feel sympathy. If a man goes into business he must accept everything he gets. I include myself in that statement as much as Sir Reginald.' But Butler added: 'I won't work for Ansett. I would rather crack stones.'[6]

Having won control of Butler Air Transport (BAT) and its Queensland Airlines (QAL) subsidiary, ATI purchased Guinea Holdings, the parent company of Guinea Airways. BAT was subsequently renamed Airlines of New South Wales, and Guinea Airways became Airlines of South Australia.

The Menzies Government recognised the need to introduce stability to the air transport industry and, as a result of the ATI takeovers, initiated the *Civil Aviation Agreement Act 1957*, which legally bound the TAA and Ansett organisations and subsidiaries to the 1952 *Civil Aviation Agreement Act* and legislated against the possibility of a third competitor entering the Australian airline market. Reg Ansett was seen as the favoured son of the Menzies Government. The airline he established in 1935 with 1000 pounds borrowed from rich grazier friends had in just over twenty years become an icon of the free-enterprise system. But there was no escaping the fact that ATI flourished because it was able to operate within a legislated system of government protection. Reg Ansett won taxpayer-backed loan guarantees when he negotiated finance for new aircraft.

The *Airlines Equipment Act 1958* established the machinery for achieving and maintaining comparable, but not necessarily identical, fleets between TAA and what became known (after the takeover of ANA)

Reg and Frank Pascoe, a long-time associate (on right).

as Ansett–ANA. Both airlines introduced turbo-prop Electras in 1959, and TAA replaced its intrastate DC-3s with turbo-prop Fokker Friendships. In July 1960 Australia–Papua New Guinea services were initiated by TAA and Ansett, and in September that year TAA took over Papua New Guinea internal services, which were previously operated by Qantas. Ansett replaced its DC-6Bs with Viscounts and purchased Mandated Airlines in Papua New Guinea, from W.R. Carpenter and Co., which had operated in the area since 1938. The *Airlines Agreement Act 1961* was further extended, and then subsequently amended in 1982.

The first pure jets were introduced into Australian domestic services in 1964, when the two airlines began operating Boeing 727s. In 1965 both Ansett and TAA lodged orders for Douglas DC-9/31, taking delivery of the first aircraft in April 1967.

On 1 November 1968, Ansett–ANA became Ansett Airlines of Australia. The following year Western Australia's MacRobertson Miller Airlines introduced Fokker Fellowship twinjets and became a wholly owned Ansett subsidiary. TAA and Ansett formed Air Niugini on 1 November 1973 to take over the Papua New Guinea services previously operated. After the country gained independence in 1975, ownership of Air Niugini was 89 per cent government- and 11 per cent Ansett-owned.

Throughout this frenetic period of takeovers and personal achievement Reg Ansett remained ever his own man: ruggedly determined and fiercely individual. He amassed a personal fortune and, as a self-made tycoon, took on the trappings of those who achieve personal riches. He became a successful racehorse owner, an influential member of various racing clubs and a close friend of Liberal politicians, and he was especially close to long-reigning Victorian Premier Sir Henry Bolte, whom Ansett would reward after his departure from office with a seat on the Ansett board. The Queen made Reginald Myles Ansett a Knight of Order of the British Empire for his services to aviation in the 1969 New Year's honours. He was for a time also a director of Hong Kong-based Cathay Pacific Airways.

Reg Ansett made his home on a large estate at Mount Eliza. Each day he cocked a snook at city commuters by journeying to and from work in a company helicopter that landed on a floating pontoon at the downtown city heliport on the Yarra River. That helicopter, according to family members, was an alarm clock for parents on the Mornington Peninsula, who knew that if their children were still at home when it went over they would be late for school.

Here was a man who loved his family and spent much time involved with his children's diverse interests while at the same time building up a business that would become an Australian icon. He loved horseracing and duck shooting, the latter a pursuit that, in those days, was unconstrained by the qualms of animal welfare groups. Yet he was said to detest cruelty to animals and at one race meeting in Melbourne 'went berserk' when one of his horses was struck across the face with a whip during a race.

Reg Ansett dreamed of owning the winner of the Victoria Derby, one of Australia's turf classics. He never achieved his objective, even though he owned some pretty smart gallopers, two of them still alive in 2002 and living on the family estate. On Saturdays he followed a particular routine if he was going to the races—one that his family found both quirky and amusing but no less so than his other attributes. Just before leaving home for the racecourse, he would have a lamb sandwich accompanied by a can of Foster's. It might have intrigued those who knew him as a tough, uncompromising businessman but the fact is that he never lost sight of his roots. Simple things appealed to him, like his favourite sausages and mash served up by Mrs Mac in the staff canteen at Ansett headquarters in Melbourne. He would return home excited about this most mundane of meals when it was his good fortune to have it.

He was a frequent visitor to the staff canteen in his time at 489 Swanston Street, sharing time with employees and building on the indomitable Ansett spirit. Reg Ansett helped foster that spirit, in the process creating the Ansett 'family' as a force in Australian business. Even at the end, employees talked glowingly, lovingly, passionately about the Ansett family, about what it meant to them, about how it had helped them through the worst of times, about how it would return stronger than ever under a new banner, then about how its spirit would live on despite the ignominious ending. And for that Reg Ansett deserves a great deal of credit. Tough and uncompromising, he nevertheless commanded respect and proved himself to be a leader of significant stature.

At home with his wife, Joan, and their three daughters—Janet, Jane and Jillian—he was regarded as a wonderful father: compassionate, loving and open. He was a tidy, organised man who would take off his tie and jacket, folding the latter, and put them with his briefcase on the same chair each evening. He would sit down with a martini or a scotch and listen as each family member in turn talked about their day. At this point, the memory of his own working day was forgotten. It would return later, when the family had retired for the night.

Just after 7 a.m. each work day, he would have a cup of tea and a piece of Vegemite toast beside the bed. He would light up his first cigarette, always an unfiltered American Lucky Strike for which he had a strong affinity. So attached to these cigarettes was he that he had them imported from the United States on a regular basis. After showering and shaving and dressing for the day's work, he would enjoy a black coffee and home-made tomato juice. When he was ready to leave, he would turn in his chair and wave his table napkin in the direction of his helicopter pilot waiting on the front lawn of the property. This was the signal to start the engine. For Reg Ansett another day with his other family was about to begin.

He was a man full of passion for the things he believed in and, thanks to his own background, he hated snobbery. He was nevertheless relaxed in the company of Melbourne's leading business figures—people like Sir Norman Myer, whom he would meet on Sundays when the two men went horse-riding together. He would often be accompanied on these occasions by Janet riding her Shetland pony, Johnnie Ray.

Reg Ansett had the capacity to leave business behind at the head office door when he left for the day to be taken by his driver, Max Humphrey, to his waiting helicopter on the Yarra. Departure time in those heady days of empire building would be determined by a phone call to the Bureau of Meteorology, which would provide him with the time of the sunset.

A man who did not suffer fools, who enjoyed the company of friends, who loved oysters, fish, duck, beef and loin chops but disliked pudding, Ansett was a man who mixed comfortably with all types. He was a canny, astute businessman, determined to build on his dream and doubtless believing that he would be carried out of the head office building when his time came. That time came not with his death, as he might have expected, but in another form of empire building: takeover fever was emerging as a new 'industry' in Australia and Ansett would not be immune to its blandishments.

Reg Ansett's reign at the airline he founded ended when the Australian-born international media baron Rupert Murdoch achieved control of Ansett Airlines of Australia on 13 December 1979. His baby was now an adult and its future would be determined by others with different agendas. He died a few days before Christmas 1981 after suffering a severe illness. A flight of Ansett aircraft saluted the airline founder by flying over the Melbourne central activities district after a memorial service at St Paul's Cathedral on 15 February 1982. Delivering the eulogy, his long-time friend Sir Henry Bolte said that his friend and fellow knight had been the best known businessman in Australia. Quoting from Shakespeare, he added: 'Some men are born great. Some achieve greatness. Others have greatness thrust upon them.' Sir Henry noted that the first and third never applied to Sir Reginald, but he added that Reg Ansett did achieve greatness.[7]

3
A REAL AUSSIE CHARACTER

IN APPEARANCE REGINALD Myles Ansett
was a tall, lean figure whose long sharp features
evoked an image of the archetypal post-war
Australian character. The Melbourne *Sun*'s Alan
Trengove said after a 1969 interview with Reg
Ansett that he 'looked more Australian than

Chips Rafferty'.[1] Thirty-three years later Alan Trengove could recall very little of the occasion, except for a framed message in bold type that was attached to a wall outside Ansett's own office. The note read:

> Nothing in the world can take the place of persistence. Talent will not; unrewarded genius is almost a proverb. Education will not; the world is full of educated derelicts. Persistence and determination alone are omnipotent. The slogan 'Press on' has solved and will always solve the problems of the human race.

Extracted from a speech by former United States President Calvin Coolidge, the words also gave some indication of the man Reg Ansett, the reporter told *Sun News-Pictorial* readers. Alan Trengove confided all those years later that memories of the wall message lingered because he had made copies of the text and given them to his children.

Trengove's interview had been a rare scoop for the reporter.[2] Reg Ansett hated personal publicity and seldom spoke to journalists. He preferred to convey his views to mates at the top end of town—the movers and shakers who occupied key posts in business and government. Many were racing mates, such as his close friend and duck shooting partner Henry Bolte, the knock-about Victorian premier and farmer. He told Trengove:

Reg Ansett and Horrie Miller

> What I have to think about are my three daughters down at Mornington. There is a lot of envy and resentment generated when people keep reading of someone like me, and I don't want that to affect my daughters. They have their own lives to live and they have to be sheltered.

Reg Ansett was then aged fifty-nine. Typical of the man, the Trengove interview was agreed to on terms that suited the interviewee more than they did the reporter. Apart from myriad business interests, Reg Ansett at that time had decided to become a fight promoter. He would stage the world bantam-weight boxing championship at Kooyong Stadium where Melbourne's home-grown champion Lionel Rose was to meet a challenger.

For Reg Ansett and his group of companies the spin-offs from staging the fight would be in the numbers of air tickets bought by interstate fight fans and the right to screen the program on Channel 0, the television station that Ansett Transport Industries had been gifted six years earlier by the Menzies Government. Channel 0, later to become Channel 10, had been the Cinderella station, always running a poor third in the

Lionel Rose and Reg Ansett

ratings to the Packer family-owned Channel 9 and the then Herald and Weekly Times Ltd's Channel 7. Channel 0 had a difficult birth. In most households existing receivers had to be converted to receive the new channel. Never having thought that a Channel 0 might some day exist, nobody bothered to include the number on the selector switches of the sets that were then in most households.

When the Menzies Government announced in April 1963 that it was granting Melbourne's third commercial television licence to ATI's Austarama Television Pty Ltd, the Opposition benches in Federal Parliament burst into uproar. Labor Party leader Arthur Calwell, no friend of Ansett before the announcement, claimed that:

Reg and the General Manager of Channel 0 on opening night.

Ansett was being given a goldmine. In addition to this licence, Mr Ansett has received substantial financial assistance grants and aid through legislative and administrative action taken over the past 13 years by the government designed to bolster Ansett–ANA and hamper TAA.[3]

Calwell, an old-time socialist politician, saw Reg Ansett as the capitalist bogey man in bed with the Menzies Government. In his attack, Calwell alleged that Ansett had prior knowledge of the licence decision and had let it be known around the country to promote an extraordinary rise in the price of ATI shares from five shillings and four pence to six shillings and seven pence. Defending Ansett, then Federal Treasurer Harold Holt replied that most Australians would form their own opinion about the government's decision. They had watched with admiration the courage and ability shown by Ansett in building up a great commercial enterprise, Treasurer Holt said, pointing out that ATI's bid had the unanimous support of the then Broadcasting Control Board.

Reg Ansett was, and would remain to his admirers, the arch-apostle of free enterprise, the living justification of capitalism, and to his enemies a ruthless, scheming go-getter, the epitome of a big business tycoon. As he told Trengove:

I am an administrator. I have been a jack of all trades in my life, but I am best equipped now to be an administrator. I can't get interested in things that I'm not basically interested in, and I am vitally interested in the aviation business. It is hard, but very exciting. And once you've been in the flying game you can't get out of it. The whole reason I diversified years ago was to strengthen the airline operation and make sure I kept it. When there were three airlines it was most desirable we had these other activities because it was a tough fight. I knew that something would happen and that we had to maintain ourselves until that day came. It did when ANA collapsed. But you must remember that for a long time the writing was on the wall for us. The Labor Government wanted to nationalise the industry and launched TAA. We will never forget this.

Trengove wrote that Ansett acknowledged that all his ventures had been grim struggles before they became profitable. He had never anticipated the complexities of television, the difficulty in building programming material and creating an image for the station.

'We refuse to accept failure. If we go into something, we have an idea of success. We are not stupid. We are not dealing with our own money. We must justify our actions all the time.' He was to add: 'I suppose it's inevitable that I should be labelled big business. Other companies have merged and many of the individuals who started big companies have passed on. But I am still here and will be for another year or two, I hope.'

> Reg Ansett was, and would remain, to his admirers the arch-apostle of free enterprise, the living justification of capitalism, and to his enemies a ruthless, scheming go-getter, the epitome of a big business tycoon.

But then Reg Ansett disclosed that 'Ansett' would not have been the name he would have given the company had he perceived what was to become of the enterprise he started; he would have chosen a much grander title. 'The fact that it is known by my name makes me better known than I otherwise would be.' Reg Ansett got distracted somewhere along the way and the eager young businessman who wanted to make his pile and retire at thirty-five somehow let the milestone pass.

But few people know that, by the late 1960s, Reg Ansett and his transport conglomerate was at the brink of collapse. Documents outlining the true state of the company's troubles were kept secret by successive governments who gave little more than lip service to the principles of the Two Airlines policy. Documents obtained from the National Archives in Canberra include the findings of a detailed government

Government assistance was needed just to keep Ansett and the then government-owned TAA operating.

investigation into Ansett's finances at the time. They formed part of a series of submissions put to the Cabinet of Prime Minister John Gorton in 1968 by the Treasury and the Department of Civil Aviation. They reveal that government assistance was needed just to keep Ansett and the then government-owned TAA operating. With Ansett near bankruptcy, 'the Cabinet accepted that by comparison with TAA, Ansett was at a considerable competitive disadvantage particularly in relation to its capital structure,' the Cabinet documents show. Senior bureaucrats warned that Ansett's published profit of $3.7 million for 1967 was 'about as high as it could be without qualification from the auditors'. On a more conservative basis this figure could well have been $1.5 million,' they reported.[4]

The depth of the crisis confronting the company had prompted Reg Ansett in November 1967 to write to the Aviation Minister Reg Swartz:

I wish to place before the government a potentially grave situation regarding the future of the two-airline policy ... The whole future of the government's two-airline agreement will be in jeopardy if corrective action is further delayed.[5]

Reg Ansett said, further, that the survival of the Two Airlines policy depended on both airlines operating comparable aircraft under similar cost structures in a stable fiscal environment. He argued that Ansett would have to buy fifteen jet aircraft over seven years, but the company would not be able to find the US$75 million price tag without a government guarantee to underwrite finance on a plane-by-plane basis in a deal similar to that obtained by TAA.

He also claimed that if different cost structures for the airlines were allowed to continue, then it would 'inevitably lead to the destruction of private enterprise in air transport'. The biggest complaint was that TAA used its own growing superannuation funds to finance business activities, leaving its private competitor to raise the money on the far more expensive money market. The

Unless steps were taken the government would have to either sell TAA to the private sector or set up a single-airline system in Australia.

government-owned airline also avoided paying a host of government charges. Another complaint was that federal politicians and bureaucrats were flying solely on the government-owned airline, leaving Ansett with very little government-funded income. Tackling the issue of a stable fiscal environment, Reg Ansett told the government that there had been an annual increase of ten per cent in air navigation charges for the previous six years and the fuel tax was the highest in the world. 'Now a substantial head tax is proposed. These costs impose an intolerable burden on an air transport system serving a nation with Australia's low population density and vast area,'[6] he wrote.

Ansett also said that unless steps were taken the government would have to either sell TAA to the private sector or set up a single-airline system in Australia. His views carried weight with the Gorton Government, and Cabinet agreed to increase by $500 000 payments, the subsidy for developmental and essential rural air services.

Further, it would underwrite a loan to the then ATI to buy an additional Boeing 727, providing the same deal was offered to the government-owned TAA. Cabinet had also recommended to ATI that its television interest should be set up as a company separate from its aviation interests.

The Cabinet had also decided it was not 'disposed' to allow increases in fare and freight charges to solve 'Ansett's short-term problems', but it would allow Treasury and Aviation Department officials to examine the possibility. Furthermore, Cabinet decided Treasury would also examine the possibility of a directive to departmental travel booking officers to ensure that ATI was considered as an alternative carrier for public servants and politicians flying around the country.

The documents show that Cabinet discussions were based on continuing the government's Two Airlines policy. Cabinet was told that ATI was in a 'parlous' financial situation, although no offence had been committed under company law. 'The Cabinet accepted that, by comparison with TAA, Ansett was at a considerable competitive disadvantage, particularly in relation to its capital structure,' the 1968 Cabinet documents reveal. 'The company would only be able to retrieve its position and become viable if the government took steps fundamentally to redress the competitive disadvantage. The disposition of the Cabinet was to move for the adoption of measures which would ensure that Ansett would be viable.'

The Department of Civil Aviation had suggested to Cabinet that the government should defer for two years any proposed passenger charges and any increases in air navigation charges and should reduce duty on aviation fuel. But aviation public servants pointed out that the proposals would be fought by Treasury on the basis that the government's policy was to make the aviation industry commercially viable. Aviation bureaucrats also suggested the two airlines could work together and pool revenue from low-frequency routes like those to Tasmania, Canberra and north Queensland.

Not all bureaucrats supported the government line or the recommendations of their colleagues. Air Chief Marshal Sir Frederick Scherger, then chairman of the National Airlines Commission that ran TAA, wrote on 28 June 1968:

I am getting the uneasy feeling that I am protesting too much, but I cannot help but be gravely concerned over Ansett's persistent and constant attempts to induce the Government to force the air travellers to subsidise the whole ramshackle empire of ATI.[7]

By the late 1970s rumours were rife within the Ansett organisation that the boss was contemplating retirement. He had achieved greatness beyond anything he could have imagined in those first years in business. He was individually wealthy, was a knight of the realm when imperial honours mattered and he had spawned a healthy breadth of business and personal interests during his lifetime.

He enjoyed bush life—the mateship that came with duck shooting and the trips each month to the family farm bordering Kow Swamp, north of the Victorian Murray River centre of Echuca. He had become an active member of the Mornington community, especially the local racing club where he would take his turn to oversee the gate on race days. But, although he still had an air of vitality away from work, by early 1979 Reg Ansett appeared to be slowing down. He walked with a stick and commentators noted in April that he had looked tired and ashen during the company's annual meeting.

His neighbours at Mornington noted that the helicopter that whisked him to the office each day was leaving much later than it did when he was younger. It was also returning from the city much earlier. He was then seventy years of age and the talk among brokers and the business community was about company succession. Fears existed that his departure would bring about the demise of the airline.

The first talk about his departure emerged in March 1972 when Sydney transport supremo Ken Thomas, of Thomas Nationwide Transport Ltd (TNT), surprised everyone by spending $11.46 million to acquire the Boral and Carpenter shareholdings in ATI, giving it a 23.3-per-cent interest in the airline. TNT followed up, offering $46 million for the remaining shares in Ansett on the basis of one of its shares for every two Ansett shares. This valued each share in ATI at $1.20. The shares swoop sparked a detailed debate in federal parliament. The Senate referred the issue to its Standing Committee on Industry and Trade. At that time negotiations between the Commonwealth and ATI for an extension of the Two Airlines policy were well advanced and had to be suspended.

Market analysts described the TNT move as a logical step for the road transport group that had moved heavily into sea transport. Its bid to take to the skies by buying Australia's second airline aroused weeks of high-stakes business drama, with the two knights, Sir Reginald Ansett and TNT's CEO Sir Peter Abeles, jousting for supremacy. It was to be a knock-down, drawn-out affair for the nation's government-protected, sole commercial airline. Federal law barred the entry of any interloper wanting to start up in open competition. The Ansett–Abeles fight became a brawl between Melbourne and Sydney interests. Ansett employees, ever loyal to their boss, bought shares and spoke out publicly against the would-be invader from across the border. Even the Ansett hostesses, whom Reg Ansett, had dubbed 'old boilers' during an earlier industrial dispute, rallied behind him.

The knock-out punch that unseated Abeles came on 26 April when Victoria's premier Henry Bolte enacted legislation in the Victorian Parliament for a select committee inquiry of the Legislative Council to examine and report on the proposed takeover. Bolte, a racing mate of Reg's, determined that the parliament should decide whether the takeover was in the best interests of the state and its economy. Members of the Upper House committee were instructed to investigate and report on whether a TNT buyout was in the public interest. Bolte's *Select Committee (Ansett Transport Industries) Act 1972* effectively froze the takeover offer until 30 November 1972. Shareholders were barred by the legislation from transferring their shares without the consent of the government. TNT had little choice but to retire hurt, leaving Sir Peter Abeles to occupy an Ansett board post that gave him voting rights restricted to just ten per cent of the costly 23.5-per-cent investment TNT had made in the airline. Like a sleeping dog Abeles would wait his time to strike when the prey was more vulnerable.

Reg Ansett had retained control of his airline, for the time being. But Bolte came under attack by federal politicians and the Sydney media. The late Peter Blazey, in his 1972 political biography[8] of the former premier, noted that TNT's Ken Thomas afterwards described Victoria as 'Ansett country'. Blazey wrote that Bolte's move was hailed as a triumph in Victoria even amidst the admission that it set a questionable precedent of political interference in the stock exchange. He told how the *Age* newspaper, in an editorial headed 'Baron of the Bourses', echoed the ambivalence of many Victorians when it condemned Bolte's political interference but ended by saying: 'Sir Henry has broken the rules, offended the financial world. But what a politician!' After Bolte retired from politics, he was subsequently rewarded with a seat on the Ansett board.

Sir Reginald Ansett might have begun to slow physically during that era, but on the business front ATI and Sir Reg remained active and kept close watch on the finances. Weekly performance sheets for each arm of the organisation were delivered to his desk each Friday. ATI was cashed up and diversified into unrelated business activities, including the purchase of a 50 per cent interest in Diners Club in Australia, a move into the insurance industry, the purchase of a 50 per cent share in the Bic pen and lighter group, an ill-fated move to acquire 49 per cent ownership of Associated Securities Ltd, and the takeover of the Avis Rent-A-Car group despite opposition from Ansett's son Bob, a child of his first marriage who ran opposition Budget car rentals.

The issue that fanned rumours of what was then believed to be a looming departure was the $300-million crash of Associated Securities Ltd (ASL). According to Ansett's friends it was the ASL debacle that forced him to carry on. True to his character, he believed he could not leave the group without first sorting out the problems caused by the ASL failure, which had cost ATI $19.5 million. Reg Ansett's friends said that he wanted to leave the company he founded on a good note, not a bad one. Unlike the beleaguered airline that continued to bear his name, Reg Ansett had been carefully preparing the organisation for the day of his retirement. At ATI in the 1970s were men like Frank Pascoe, Ralph Cooper and a strong second-line leadership, well able to run a corporation with assets worth $109 million, sales of $500 million and profits of nearly $20 million a year. Waiting in the wings were TNT and Sir Peter Abeles.

ATI remained the perfect takeover opportunity. Its shareholdings—apart from the TNT block—were widely spread. Sir Reginald held only a little more than one million shares, or 1.3 per cent of the capital. And following the ASL failure the price of the company's shares slipped dramatically to $1.19, while having an asset backing exceeding $1.30.

Ansett, with its wide interests in airlines, road transport, television, hotels, credit cards, pens and lighters, not to mention other areas, was a soft target that could be bought and the spoils divided and sold by any corporate raider. Such a fate was not far off in those first months of 1979.

4
TAKING HEAVY FLAK

ANSETT AIRLINES FLEW through a storm-
filled last year of the 1970s. Shareholders had
been unsettled by concerns about Reg Ansett's
ability to continue to work and keep abreast of
what was then a diverse and vast conglomerate
of transport, hotel, manufacturing and finance

and insurance groups. The airline, then valued at $203 million, comprised only about half of the total value of the ATI group.

The first storm struck in March when ATI reported its December-half profit result, where an $11.3 million profit was eroded by a $9.4 million loss attributed to the collapse of the New South Wales-based finance house Australian Securities Limited (ASL). The ASL stake had been bought not long before from the Bank of Scotland. Reg Ansett and fellow director Henry Bolte were made to confront the full glare of a securities investigation launched by the government of New South Wales.

While the ASL scandal worried investors, equally damaging was an Equal Opportunity dispute that crept up on the company like a squall and then blew out into a force-10 gale. Deborah Wardley, a skilled 26-year-old pilot, was being refused a job with the airline and Ansett's growing segment of female travellers were outraged. Wardley would fight and eventually win Australia's most celebrated sex discrimination case against the airline, which would lose at every legal stage, including an appeal to the High Court. Wardley eventually won $14 500 damages from Ansett, as well as a court order that the airline pay her $40 a day until it was prepared to give her a job.

The case built into what became a year-long stand-off between a young woman determined to pursue her chosen career and an elderly man equally determined to hold on to male ideals from another era. Reg Ansett might have been a loving husband and a caring father, but he wasn't going to allow women to take command of his aircraft; that was a man's job as far as he was concerned, and that was that. But Wardley would not go away, and her case became a *cause célèbre* for feminists, who promoted a boycott by women travellers.

Even before the Wardley case and the ASL losses had driven down the price of Ansett shares, and when first-half accounts were published that March, analysts were trying to work out where to lay blame. In reference to the ASL case an unidentified director admitted to various journalists: 'We calculated wrongly. We did our figures very quickly, very late at night. They were wrong.' But nobody sought to direct the blame at the boss in the driving seat. Reg Ansett was at that point unassailable but the old man's reputation would not remain untarnished. The *Australian* reported on 31 March that investigators from the New South Wales Corporate Affairs Department had interviewed Reg Ansett and Henry Bolte over their involvement in the ASL disaster. Both were rich men and could well afford the ASL setback, but little people, such as retired jockey Ron Osborne from Melbourne's outer western suburb of Werribee, Leslie Pound of East Ivanhoe in Melbourne's east, and the Reverend Donald Haddy of the Victorian bayside suburb of Seaford, were thousands of dollars out of pocket and angry. Osborne had put $2000 from his 22-year RAAF severance pay into ASL; Leslie Pound invested $5000 in ASL debentures; and the Reverend Haddy had put $3000, inherited from his mother's estate, into the finance group, and had told the *Australian* that he was deeply worried. 'When Sir Reginald Ansett and Sir Henry Bolte went in I breathed a sigh of relief. Now it leaves a nasty taste in one's mouth.'[1]

Ron Osborne and Leslie Pound had invested not only money but also their faith in the ability of the two knights to back a financial winner. Osborne was reported as saying: 'I always looked up to Ansett and Bolte—especially Bolte, the former Premier. But they have let me down.' Leslie Pound added: 'I had steered clear of ASL early on, but when Reggie went in I thought he'd pump in all his finance and pull them out. It was a calculated punt. I am sure that other investors were influenced by him too.'[2]

> '**I always looked up to Ansett and Bolte—especially Bolte, the former Premier. But they have let me down.**'

From that moment shareholders tightened their seat belts, realising they were in for a very rough flight. The first sign of things to come emerged in the last week of June when Sir Peter Abeles began buying shares and lifted TNT's interest to 13.9 per cent. Within days heavy trading in Ansett shares flared on national share markets. The trading volume accelerated further when the 'raider from the West', Robert Holmes à Court, bought a parcel of 200 000 shares on 5 July to grab 4.1 per cent of the company. This pushed the stock to $1.28, a rise of 5 cents.

Two knights: Sir Reg Ansett and Sir Peter Abeles.

The battle for control of Ansett was being waged in earnest and observers tipped that TNT, with 13.9 per cent of the company, would grab 20 per cent of the diversified transport group. The share price rocketed. Melbourne broker J.B. Were was bidding $1.58, a 13-cent rise, and spent about $3 million to snap up a 2 per cent holding on 7 August. The following day Robert Holmes à Court revealed that he had almost doubled his Ansett portfolio to 7.71 million shares, gaining about 10 per cent of Ansett's capital. His Bell Group wanted a 20 per cent stake.

The play for Ansett continued throughout August, as TNT, Holmes à Court and the then Ampol Petroleum played their cards in what became a high-stakes game of bluff and gamble. Just as Holmes à Court showed his cards to seek a 20 per cent stake, Ampol countered with a different hand, revealing that it already had 3 per cent of ATI—probably 5 per cent if that day's purchases were counted. The share price jumped 17 cents to $1.62 in Sydney and peaked at $1.65 in Melbourne, with 3 million shares traded nationally on 7 August.

The Friends of Ansett, who included Sir Reginald and the AMP Society, entered the market on 8 August. They picked up 5.7 per cent of the company in a single trade of 4.06 million shares, paying $7.3 million, or what was then the very high price of $1.80 a share. The move scared Holmes à Court and he withdrew from the market as soon as Potter Partners, ATI's regular Melbourne broker, made the announcement.

Buyers turned over 7 million Ansett shares worth $12.2 million that day, but Holmes à Court's Bell Group had edged its holding to just over 12 per cent before the withdrawal. Ampol ended the day with about 6.5 per cent, but claimed that it was buying for investment purposes only. The following day bidding slowed, with Ansett friends buying 2 million shares at $1.70 in a single trade in Melbourne, and owning 8.1 per cent of the company after further on-market buys by the day's close.

The dogfight for control of Ansett became a four-group affair, with TNT, Holmes à Court, the Friends of Ansett and Ampol controlling a third of the capital. At the end of the first week of the 'war' nobody was prepared to name the likely victor; loyalty was in short measure and the market commentators refused to speculate on which groups might combine to take control of the organisation. Neither had the possibility been written off that Reg Ansett might return to the market and launch a counter-strike. Bell was repulsed for the moment, but Ampol was at that point continuing to build its stake, having secured over 15 per cent of ATI the previous week at a cost of $20 million.

Reg Ansett counterattacked after the weekend break to defend his then $150 million empire, launching through his Friends of ATI a $20-million bid for 20 per cent of Ampol. Just when some observers were prepared to predict a union of TNT and Ampol interests, the wily, old-dog tycoon had proved he was still good for one more fight. He landed heavy punches on Ampol chairman Ted Harris, securing his Ampol target of 20 per cent in three days of impressive trading.

At 5.15 p.m. on 15 August, ATI announced: 'Ansett Transport Industries Ltd has purchased in the course of the past three days slightly in excess of 20 million shares in Ampol Petroleum. This statement closely imitated another Ampol statement issued at 10.30 that morning: 'Mr A.E. Harris, of Ampol Petroleum Ltd, announced that Ampol had today reached its target of 20 per cent shareholding in Ansett Transport Industries.'

Reg Ansett had grabbed back the initiative in what was a titanic battle for control of the company, at that moment pulling off what many observers believed to be impossible. His lightning raid had routed Ampol and won him back control of the company. Not only had he gained a strategic foothold in the camp of an enemy, but on the same day it was apparent that he had secured the full support of Sir Peter Abeles and TNT. Four days later Reg Ansett and Ted Harris called a truce, announcing an agreement not to buy or trade in further shares of each other's companies.

But it was to be only a temporary ceasefire; a bigger and more decisive battle loomed on another front. Four weeks later Rupert Murdoch, the Melbourne-born international media magnate, came home from the United States to attempt to buy from Reg Ansett Melbourne's Channel 0. Rupert Murdoch was making his move two months after his News Limited group of companies had spent more than $17 million to win control of Channel 10 in Sydney. The first sign that a new player had entered the game for Ansett came on 21 September, when Sydney broker Wallace H. Smith bought 2.7 million shares at $1.82—2 cents above the peak of the previous month—on behalf of a then mystery buyer. The same mystery buyer continued to bid and within days had secured 3.2 million shares, representing 4.2 per cent of Ansett. All up, the stake had cost $5.8 million.

The buyer was ultimately identified as News Limited, which by 16 October was prepared to bid $2.25 for ATI scrip, almost $1 a share above the price at which Ansett stock had been quoted three months earlier. Business commentator Terry McCrann noted:

> At this level, well above any previous ATI price, the company is valued at a staggering $175 million. Mr Murdoch's takeover of Channel 10 was highly controversial. He moved into the market before getting approval from the Broadcasting Tribunal. He also seems prepared to risk another public brawl in winning approval to takeover Channel 0.

McCrann went on: 'He [Murdoch] can throw in his lot with Sir Reginald in return for Channel 0; he can buy out Mr Holmes à Court and join forces with Sir Peter Abeles, of TNT, to take control of ATI; or he can persuade Sir Reginald to give him a seat on the ATI board.'[3]

The Murdoch purchase brought to a head the need to resolve the future of ATI; that agreement was reached at a meeting at Cavan, the Murdoch-owned country property near the town of Yass, outside Canberra, on the weekend of 27 October. News Limited had made clear that its prime purpose was to acquire a television station: Rupert Murdoch was first and foremost a publisher of news and he told reporters at the outset that he did not intend to buy an airline.

Reg Ansett's chances of keeping control of the company he had started were not helped either by the release at the end of September of ATI's full-year accounts, in which the company bean counters had employed 'creative' accounting to keep the ASL losses— by then calculated at $19.3 million—out of the Profit and Loss account. While the loss could not be concealed, McCrann wrote on 29 September: 'Sir Reginald has managed to find some hidden fat in his planes to neutralise the impact of the ASL loss.'[4] The Ansett Board had, instead, carefully included the ASL write-off against a list of unappropriated profits, and had revalued some of their fleet of old planes. The accounts disclosed that the residual value of old DC-9/30 and Boeing 727/100 aircraft had been set at 33.3 per cent of their original values, not 20 per cent as were other aircraft. The following month the Victorian

> **Reg Ansett was pondering his future ... Having returned [from a shopping trip] with a pair of business shoes ... Lady Ansett told him that they would not be needed and he should have bought sports shoes instead.**

Supreme Court ordered ATI to employ Deborah Wardley.

Reg Ansett was pondering his future. He acknowledged as much in a quip to reporters about a shopping trip he had made for new shoes on his wife's orders. Having returned with a pair of business shoes, he said Lady Ansett told him that they would not be needed and he should have bought sports shoes instead. A few months earlier Lady Ansett had told the

Melbourne *Herald*: 'Of course I would like to see him retire. Any woman would like to see her husband retire. I would see more of him and I would like that, but I would never force the decision.'

An account of the events at Cavan emerged at a subsequent hearing of the Australian Broadcasting Control Board (ABCB) that ruled on the right of News Limited to seek the Channel 0, later Channel 10, licence. Business writers also outlined the event in reports that editors moved from the back pages of their publications into the news columns. Present were Robert Holmes à Court, Sir Peter Abeles and Rupert Murdoch. Reg Ansett did not attend.

The question was who would buy and who would sell their shares in ATI. Holmes à Court held 15 per cent and; Sir Peter Abeles, through TNT, 20 per cent. Rupert Murdoch held about 5 per cent and appeared to have some control over the sale of shares held by 'friends' at two London-based merchant banks, Morgan Grenfell and Hambros. Robert Holmes à Court wanted to buy. Of the three men, he had been hand-picked by Reg Ansett as his company heir, provided that he merged his Bell Group of companies with the transport interests of Ansett. Holmes à Court would later acknowledge to friends that Murdoch and Abeles had appeared to have discussed this possibility beforehand and were prepared to sell to the Western Australian.

Rupert Murdoch's motive was to gain control of the Ansett-owned Melbourne telecaster. It was a long-held dream that soured a year later after an adverse ABCB decision. At Cavan, Rupert Murdoch sought from Holmes à Court first right of refusal for the Melbourne channel from whoever ended up in control of the company. The price of the two stations was purported to be about $40 million—Ansett also owned TVQ-0 Brisbane. No commitment was made to sell.

The three met again at Ansett headquarters on Tuesday, 30 October. They decided that Holmes à Court would buy out Murdoch, Abeles and the 20 per cent held by Ampol, would merge the Bell group with ATI, and would become ATI's chief executive. But in the weeks that followed, Reg Ansett got cold feet, and spent the next month trying to back out of the arrangement. Holmes à Court held firm and would not compromise.

Rupert Murdoch, too, had become anxious and wanted the cash for the ATI shares he was selling. He had realised that his hopes of getting the Melbourne channel were slipping away by the day, and that the price Holmes à Court had set for both stations at the Cavan meeting was 'ridiculous'.

'It dawned on me,' he subsequently told the broadcasting tribunal, 'that this was not worth the gamble. If one was going to make any move into Melbourne it made much more sense to make at least one attempt for the Herald and Weekly Times.' The Herald then owned HSV Channel 7; and ownership of the country's biggest publishing group (at that time) would give Murdoch his two-state television network. That first News bid for the Herald group, which included the major newspapers in Adelaide, Brisbane, Hobart and Western Australia, was launched on 20 November. The publishing tycoon was portrayed as seeking to reclaim a denied inheritance: his father, Sir Keith Murdoch, had been a great and respected CEO of the Herald organisation, a man so loved by his staff that they later honoured his memory with a bronze wall plaque; it remains to this day in the foyer of the newspaper's Melbourne headquarters.

Murdoch went close to pulling off the Herald and Weekly Times (HWT) quarry. The Fairfax Group, then involved in a strategic alliance with the HWT organisation through a Melbourne–Sydney connection, was buying Herald shares at a peak of $5.52 but it eventually ran out of resources. When the Trade Practices Commission entered the fray Rupert Murdoch became nervous and pulled out of the action, dumping his new holding. Nevertheless, he was left with a still-handsome second prize: a $3-million increase in wealth from his share transactions.

Market rumours then began that Reg Ansett was not going to proceed with his agreement with Holmes à Court. Rupert Murdoch was playing tennis at the home of former tennis great John Newcombe on 29 November when the phone rang. He took a call from Holmes à Court who was about to decide whether to sell his then crucial 15 per cent stake in Ansett. Was Rupert interested? Holmes à Court rang off, saying he would call back in an hour.

Holmes à Court had been sparked into making the call by a news item on television: Reg Ansett appeared to have gone back on the deal he had done a month earlier. The news report indicated that ATI would not buy the Bell Group. Reg Ansett still wanted Holmes à Court to fill his chair, but as a paid employee. An agitated Holmes à Court went to see Reg Ansett in his Swanston Street office, refused a calming whisky and left soon after for his hotel room. From there he rang Murdoch back. 'The shares are yours,' he told him. 'How long have I got to decide?' the newspaper baron asked. 'The length of this call,' snapped Holmes à Court, still angry. Murdoch bought and the rest is history.

Reg Ansett fought a losing rear-guard action, refusing to register News Limited's share purchases and then complaining to the Fraser Government's Minister for Posts and Telecommunications, Tony Staley, and Attorney-General Peter Durack that News was in breach of the *Broadcasting and Television Act*. ATI argued that nobody could hold more than 5 per cent of more than two television stations. ATI already had two stations and News had TEN Sydney. Murdoch had previously spoken to ABCB chairman Bruce Gyngell and was assured there would be no problem as long as he sold one of the three stations within a reasonable time.

The Ansett–Murdoch war was fought out during the first two weeks of December. Sir Peter Abeles, who had been overseas during the last weeks of November, flew in from New York on 7 December and immediately bought Ampol's 1.75 per cent ATI holding. Later that day ATI director, and long-time friend of Reg Ansett, Sir Cecil Looker confronted TNT executives and asked whether the group was making a bid of its own. The following evening he telephoned Murdoch in London, and asked if he wanted to run ATI and become chief executive.

The announcement was made that Sir Peter Abeles would be joint chief executive with Rupert Murdoch. Reg Ansett saw the writing on the wall.

On 13 December ATI agreed for Ampol to sell its ATI shares to News, giving the Murdoch interests 47 per cent of the Ansett organisation. Rupert Murdoch would become CEO, Reg Ansett would keep face and remain a non-executive chairman and ATI would sell the Brisbane station. Under-takings were given to the Ansett Board that the company would not be dis-membered. It remained only for the Ts to be crossed and the Is dotted.

TNT bought out the minority shareholders and on 23 January 1980 an announcement was made that Sir Peter Abeles would be joint chief exec-utive with Rupert Murdoch. Reg Ansett saw the writing on the wall: he was no longer able to make the key decisions. He sold his Ansett shares at $2.50, and departed with $5 million and the Riverina station property Brewarrina in New South Wales. It was forty-four years since he had start-ed the company and a month before his seventy-first birthday.

Questions then arose about how these two very different men could work harmoniously—Abeles the chain-smoking, cigar-loving heavy drinker and Murdoch the diet-conscious, super-fit, deal-making dynamo. Abeles told reporter Philip Chubb of the *Age*:

> His [Murdoch's] drive is incredible. I have always thought that I was a hard driver, and all of a sudden I realise that I am relaxed compared to his incred-ible energy. Murdoch is one of the most polite and nicest persons to deal with. One never feels unpleasantness. Working with him is the most interesting human experience. It can only work out if there is no jealousy in either of us. And we are both busy men and, if anything, want the other to do more. One has to trust the other and we have trust.[5]

And work out it did. Sir Peter took responsibility for overseeing the road transport aspects of the Ansett group while Rupert, naturally, watched over matters concerning television. In the running of the airline, their roles were not so clearly defined.

5
NEW PLANES, NEW FUTURE

THE FIRST CHALLENGE for the Ansett twins—News Limited and TNT—was to make urgent decisions about the choice of a new fleet of wide-bodied aircraft to replace the carrier's aged Boeing 727 tri-jets and Douglas DC-9 twins. The distraction caused by the long takeover took its toll on the operating performance of the airline, prompting fears that TAA would attempt to lead the market by showcasing the latest in new aircraft. Decisions involving the purchase of a new fleet and other capital equipment vital to the economic well-being of the airline had been put on hold for the duration of the takeover. Reg Ansett had his future and that of the airline to consider, and would not be rushed into a decision to spend hundreds of millions of dollars simply because TAA had done so. A former Ansett director said the delay was:

typical Reg. He would go around and talk to all the top people and still have trouble making his mind up. But when he did, right or wrong, he wouldn't brook further argument. Pig-headed, stubborn, call it what you like. But my God, it was frustrating.[1]

Now that they were at the helm Rupert Murdoch and Sir Peter Abeles aggressively pursued deals with Boeing and European Airbus, paying large cash deposits to both companies to reserve spots on their production lines. Would they buy Boeing's untried and yet-to-be-flown 767 aircraft or the A300 that TAA had ordered from France? In the end, just like buying a car, the deal swung on a matter of which group could come up with the best finance package. Rupert Murdoch and Sir Peter Abeles settled on a $400 million deal to re-equip Ansett as an all-Boeing fleet, rejecting approaches by the European Airbus consortium to duplicate TAA's order for four A-300s. The pair chose the untested 767, still on the drawing boards at Boeing's Seattle factory. In 1981 the airline ordered a further twelve Boeing 737 mini-jets and four more of the popular workhorses of Australian aviation: the Boeing 727. The aircraft purchase was then the biggest in Australian aviation history and the fifth-largest ever placed with Boeing. It was financed at an 8 per cent interest rate by the US Government-owned Export Import (Exim) Bank. For a time the deal sparked a political scandal after US senators who were opposed to the then Carter administration charged that the US$290 million (A$400 million) funding was granted in exchange for President's re-election endorsement by the News Corporation-owned *New York Post*. News, TNT and

Graeme McMahon.

Ansett denied the alleged impropriety. As Sir Peter Abeles said in a letter sent to one of the senators, William Proxmire:

> We believe you have not been informed that this company has dealt with Exim Bank through many financing transactions over the past 15 years (as has its primary competitor, TAA), and it is exceedingly unfair you should suggest improper use of political influence was involved in negotiation of these loans.[2]

The bank's chairman, John L. More, Jnr, responded: 'I'm vehement in support of US exports and I'm vehement in support of President Carter, but I don't put the two of them together.'[3] A subsequent US Senate inquiry cleared the parties of any charge of political impropriety.

As Ansett's then assistant general manager of that era, Graeme McMahon, recalled:

> with the arrival of Abeles and Murdoch things took a diametrically different approach. Reg Ansett lived through the era when airlines were stringently regulated businesses. You were required to work and not rock the boat. It was a system designed by government for both companies to have 50 per cent of the market. When Abeles and Murdoch arrived, they were heading towards deregulation, because America was deregulated in 1979. Hardly a day went by that someone wasn't doing a comparison of how expensive air fares were in Australia compared with what people were paying overseas.[4]

McMahon, who in 1989 took the top job as general manager, soon realised that Abeles and his publisher partner were preparing early for deregulation. The first signs of a break in the nexus of the historic Two Airlines policy meant that Australia's two carriers, which had long flown the same planes and had the same timetables, would fly different planes and operate separate schedules. The three-year wait for the 767 meant that Ansett would compete against TAA's Airbus with small planes and on a more comprehensive flight schedule.

For the first time air travellers would have the opportunity to make a choice of aircraft. Under the then anachronistic agreement with the Federal Government, both airlines had to provide near-identical passenger capacities on each route. By using 737s to compete with TAA's much larger Airbus on the Melbourne–Sydney route, Ansett would fly three additional schedules. The move, seen by many as a vital first step in the journey towards airline deregulation, boosted competition and ended the parallel scheduling that was detested by the vast majority of regular travellers. But Ansett's use of the 737 against the larger capacity Airbus increased cost pressures for the privately owned airline and gave the government carrier an opportunity to build a war chest.

McMahon soon realised that Abeles and his publisher partner were preparing early for deregulation.

With new wide-bodied aircraft TAA was handed a unique opportunity to rout its traditional enemy in that sales war for travellers, but it was a one-off chance that TAA failed to exploit. While the Two Airlines policy afforded Ansett some protection, barring the government carrier from using fuel savings to undercut the cost of fares charged by its rival, TAA introduced the Airbus into service during an economic recession when the numbers of people making air bookings had dived. The Two Airlines policy also required that TAA match and maintain the same fare on all routes that it flew with Ansett—irrespective of the new economies achieved from a hi-tech aircraft and the savings on fuel. But the issue troubling Canberra in those first years of the 1980s was not about fuel and air fares; it was that Ansett would have thirty-two planes when its new planes were delivered, compared with TAA's twenty-two.

The bigger fleet enabled Ansett to take market share from TAA. By putting more aircraft in the air, Ansett was able to surround a TAA Airbus service with two Boeing 727s or three 737 flights. A Melbourne–Sydney TAA flight at 8.00 a.m. was surrounded by Ansett flights at 10 minutes to 8, 8 o'clock, and a third flight at 8.10 a.m. Ansett ran full page newspaper advertisements featuring clocks that emphasised its far more numerous flight schedules. Television commercials showed rooms filled with empty chairs, one bigger than the other that took much longer to empty. Within weeks the passenger share between Ansett and TAA changed, with Ansett having snared the advantage.

Ansett fired the first shots in the battle for bums on seats with a humble sandwich. The Abeles–Murdoch partnership wanted a bigger share of the market, and a sandwich designed by widely published cookery expert Margaret Fulton was giving the flying public the first ever chance to choose one airline in preference to the other for reasons other than carrier brand.

Sydney's *Sun Herald* compared the service that January[5] and reported little difference other than the Fulton sandwich, which the writer described as a microscopic slice of olive, four slices of cheese, one slice of cucumber, two bits of pickle, a tiny chunk of tomato, two oblong bits of ham and a lettuce leaf between two pieces of brown bread. TAA's tea break, by comparison, was said to have been a dull affair: a hot cup of tea and one cream biscuit or two sweet biscuits. TAA had been caught unawares by the Fulton Ansabox, a simple lunch pack—not all that different from the Saturday sandwich—which subsequent generations would not believe caused shock waves for Australia's multi-million dollar airline industry.

TAA counterattacked in March, offering half-price travel. Days later Ansett joined the first-ever discounts battle. TAA had been granted government approval to operate a 40 per cent year-round discount fare instead of the maximum 169-day advance purchase that had previously applied. Ansett hit back with a 40 per cent discount offer on seats booked 40 days in advance. When TAA announced a half-price ticket giveaway that May, with 2800 discounted seats, Rupert Murdoch told a Melbourne radio program: 'We are not going to match that.'[6] But he added: 'We are delighted by the response we have got from the public. We have given the public meals and drinks, better service, better morale and already from having only had 45 per cent of the business we have gone to 51 or 52 per cent. Two days last week we had over 53 per cent of the business … people respond to better service and a sense of competition.'

Ansett again hoisted its battle flag in the war for the skies on 24 November. On this occasion it was in the form of a photograph of a skimpy cabin curtain draped over the curves of a glamorous blonde model, Celeste Billings. Posing with her barely concealed 'essentials', Miss Billings stood barefoot in an aircraft aisle, her long legs naked, surrounded by seated male passengers. Alongside were the words: 'If the hostess was out of uniform would you know which airline you were flying with? … Until recently probably not.' The ad was blatantly sexist, and certainly riled feminist groups such as the Women's Electoral Lobby as well as certain members of the then Airline Hostesses Association (AHA).

Posing with her barely concealed 'essentials', Miss Billings stood barefoot in an aircraft aisle, her long legs naked, surrounded by seated male passengers.

However, as a one-off advertisement (it was never intended to appear on more than that one occasion) it stirred up sufficient comment to achieve its purpose. Ansett wanted customers to know that, from the following June, it would begin to offer Australians the right to make a choice of aircraft before flying. AHA vice-president Wendy Abbott took a more realistic view, ending any threat of likely industrial action with: 'We don't disagree with the intent of the advertisement because it was very well done, but we do disagree with the high stress on the sexist side of things.'

Ansett under Abeles and Murdoch had already won points as an employer cognisant of the status of women by lifting all bans on Deborah Wardley joining its force of pilots after her fifteen-month court battle. She flew for the first time with Ansett on 16 January 1980, within weeks of their takeover, as the first officer on a Fokker Friendship aircraft between Alice Springs, Darwin and Tennant Creek. Later in the year, yet another female, 28-year-old Felicity Bush from Sydney, who had logged 1600 hours in light aircraft, joined the flying staff of Ansett as the carrier's second female pilot. With Wardley, she would pave the way for others.

The marketing departments of both carriers had metaphorically loaded their guns and fixed their bayonets and were entrenched in all-out warfare. Ansett Airlines had nudged its way past TAA in the campaign for passengers. By 30 June 1982, Ansett had carried five million passengers for the year, compared with TAA's 4.8 million. TAA counterattacked by dumping its advertising agency of twenty-two years, giving the annual $5 million account to John Clemenger, and added some frills, such as ABC radio, to its flight programming. The solid competition had caused each carrier to emerge with a different character.

Apart from the new planes, old 727s had been repainted and had undergone million-dollar refits. Flight attendants ('hostess' or 'hostie' were politically incorrect terms and no longer acceptable) had gone back to school to learn new and more polite ways to treat their passengers. In Ansett's case, uniforms had been replaced with an Adele Weiss designer outfit.

By then, TAA had the Airbus, but Ansett wooed customers by persuading them that an Ansett ticket would take them to their destinations on a brand-new airline. General manager marketing Tom Dery was to argue that frequency was more important than bigger, wide-bodied aircraft, and Ansett had more flights, more often. As well as retraining cabin staff and spending more on food, Ansett sought to simplify on-ground passenger movements. The carrier pledged to be more consumer-orientated than product-driven. The strategy worked, helped in no short measure by the introduction in 1981 of the Golden Wings Club, which recruited 9000 fully paid memberships to its club-like serviced lounges in its first year.

Ansett had also embarked on a cunning strategy to build relationships with regional carriers, including Hazelton, Kendell, Skywest and

Boeing 767

Aeropelican, which would be bought out and become subsidiary operations. Like an ageing dowager, TAA donned a new face and tried to be competitive, withdrawing from uneconomic services to Newcastle, Albury, Devonport and Wynyard. Cargo was about the only area of the industry in which it could claim market dominance.

That July, TAA's problems caused the government to call in consultants to examine the feasibility of selling all or part of an airline shy of operating capital and in need of a huge cash injection to finance its employees' superannuation program, which had gone unfunded and had been ignored for too long by successive governments. By May 1983 TAA had reported its first loss in thirty-one years: $7.9 million. This was reduced to $494 000 after accounting for abnormal and extraordinary items arising from the sale of obsolete aircraft. The taxpayer would not get a dividend. By comparison, Ansett's profit for the same period amounted to $25.9 million, which had been boosted to $32.9 million by the sale of aged DC-9 aircraft, engines and spares.

Ansett's answer to the TAA Airbus—the 201-seat Boeing 767—touched down for the first time in Melbourne from the Seattle factory on 4 June 1983, and was followed the next month by three more aircraft, with a fourth entering Australian service that August. By then, both carriers were fighting for market share on a customer base that had slipped 10.5 per cent that year on the high-density air routes.[7]

Using the smaller 737-200 aircraft Ansett maintained market leadership, ferrying 1.064 million passengers during that March quarter, compared with the 1.043 million who travelled with TAA. Ansett carried 50.49 per cent of Australian domestic airline passengers; TAA claimed a 49.5 per cent market share. The battle of the skies extended to new routes between Hobart and Christchurch, and there was a short-lived attempt to win Asian tourists, with a flight that took a party of VIPs from Townsville to Singapore in a much-publicised trip in May 1980.

But just when hopes for Ansett to become Australia's second international airline began to rise, a Federal Cabinet row intervened to put a damper on things. Transport Minister Ralph Hunt was overwhelmingly defeated in his attempt to persuade the Cabinet on 9 May to give Ansett two overseas routes: Hobart to Christchurch and Townsville to Singapore. He was stopped by the Cabinet old guard, led by the protectionist Peter Nixon who argued persuasively that to give Ansett services into Singapore would cause problems on a delicately negotiated low-fares package between Australia and member countries of the Association of South East Asian Nations (ASEAN). Nixon had first-hand knowledge of the problem. It was the only policy he promoted to the Asian nations during his term as transport minister. He had barred ASEAN airlines from selling low fares on the lucrative London–Australia market, thus causing a major diplomatic rift. The Cabinet rebuff for Ralph Hunt forced him into making an abrupt about-face on his earlier support for launching Ansett as Australia's second international carrier.

Ansett had argued that its smaller Boeing 727 aircraft were better suited for the routes, and had staged the proving flight as part of a concerted push, in an election year, to force the Federal Government—with the support of the Queensland Government, also facing an election—to change the aviation policy. The carrier pursued its 727 strategy, claiming that it would be uneconomic of Qantas to divert parts of its all-747 fleet for short runs between the Australian mainland, Singapore and New Zealand.

There were other considerations, too: as an international airline, the value of Ansett and its potential profits would be considerably higher. Ansett's plan to fly a direct Townsville–Singapore link was also countered by arrangements that Qantas had made with Thai International to fly a DC-8 service from North Queensland, prompting accusations by Ansett's fiery policy director Bryan Grey that Qantas was giving away jobs that should go to Australians. Qantas then did a deal for a Singapore service that was to be run by TAA, should the government change its single over-seas airline policy. Grey, who founded the short-lived Compass Mark I airline in the early 1990s, fired off charge after charge against Qantas and TAA in what became a long-running war of words.

The *Australian*'s political correspondent Malcolm Colless revealed that the government was considering a proposal to provide Qantas with a subsidy of $1 million a year to fly the Hobart–Christchurch service. Rupert Murdoch told Prime Minister Fraser that Ansett would provide the service without a subsidy. An offer that seemed too good to refuse was turned down at the 8 May Cabinet meeting that decided Ansett must wait at least another year before its international ambitions could be fulfilled. But Ansett got its chance to fly offshore the following December when the government finally agreed to allow it to fly the HobartChristchurch link under a code-share arrangement with Qantas.

By early 1982 Sir Peter Abeles was running the airline on a day-to-day basis. He had told the *Australian* news-paper in April that cost and profit con-trols had been tightened since the takeover from Sir Reginald Ansett.

People have learned one thing: that we came not as wreckers but as builders.

It is correct that Rupert Murdoch is a distant partner in the airline. I am run-ning the airline, there is no question that Rupert runs the television stations, but all major decisions are made jointly. My first job was to settle down the organisation and build it back into a fighting team ... I believe that has been achieved. People have learned one thing: that we came not as wreckers but as builders.[8]

Sir Peter had been quick to learn where the profits were in the airline business. He was briefed by senior executives on how the business ran. They told him that he was operating an airline in a regulated environment where each carrier was locked into having 50 per cent of the market; no matter what occurred, each airline could expect to better its rival by no more than a few percentage points in the battle for customers. Senior staff of that era recalled Sir Peter's response: 'Well, if I am going to have half, I want the ones in navy blue suits.' He didn't want the tourists who were buying the discount fares. Sir Peter was determined to fill his planes with business passengers who would pay full fare.

ATI had prospered and by September 1983 the Ansett twins were beginning to reap rewards that would add black ink to the bottom-line accounts of News/TNT. Their biggest reward came after $150 million was gained from asset sales.

With the new Boeing fleet delivered and aircraft loans fully drawn, Ansett had been restructured and a decision was made to distribute retained earnings. TNT/News and a handful of minor shareholders would receive a $1.95 a share special dividend that was funded from the $13.2 million obtained from the sale of Channel 10 Melbourne to the Murdoch-controlled News Limited. The 50 per cent stake in the Avis car rental group had also been sold, along with shares the organisation had in Ampol Petroleum and the Cooper Basin resources group, Santos Ltd. ATI contributed almost a quarter of the $87 million profit posted by News in 1983–84, having revealed a net profit of $44.2 million. Ansett had generated earnings of almost $100 million each for the News/TNT partners, rewarding them well for buying the company.

6
THE NOAH'S ARK FLEET

THE 1985 PARIS Air Show would prove a watershed in the fortunes of the Ansett group of companies and the economies of operating the airline. Sir Peter Abeles returned from the event having spent $1 billion on seventeen A320 airliners from Airbus. With an all-Boeing fleet less than five years old, Ansett, through Abeles, was building what a subsequent CEO would describe as a Noah's Ark fleet and a huge headache for management. Spare parts, engines and tooling would all have to be duplicated to maintain the various makes of aircraft. As one company finance chief would lament years later: 'pilots and maintenance staff had to be certified on each set of aircraft. And once someone got a certificate they always got a pay rise.'

The orders that Abeles brought home from that trip to the French capital included an additional seven F50 Fokker turbo-prop aircraft, a refinement on the company's Friendships that had done sterling work servicing outback ports and Tasmania during the 1960s and early 70s. The airline was spending a total of $280 million on twenty-two aeroplanes. Abeles told friends that he would use some of the A320s on Australian air routes but others would go into an organisation that the TNT–News partnership was starting with the purpose of leasing aircraft and aviation expertise to airlines in other countries. The seven additional F50s would be delivered directly to the TNT–News Corp Seattle-based subsidiary Corsair for leasing to other airlines. Abeles admitted that no plans had been made to integrate the A320s into the Australian fleet, but, he told local aviation writers travelling with the Ansett party, 'we will use them to best advantage'.

Sir Peter Abeles' spending on myriad aircraft types reflected the type of airline Ansett was in those days before deregulation. The carrier had become the nation's second major airline by a series of takeovers; small regional rivals were folded into the Ansett conglomerate, each flying different types of aircraft that best suited their requirements. MacRobertson Miller, later to become Ansett Western Australia had flown F28, 50 seat jets, switching later to the 76-seat BAe 146. Ansett Airlines of New South Wales flew F27s and then F50s. When the company was brought together all those aircraft types were brought into the single fleet. Similarly TAA, in the 1970s and early 80s, had A300s, 727s, DC9s, 737s and F27 aircraft. TAA also operated BAe 146 aircraft, through a contract arrangement with National Jet. TAA also bought Southern Airlines with Dash 8 aircraft. But come deregulation both Ansett and Australian Airlines needed to rationalise costs and needed aircraft with common cockpits, as well as a full range of engines and other spares that could be used across their fleets. This rationalisation didn't happen at Ansett.

Seventeen years later Ansett executives continued to rue Sir Peter Abeles' purchases, not only in aircraft purchases but in lavish spending on other Ansett properties, such as a multi-million dollar revamp of Hayman Island, which Reg Ansett had bought in the late 1940s. In the heady 1980s, Sir Peter Abeles decided Australia needed a large, superior hotel in the tropics and bought a marble mine at Chillagoe in North Queensland to ensure that there would be no shortage of prestigious rock for the project. Pink marble for the hotel's main foyer was imported from Italy but this was not to be a hotel where the marble stopped at the foyer: it stretched to the sea. Abeles spent $300 million on redeveloping Hayman Island, making it the only Australian resort hotel to be classed by the 'Leading Hotels of the World' organisation as a true five-star resort. It was sold off in the late 1990s for less than a third of that amount.

Born Emil Herbert Peter Abeles in Vienna on 25 April 1924, the former migrant who became an Australian transport and media baron had been a victim of wartime Nazi persecution and came to Australia in the mid-1950s. With fellow new arrival George Rockey, he bought a truck on hire purchase ... and prospered.

By 1967 their group Alltrans had merged with Thomas Nationwide Transport (TNT) and was operating five hundred trucks. As a result of that union, Abeles guided TNT's expansion into New Zealand, Canada, Africa, Britain, Brazil and the United States in the 1970s. His personal wealth grew, partly through a property portfolio in partnership with Sir Arthur George. Abeles' closest colleague and confidant at TNT was Fred Millar, who became chairman of Abeles' own personal company.

The close business association with Rupert Murdoch resulted from the 1979 Ansett takeover, when News Limited and TNT gained control of the airline and its portfolio of diversified assets. Many of his friends in the 1970s were journalists, media proprietors and media managers, but he was known for friendships with politicians and was knighted by the New South Wales Askin Government in 1972. Later, when Sir Robert Askin retired as premier, he joined Abeles' TNT board of directors. A 1970s meeting over waterfront issues with Bob Hawke, who was then president of the ACTU, cemented a friendship between the two but the Abeles connection was something of a mixed blessing for Hawke. After the end of the 1989 domestic pilots' dispute, Abeles remarked: 'people said I was a union breaker'; and when he died on 25 June 1999, Fairfax newspapers reported:

> Many Labor voters saw the relationship [with Hawke] as unfortunate. This perception was heightened when in the early 1980s Abeles was accused—during a US court hearing—of having bribed a Mafia figure to ensure peace for TNT on the waterfront. A TNT executive denied the charge. Supporters of Sir Peter later pointed out that anyone wanting to engage in the transport business in the US had to deal with the Teamsters Union and that this union had close links with the Mafia. In 1997, Sir Peter said: 'You can't run a road company in America without having a brush with the Mafia ... we paid the Mafia officially.'[1]

Sir Peter's reign over what became his Ansett fiefdom eventually ended in 1992, when he was forced out as chief executive of TNT and left virtually powerless as deputy chairman. On the fateful afternoon of 30 August 1993, he led a walkout by five TNT directors amid a board split over the company's third yearly loss of more than $200 million. A group of directors wanted to raise more money to buy time to cut the losses and others backed Abeles, who wanted to float its European business and separate the profitable operations from the loss-makers. Abeles' grip had already been weakened when he was out-manoeuvred by TNT's finance director, David Mortimer, who took his place as chief executive a few months earlier. The board split was Sir Peter Abeles' final attempt to reassert his influence. He lost. His long-time friend and TNT chairman Fred Millar backed the Mortimer plan to raise fresh debt. Abeles never forgave him.

The walkout would also result in the loss of his fiefdom at Ansett. He had been protected in his post as joint chairman and managing director because of TNT's 50 per cent shareholding but his loss of support at TNT and his replacement by David Mortimer on the Ansett board gave the opponents of his mismatched fleet acquisition program a means for removing him.

A year later, in 1994, Abeles' ten-year term as a director on Australia's Reserve Bank board also ended. After Ansett his main business interest had been Abakus Aircraft & Aviation Specialists, which he ran with former TNT colleague Paul Keen. The company dealt in aircraft leasing and represented British Aerospace in Australia.

A successor at Ansett, Rod Eddington,[2] publicly acknowledged Abeles' role with the company, noting that Sir Peter had made a significant contribution through his 'strong personal commitment to, and insistence on, customer service excellence' and adding that his predecessor had also led the company's thinking on the need to embrace domestic airline deregulation during the late 1980s. Eddington, who was later openly critical of Abeles' fleet purchases, carefully avoided any comment about the myriad operational problems caused by the mismatched aircraft purchases during the Abeles era. James Strong, one-time Qantas chief executive and managing director, had fond memories of his former rival:

> I found him to be an astute, charming and engaging person who was a pleasure to know and deal with. Peter was a larger than life figure and a great personality.[3]

A common story told by those who once occupied the seventeenth-floor mahogany row offices in the Melbourne head offices of Ansett was that Abeles would attend the air show in Paris, sip the offered champagne in the hospitality tents and buy aeroplanes. Nobody would know what he had done until he got back when he would tell someone: 'By the way, we're now flying a new brand of aeroplane.' Among those purchases was the British Aerospace 146, a high-winged four-engine jet built in the United Kingdom that had a troubled life with Ansett Western Australia. Australian pilots regarded the planes as real dogs, citing their propensity to emit fumes into cabin areas, their lack of ceiling and their slow performance. One expert quipped: 'They had only four engines because BAe couldn't fit eight on the bastards.' On one of his overseas visits Sir Peter Abeles stunned the aviation industry by placing orders and lodging options for seventy-two of these aircraft—the factory's entire 146 production for five years and a deal costed at $2.1 billion. A long-term Ansett executive remembers Sir Peter's defence: '"I got a great deal" was his only reply.'[4]

Former Ansett operations staff acknowledge that, regardless of any deals Abeles snared, his acquisitions were worthless because fleet needs and aircraft evaluation did not occur beforehand. They charge that Abeles ignored the fundamental principle of planned acquisition and careful integration of new aircraft.

By the late 1990s passengers travelling on the airline's main east-coast routes might fly in a 737, a 767 or an A320. But if any one of these aircraft broke down and the replacement was another make, the crew would not be able to fly the replacement on the next leg of the service because they were certified only for the grounded aircraft. Huge expenses would be incurred by chartering a business jet to rush a qualified crew to the airport in question. While the problem might have gone unforeseen by an airline chief liberally wining and dining in Paris, it was an unnecessary complication that festered in the accounts of the company. 'There was too much complexity,' Ansett's former chief of airline operations Captain Trevor Jensen said. 'We had a range of 737s, up to twenty A320s and about eleven 767s.'[5]

Boeing 767.

But in 1985 Abeles had a bold plan to create a whole new market for new aircraft and create profits as a middleman financier. Out of that arrangement emerged Ansett Worldwide Aviation Services. AWAS was 50 per cent owned by the News Corp subsidiary Twentieth-Century Fox and 50 per cent by Alltransair Nevada Inc., a subsidiary of TNT Ltd (USA). In just over two years AWAS had become one of the toughest competitors in international aircraft leasing. By 1989 it had up to 150 aircraft on lease or on order from factories, ranging from the fifty-seat Canadair Regional Jet to a 260-seat Airbus A 300-600—in other words, more aircraft than Ansett then flew in Australia on routes which it had been allowed to operate as a newly arrived domestic carrier in New Zealand, combined with the fleet used by its then subsidiary East–West Airlines. AWAS customers would include America's TWA, France's UTA, British Midland and Brazil's Varig. In the 1990s AWAS was shooting for big profits, with a drive to win entry into new markets that had begun to open in eastern Europe. But the oper-ation eventually struck hard times after a downturn in world aviation prompted the cancellation of new aircraft orders. AWAS was among a string of non-core assets that were later disposed of in a restructure of the carrier and it was acquired in 2000 by the merchant banker Morgan Stanley.

For a long time AWAS had proven itself an invaluable associate of its Australian cousin. AWAS pumped into Ansett Airlines $100 million in 1991, followed by a further $100 million to help the Australian carrier ride out an economic recession that caused cutbacks in domestic business and holiday travel in 1992. The fortunes of the carrier—along with rival TAA, which by then had been renamed Australian Airlines—had nose-dived in the early 1990s as a result of a six-month-long pilots' strike and the added complication of new competition from the popular start-up carrier Compass Mark I (which itself went broke and almost took Ansett to the wall in a price war that introduced air travel as an affordable option to the 'mum and dad' traveller).

It was, however, the pilots' strike that provided real proof at the time of the Ansett group's strengths in the aviation industry. Sir Peter Abeles was able to rely on support from Prime Minister Bob Hawke, a friend of long standing. Hawke—like one Labor leader before him, who sent troops into the mines to break a protracted coal strike—co-opted the RAAF to help run the nation's air services and ferry the stranded. Ben Chifley incurred the disfavour of Labor's stalwarts for using the army against unionists, but when Hawke ordered RAAF Hercules and planes from the VIP fleet to work as a co-opted airline, there was scarce community support for the already well-paid pilots who had walked out and later resigned their jobs over their disputed claim for a 29-per-cent pay rise.

Whereas Australian Airlines, the government-owned domestic carrier, was forced to rely on a handful of management pilots and new recruits hired from overseas as strike breakers, Ansett was able to call on international air connections to become airborne again. Ansett leased two Boeing 737-300s from the United States—with pilots from America West, of which it owned twenty per cent and was the major shareholder. What few people knew was that these planes were owned by Ansett Worldwide Aviation Services. One of the best kept secrets of the period was that Ansett Australia sent aircraft to America West for the duration of the strike which were used for pilot training. The deal with America West gave Ansett an edge against the opposition, and gave them pilots when they were a commodity in short supply worldwide. America West sent planes and flight crews to Australia. When the strike ended, 24 foreign pilots were flying for Ansett. From Europe, Sir Peter had also drawn on the resources of his native Hungary; the country's national airline Air Malev provided crews to fly BAe 146s in Western Australia.

At home Ansett called on help from affiliated regional carriers, Kendell Airlines among them, which were able to continue skeleton services on some primary routes. Even Australian Airlines found itself with a Boeing 737-300 leased by AWAS to the French charter group Aeromaritime.

The pilots' strike, lasting from late July 1990 to March the following year, became a stand-off between Peter Abeles and the head of the Australian Federation of Air Pilots Brian McCarthy. The mistake the pilots made was to resign their jobs in a mistimed strike tactic. Had they remained on strike, and not quit, it is doubtful that Ansett would have been able to maintain both the support of the government and the rest of the trade union movement. It was a strike the pilots could not have won after this move. Both the Federal Government and Sir Peter Abeles had pledged to peg prices and incomes according to an accord agreed to at an earlier business, union and government summit in Canberra. As the strike raged it became clear that it was a matter of the pilots versus Sir Peter Abeles and his close friend, the leader of the government. Abeles was able to persuade the government that it should compensate the airlines for the wages of staff stood down and left idle for the duration of the stoppage.

In the year leading up to the pilots' strike Ansett had encountered a series of damaging industrial problems over the introduction of the A-320 Airbus, with flight attendants first demanding an extra crew member in the cabin. Pilots, long used to having flight engineers watching an extra switch panel, had objected to two-man flight crews in what was a whole new generation aircraft. Ansett then lost direction, enabling Australian Airlines to snare an advantage, albeit a temporary one until the initiative of the private-enterprise carrier came to the fore when the pilots withdrew their labour and attempted a total shutdown of services.

Former general manager Graeme McMahon took Ansett through the period of new competition created by the start-up carriers Compass I and Compass II and later negotiated arrangements with the Hawke

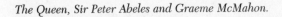

The Queen, Sir Peter Abeles and Graeme McMahon.

Government during the pilots' pay strike. 'At the end of Compass Mark I,' he later said, 'finances were pretty shaky. But it was more the pilots' strike that caused problems for the airline.'

The pilots' dispute cost the company a couple of hundred million dollars and really depleted the finances. It got in the way of us getting ready for deregulation. The United States deregulated in 1979, and like ourselves, they had a heavily regulated market with a set number of carriers licensed to fly across state borders. We had two and they set the pace when they deregulated and we went over and studied what happened. We were putting a lot of things in place to get ready for deregulation when the pilots' dispute blew up and that put us back on our heels considerably.

From the day they went on strike we started to negotiate for the RAAF to be able to carry some people and for restrictions to be lifted on international airlines carrying domestic traffic. That got people moving and then we started to bring in the overseas aircraft to try to give us some lift until we could get some pilots of our own back in the sky.

The biggest problem was that the pilots weren't licensed to fly in this country. We had to get them endorsed to fly in the Australian environment and that proved to be enormously difficult. An America West 737 with its crew would first have to fly with an Australian-approved pilot doing a proving flight over each route before they were allowed to fly the same route with passengers.

There were no Australian pilots to do the proving flights, so really there was just a huge amount of work to negotiate with the government to find ways and means around it. We got there. It took us a while, but we got there.[6]

Many smaller communities lost their air links. Alice Springs did not have a regular airline service from the time the strike started. The first flight to the Outback town came after 111 days. Tourism disappeared from the region. At Cairns, the new high rise Hotel International had to close and most of the traders operating from shops in an arcade beneath were broke.

The airlines recovered and by the time Graeme McMahon retired in 1996, Ansett was making good profits. Although the company had

Commemoration of first flight in 60th anniversary celebrations.

bounced back, McMahon believes that many smaller communities have not recovered from the decision to deregulate the airlines.

The long-standing Two Airlines policy also carried obligations for the airlines to fly to places like Alice Springs, Rockhampton and Mackay and Launceston. But when deregulation came about that obligation disappeared and service frequencies to these ports dropped. In some cases, this was followed up by cutting back the size of the aeroplane and still later, replacing what had been a mainline Ansett service with a Kendell or Hazelton regional service. Communities lost their pure jet connections; these were variously replaced with propeller-driven aircraft, thus downgrading services. At the time of the pilots' strike Ansett scrapped its services to Tasmania and sold off its Fokker 50 fleet.

'That's why today you're seeing places such as Rockhampton and Launceston and so forth not being properly served by the airlines,' says Graeme McMahon.

People will look back at the history of a state like Tasmania. They will see that Launceston and Hobart got equal service from Ansett and Australian under the Two Airlines policy. But Launceston suffers because the airlines are no longer obligated to fly there with big equipment.

McMahon was prepared to bet that Hobart would go ahead economically despite Launceston having the better airport and the city's closer proximity to Melbourne. Concluded McMahon: 'The pilots' strike might have done a lot of damage, but nobody can doubt the fact that deregulation exacerbated a whole range of issues.'[7]

BATTLING THE ODDS

WHEN AIRLINES WERE deregulated in
Australia at the beginning of the 1990s Ansett
was ill-equipped for a prolonged fares war
against Australian Airlines and rival start-up carrier Compass. Ansett was already burdened with
a $2 billion debt and the mismatched fleet that

cost a king's ransom to operate. The Ansett strategy at the time, according to senior executives, was to king-hit Compass with discounting blows that would knock holes in the new carrier's finances while Australian Airlines sat back as a spectator.

The carrier was also hamstrung by the refusal of the unions to negotiate more flexible agreements. The unions refused to allow the airlines to use part-time and casual staff or have permanent staff working split shifts. The best example was the Ansett operation at Mount Isa, where the airline's resident staff would service the one jet flight a day into the town. They had to be paid for eight hours, irrespective of how little time they spent servicing the incoming or outgoing aircraft. When Compass Airlines launched a single daily service into Cairns, the start-up carrier was permitted by the unions to employ part-time workers. Compass won a dispensation from the unions because it was creating new jobs. The result was that Ansett shut down its operations at Mount Isa and Ansett jobs were lost.

With two A-300 Airbuses leased from Britain's Monarch Airlines, Compass took to the skies on 1 December 1990. Within months the Compass fleet had grown to five as Melbourne and Sydney 'battlers' grabbed the opportunity for a first-time visit to Perth for $99 or $198 return. Cheeky ploys, such as offering two tickets for one, followed. Meanwhile, Compass boss Bryan Grey watched his dream collapse in a cash flow nosedive.

Ansett, too, was on its knees at this time. It is said to have had only weeks to run when Compass folded at the end of a twelve-month ticket price honeymoon, giving it back much-needed customers. Compass Mark II was launched soon afterwards but the goodwill that Grey had earlier generated could save neither its namesake nor its founder Douglas Reid, who was found guilty of fraud and jailed. Ansett Airlines lost $50 million in that first year of deregulation.

While Compass Mark I and Mark II came and went, and airfares hiked back to budget-breaking prices, some benefits lasted. Loyalty programs and cut-price holiday tickets evolved, whereby fare and accommodation packages could be bought for not much more than the cost of a single airfare in the dark days of market regulation. Airline travel no longer meant putting up with planes taking off moments apart and a situation in which only the cabin service, aircraft livery and the flight attendants' uniforms were different.

Two months before Compass Mark I began flying, Ansett and Australian first cut their fares to counter the harsh impact of a recessionary economy. Other shake-ups followed on sectors not flown by Compass. When Australian Airlines took off with flights to Yulara in Central Australia, Ansett matched its competitor by upgrading the sector using a bigger aircraft, Boeing 737. In a chessboard-like series of moves, other services were withdrawn from different regions of the Northern Territory. When Australian pushed into Queensland's Sunshine Coast, Ansett checked the opposition by using a low-cost feeder operation run by sister carrier East–West Airlines.

The game plays that emerged in that first year of deregulation were not so much about where planes went but how they got there. Both carriers moved their bigger planes off the low-capacity routes and introduced more economical, smaller aircraft. Ansett achieved the route flexibility it needed by revamping the operational sphere of NSW-based Ansett Express into a whole east-coast-of-Australia Fokker operation. Other initiatives saw Australian Airlines buying the Queensland regional carrier Sunstate. Adelaide-based National Jet wet-leased (rented on commercial terms) aircraft and crews to Australian and created Australian Airlink, which serviced both major towns and isolated ports across the Northern Territory and parts of Queensland.

In 1982 Ansett acquired the regional carrier Kendell for $1.5 million. It was repaid handsomely by 1996 with a profit upwards of $10 to $11 million per year. 'A really nice little business until it came under Air NZ management,' was how it was confidentially described by one former executive. In the financial year 2000–2001, Kendell lost in excess of $70 million.

But any chance Ansett had of long-term survival was stacked against it by the Keating Government when the operations of the two government carriers, Australian and Qantas, were merged in 1992. The Australian domestic airline market was no longer a battleground between two equal-

Ken Cowley, Sir Peter Abeles and then Prime Minister Paul Keating.

sized players. Heavyweight Qantas had entered the ring against the welterweight Ansett. Coupled to the size difference, the government rigged the odds in favour of Qantas by forgiving debts totalling $700 million. These actions mirrored the similar complaints made by Ansett to the Gorton Government in the 1960s; namely, that the Federal Government continued to favour its own carrier and create an uneven playing field. The 1992 budget-eve government decision meant that the merged Qantas international-domestic operation had been given a helping hand by government to become the dominant Australian airline.

As often happens with mergers, the new Qantas lost sight of the main game while its management struggled to sort the job cuts and myriad transfers. While well-versed about running an airline in the highly charged and competitive atmosphere of the international market, the Qantas team made mistakes as it tried to come to terms with the short-cycle operations of a major domestic carrier. Ansett reaped temporary profits, but these were nipped in the bud once Qantas got its act together and became a formidable opponent. After that, things were always going to be tough for Ansett.

Ansett reported a $59.5 million profit in 1992–93—a $150 million turnaround from the $91 million loss of the previous year. Ken Cowley, Australian chief of News Limited at the time, actively involved himself in day-to-day airline operations, succeeding Rupert Murdoch in July 1992 as joint chairman with Peter Abeles. Three months afterwards, Abeles was gone and News and Cowley had total charge of the airline. The Melbourne *Age* reported on 11 September 1993: 'Industry analysts say tough management by the executive chairman, Ken Cowley, has driven the company back into the black.' While the figures may well have been influenced in no short measure by the effects of the changes at Qantas, the newspaper quoted one analyst: 'Ansett was a troubled airline for so long it had forgotten what upside was. But when News put Ken Cowley in charge even they were surprised how successful he was.'

A closer analysis of passenger statistics shows that Ansett gradually lost its 50-per-cent plus market share while Qantas expanded at a far greater rate the domestic business formerly run by Australian. According to annual report figures, Qantas achieved 45 per cent growth in domestic passenger numbers in the six years from 1993 while Ansett had managed only 16 per cent. Worse still for Ansett, passenger growth remained static for the last three years of the 1990s and slumped alarmingly to around 38 per cent after public confidence was undermined when its 767s were temporarily grounded at Christmas 2000 and again the following Easter. Qantas domestic also enjoyed more practical benefits from the new arrangement by being able to co-opt additional capacity from planes that were surplus to international fleet requirements. Ansett managers, meanwhile, would spend frenzied hours rearranging flight schedules whenever they were required to bring additional or replacement aircraft into service.

While official passenger figures for the 1993 June quarter[2] showed that Ansett retained a significant edge over Qantas, the turning point in the battle had arrived. Geoff Dixon, the wily marketing whiz who would later chart himself an enviable career at Qantas, was then marketing director of Ansett. Formerly with Australian, and having given that airline its 'You should see us now' marketing campaign, he had switched companies and was luring travellers to Ansett with the mystical sounds of the Irish popular singer Enya. (Later, at Qantas, he would capture the imagination of world travellers with a promotion featuring the Peter Allen hit 'I Still Call Australia Home' being sung by young multicultural choristers in sought-after overseas travel spots.)

The financial market maintained that a well-handled Ansett could become a consistent profit earner. Tourism was growing, the demise of Compass had helped, load factors had improved and yields were getting better. Cowley and his successor Rod Eddington, a former Western Australian and one-time Rhodes scholar whom News recruited from Hong Kong's Cathay Pacific Airways, disposed of non-core assets, beginning with the removals business Ansett Wridgways. Between 1999 and 2000 almost $350 million was raised from the sale of assets that included the door-to-door delivery business Ansett Air Freight, Hayman Island, Pacific Aviation, Whitsunday Connections, Inflight Kitchens, and shares in Diners Club and travel firms Carlson Wagonlit Australia and Europe's Equant NV. Also sold were Ansett's substantial interest in the insurance firm, Transport Industries Insurance Co. as well as interests in New Zealand's Rex Aviation, Ansett New Zealand and ANEX Ltd (formerly Ansett Air Freight). The pair rebuilt the Ansett balance sheet as their first priority. Aircraft fleet changes could occur only when the airline operation had been stabilised. The view was that the 'Noah's Ark' fleet might be costly to operate but at that time it was safe, serviceable and still offered passengers a comfortable journey.

To keep pace with Qantas, $1.6 billion was spent on upgrading the terminals at Sydney's Kingsford Smith Airport and Melbourne Airport, on replacing computer systems to track earnings per passenger kilometre, and on leasing a mix of new Boeing 767 and Airbus A320 aircraft for the main routes. The acquisitions increased the Ansett fleet to 12 widebodied 767s supported by 22 Boeing 737s and 19 Airbus A320s. A further $1.6 billion was committed to reducing debt.

Speculation that News was keen to sell surfaced after Rupert Murdoch advised shareholders in the 1991 annual report: 'Whilst it [Ansett] seems an unlikely asset for our company ... we have no alternative but to stay with it and support its management through these temporary difficulties until the climate changes.' Gossips speculated that News would sell the carrier into a public float, prompting suggestions that this could happen after a partial sale to a major carrier, such as Japan's All Nippon Airways (ANA).

A secret suitor did exist and it was none other than British Airways. It has emerged that, before acquiring its 25-per-cent stake in Qantas, BA expressed strong interest during the early 1990s in talks held in London between the CEO of the British carrier and two senior Ansett executives. It is known that these 1992 discussions came undone when Sir Peter Abeles failed to respond to further approaches from the British carrier.

News remained keen to rebuild and expand its investment and launched a new chapter in Australian aviation history at 6.25 p.m. on 11 September 1993, when a 767 aircraft, registered AN 219, cleared the Sydney Airport runway en route to Bali. Ansett could at last claim status as an international airline, achieving what previous governments, through the Two Airlines policy, had too long denied its founder. Bali was among a string of routes—including Malaysia, Hong Kong, Japan and Singapore, Taiwan, South Korea and Thailand—that Ansett International would service. Said former general manager Graeme McMahon: 'We took the view right at the very beginning that we should start quietly.'[3] Ansett was primarily a domestic operation and Bali flights were a chance to test the international market. The first flights were made at weekends by planes drawn from the domestic fleet because at that time they normally stood idle.

> At 6.25 p.m. on 11 September 1993, when a 767 aircraft, registered AN 219, cleared the Sydney Airport runway en route to Bali, Ansett could at last claim status as an international airline

Questions were being asked about planned fleet expansion. Would Ansett International become an all-747 carrier? Where would the debt-ridden group get funds to buy new aircraft? McMahon gave little away. 'We haven't decided what type of aircraft we need and we haven't decided whether we will buy, lease or hire,'[4] he said.

These questions were answered on 24 August 1994 when Ansett leased from Singapore Airlines a 747B-300 series aircraft. Repainted in Ansett livery and given Australian registration VH-INH, the ten-year-old plane was reborn as the Ansett *Spaceship* and would fly between Sydney and the Japanese port of Osaka. A second aircraft was acquired soon after-wards, and both were later upgraded with 747-400 series fitted with seat-mounted video screens to attract further custom.

But that first 747 and Ansett's respected reputation for aviation safety almost came to grief two months later, on 19 October, with a nose wheel failure on the runway of Kingsford Smith Airport, at Sydney's Mascot. The airline, as well as officers from the Civil Aviation Safety Authority (CASA), were censured subsequently by the Bureau of Air Safety Investigation (BASI). In its investigation of Ansett, BASI uncovered crew training flaws for the new overseas operation. Having chided some of the crew, the safe-ty agency then admonished the carrier. 'A review of events associated with the introduction of the B747 indicated that organisational factors involv-ing Ansett and the Civil Aviation Safety Authority led to a situation where there was increased potential for an accident of this nature to occur,'[5] the agency reported. These factors included deficiencies in the procedure for introducing new aircraft into service. Reporting that improved manuals and training were needed, BASI further noted that some regulatory requirements were neither observed nor enforced.

The jumbo had taken off at 10.07 a.m. with 275 passengers. An hour into the flight, when the plane was over south-east Queensland, an oil leak was discovered in the number one engine, prompting the pilot to dump fuel and return to Sydney. Everything continued normally until the landing gear was selected and a warning horn sounded. The BASI report stated:

> The flight crew unsuccessfully attempted to establish the reason for the warn-ing. Believing the gear to be down, the crew elected to complete the landing, with the result that the aircraft was landed with the nose wheel retracted. There was no fire and the pilot in command decided not to initiate an emer-gency evacuation.[6]

The damage bill for that 810-metre slide down that Mascot runway exceeded $3 million.

After the accident Captain Trevor Jensen was recruited from Qantas to take charge of training and operations. On coming aboard he remarked to friends: 'They had a hotch potch of manuals ... What I had was a big aero club. They did, however, have an excellent check and training manual which was typical of an aero club.' After five years under his stewardship, Ansett training was recognised as world's best practice.

Trevor Jensen

In the beginning, Jensen's problems were compounded by union agreements that required some 767s to be flown by three crew—the pilot, a co-pilot and a flight engineer whose job had been rendered obsolete by technological advances. Peter Abeles had promised the flight engineers jobs for life irrespective of what happened with automated flight and computer technology. A determined Jensen brought the issue to a head by ordering the cables to the engineer's panel cut and for the planes to be converted to two-crew systems. Jensen would argue in the Arbitration Commission that Qantas was able to fly without engineers while an Ansett 767 taking off beside it would have an engineer aboard. He told the commission: 'We had the extra cost of a man who was getting a hundred thousand dollars a year for sitting on the flight deck and adding no value to the operation.' Guaranteed overtime granted to aircraft loaders was a further management headache, lifting their pay in some cases to $90 000 a year with upwards of twenty to twenty-five hours a week additional work and overtime.

News–TNT was by 1995 looking for a buyer. The most likely suitors included ANA of Japan, a Singapore Airlines partnership that promised a much-needed capital injection of $300 million, and a deal with Air New Zealand that the Keating Government had a year before promoted under an 'open skies' accord with its opposite number in Wellington. Keating encouraged Air NZ to buy into Ansett rather than subvert the accord by cherry-picking custom from both Australian carriers. A key objective of the accord was to consolidate Australasia's airlines into two groupings, but

Former Air NZ CEO, Jim McCrae, and Sir Selwyn Cushing.

it was up to the individual companies to arrange their marriages. Air NZ refused to commit to any equity alliance being pushed by Canberra and Australian Transport Minister Laurie Brereton hit back by threatening to cut off landing rights to the Kiwis.

The issue was not forgotten across the Tasman. When Ansett crashed eight years later, acting Air NZ chairman Jim Farmer claimed the Australian Government had forced Air NZ to buy its first 50 per cent stake by reneging on the 'open skies' policy. He argued that the move disrupted an Air NZ plan to launch its own low-cost domestic airline as a third carrier in Australia. In a sworn affidavit later tabled in the Australian Federal Court, Farmer said: 'At the eleventh hour the Australian Government blocked that proposal after Qantas had reportedly urged it to do so.' Farmer's evidence wasn't given much credence by ordinary Australians who perceived it to be a classic piece of Aussie bashing, typical of remarks expressed by Kiwis envious of those living on the big island across the Tasman. The decision to expand was further influenced, Farmer later claimed, dismissing his earlier argument, by the belief that Air NZ needed to obtain direct access to the Australian market[7] or remain a small, regionally isolated airline. Air NZ had to obtain critical mass from the feeder links from and beyond the Tasman; otherwise it would lose its independent status and have trouble competing effectively.

Talks between Air NZ and News lasted for months but collapsed the following July when Air NZ CEO Jim McCrae proposed that Air NZ, News Corp and TNT form a three-way consortium as equals. Knowing that TNT was cash-strapped and in trouble, the Air NZ board was not about to do deals and run a business with a near-broke partner. Air NZ was now passing up, for the second time in two years, an opportunity to acquire the News stake at near fire-sale prices. Instead Kiwi sights turned to a buyout of the TNT interest and Air NZ initialled a $425-million deal in November 1996. They paid TNT $200 million cash at the time of signing and agreed to acquire TNT's remaining stake for $225 million by February 1998. Ansett got $200 million as an immediate capital injection after News refused to countenance a straight sale of the TNT interest and forced the Kiwis to inject a further $150 million, topped up with an additional $50 million from News. But air route protocols meant that the overseas routes flown by Ansett would have to be warehoused. Fifty-one per cent of Ansett International was hived off to International Airline Investments Holdings, a syndicate of institutions controlled by the Australian insurance giant AMP and County NatWest Australia Investment Management. News Limited became the sole owner of Ansett New Zealand to comply with competition rules across the Tasman.

Air NZ got three seats on the Ansett board—filled by then chairman Bob Matthew, CEO Jim McCrae and chief financial officer Robert Nazarian. John Curtis, a resident Australian director, was subsequently appointed to replace Matthew who quit in May 1998. McCrae was appointed deputy chairman of Ansett. But News Corp's majority stake ensured that Ken Cowley would continue to wield control as executive chairman, until the post was filled in 1997 by Rod Eddington who had joined the News Limited board in Sydney after turning around the fortunes at Cathay Pacific. Fast forward five years and it is worth noting that only Curtis remained a director of Ansett after July 2000, when Air NZ bought out the remaining News stake. McCrae and Nazarian left ten days apart, on 7 and 17 July 2000 respectively, and Curtis resigned eight months later, on 5 March 2001. The loss of this combined corporate knowledge would seriously impair the running of the airline.

The first opportunity News had to sell came in March 1999 when Singapore Airlines agreed to pay $500 million for the Australian carrier, but only after the Ansett operation had passed detailed checks in due diligence. Singapore's accountants and lawyers were allocated an office and access to the required files and registers—a privilege accorded Air NZ when it had bought the TNT stake five years earlier. It is now known[8] that Air NZ also requested, and was granted, permission for two senior managers to have access to the due diligence room while Singapore was conducting its checks on the Australian carrier's finances. This information conflicts with an account of the sale process that acting Air NZ chairman Jim Farmer gave to the Australian Federal Court on 9 October 2001. In a sworn affidavit Farmer testified: 'Air New Zealand exercised its pre-emptive right in February 2000 after very lengthy negotiations in which News Limited refused to allow normal due diligence to take place, completed a conditional contract to acquire News Limited's shareholding [sic].'

Irrespective of whether Air New Zealand had total or partial access to the data available through the process of due diligence, its board—through Matthew, McCrae, Nazarian and later Curtis—was afforded total access to the books and affairs of the company in their respective roles as directors of Ansett Transport Holdings. The feeble excuses offered by Farmer in his affidavit, and New Zealand's prime minister Helen Clark's comment that Air NZ had 'bought a lemon', seemed more like sour grapes than a genuine reason for the eventual collapse of Ansett. Ms Clark and the directors of Air New Zealand appear to have been engulfed by a culture of denial, never once suggesting that they too might have been at least partly accountable for what happened in Australia. They have variously blamed Eddington, News Limited and the Australian Government, but never themselves. As one senior source from Ansett said: 'The impression you get is that when they got their hands on the levers they didn't have what they thought they had. They went to the show, bought a dog and got it home and saw that it was sick.'[9]

Both McCrae and Nazarian knew as much about the affairs of Ansett as any of the News directors; indeed they are remembered for their active and lively interest in the activities of the airline. McCrae attended all eight directors' meetings in 1999. Nazarian was at four and attended a further four meetings of the carrier's audit committee. Both Air NZ and News directors had access to the same board papers, filled with financial numbers, service numbers and staff numbers that tracked the progress of the company in excruciating detail. A standing offer made by Eddington to the directors was: 'if you need any information as a director for the running of this company, tell me and I will ensure that it is in the board papers'.

Eddington spent three and a half years as executive chairman of Ansett. He is widely credited with having worked miracles with the finances. When he arrived, Ansett had just recorded a $35 million loss. The following year Ansett reported a $156.8 million after-tax profit, achieving a $191.8 million turnaround.[10] Eddington devised what was dubbed the Great Business Plan, which focused on getting Ansett to annual profits of 10 per cent. The 1998–99 target was a modest 3 per cent profit margin that came in at 4.6 per cent after the books were audited.

The figures for the 1999 fiscal year were impressive: net debt was reduced to $817.4 million; down from the $2.7 billion of the Abeles era; shareholder equity had improved 30 per cent to $697.4 million; net interest expense was reduced 22 per cent; and the debt-to-equity ratio had improved to 54 per cent against 70 per cent a year earlier. That these results could be achieved from what was an insignificant 0.3 per cent increase in passenger numbers says much about Eddington's decision to focus on core operations and hone operating efficiencies.

The general view expressed by aviation observers was that Ansett would have been a different concern, with a modern fleet, had Air NZ not blocked Singapore Airlines' $500 million bid for the carrier in 1999. As one senior airline chief noted: 'The Singaporeans would have made Ansett one of the world's best airlines with a new fleet of aircraft; that would have been a terrific outcome for Ansett.' But Air NZ exercised the pre-emptive right to acquire full control of the airline that it obtained from News at the time of the TNT purchase.

Singapore wanted to keep Ansett alive and gain access to the lucrative feed for its overseas services that would flow from operating within the Australian domestic market. Singapore's CEO Dr Cheong Choong Kong (C.K. Cheong) had personally negotiated an arrangement that would have allowed Eddington to stay at Ansett and hold his 1997 appointment as deputy chairman of News Limited. But the Kiwis would not entertain the arrangement. They wanted control of the airline that dwarfed their own. Air NZ, with eight 747s and thirty-three other heavy aircraft, was buying a business with a fleet in excess of 130. In a deal akin to a mouse swallowing an elephant, the directors agreed in February 2000 to pay $580 million (NZ$744 million) to News, with a further sum, equal to 10.5 per cent of the shares on issue based on a ninety-day average of the combined group's market value, after two years.

Observers estimated that the Kiwis would be paying A$700 million for what News was willing to sell to Singapore at a $200 million discount a year earlier. Why Air NZ chose to pay was never explained, nor was any reason given why McCrae was singled out for the top job in the merged entity. Eddington was to be second in command and was told by Air NZ chairman Sir Selwyn Cushing that he would get the post when McCrae retired eighteen months later. But the Australian would not entertain the arrangement and is said to have replied: 'Why would I want to be second in command to Jim McCrae when I can work for Rupert Murdoch?' At the time Eddington was second in charge of News Limited and deputy to Lachlan Murdoch, chairman of the publisher's Australian operation. News executives were aware that Eddington had for several days been thinking over an offer to become chief executive of British Airways. He had little respect for Cushing and allegedly told him: 'I'll make it easy for you. I'll go.' In reply Cushing was said to have responded the 'That's jolly decent of you. Thank you, Rod,' before turning his back on the man Sir Colin Marshall, chairman of BA, had earmarked as the fix-it specialist who could resolve the dire economic problems confronting Britain's flagship carrier.

Eddington left Australia in the months before the sale of Ansett became final. On the eve of his departure he addressed key staff, telling them: 'Well folks, we are out of the swamp, but we are not yet above the high watermark. We have reduced our debt, focused on our core business and made solid progress.'[11] He was leaving for a new job, a massive annual salary and the added luxury of a posh company house in high-rent Eaton Square in the heart of London where his executive talent was recognised.

8
A DYING CHILD

BUYING ANSETT OVER-STRETCHED Air New Zealand's finances and left the merged operation vulnerable to severe economic pressures. The Kiwi parent spent almost $300 million dollars keeping the carrier aloft during ten hectic months of the discount war against Qantas and the newly launched start-up carriers Virgin Blue and Impulse. The two budget operators took to Australian skies when Ansett was rudderless, lacking a permanent CEO and a proper first-line team of senior management. Impulse launched in June, within weeks of the cross-Tasman merger. It lost the fight and its Boeing 717s and their crews were acquired by Qantas. Virgin Blue burst on to the Australian scene two months afterwards, in August 2000, and has to date lasted as a miracle survivor.

Virgin organisation founder Richard Branson was able to spin off his highly successful European strategy and to launch in Australia with the blue nametag. He brought a handful of mostly second-hand aircraft to Australia, operated from premises built by a generous state government, and through the commitment given by key executives he created a substantial business quite rapidly. It was, indeed, good enough to allow him to knock back an offer of $250 million from Air NZ.

Whereas Virgin Blue to this day continues to operate out of low-cost temporary buildings at Melbourne and Sydney airports, Ansett flew from high-rent terminals. Simple economics proved that Ansett, with its old planes, a huge staff of 15 000 and high fuel charges, could not survive in that economic climate while the operation bled cash at the seemingly unbelievable rate of A$2.4 million (NZ$3 million) a day, reaching A$16.8 million (NZ$21 million)[1] a week at one point. Ansett executives had to swallow an unpalatable $200 million loss for the year to 30 June 2001—'most of which', declared a New Zealand Treasury document on 20 June, 'is likely to be attributable to its Ansett operations.' 'Mum and dad' investors holding the carrier's scrip were kept in the dark until September when a cash-for-equity plan with major partners Singapore Airlines (SIA) and Brierley Investments (BIL) fell apart. A-shares that had sold in April 2001 for NZ$1.06 and B stock that brought NZ$1.51 were worth little more than the price of confetti by September. The B-scrip would slump to A$0.21 (NZ$0.26) before being suspended by the Australian and New Zealand stock exchanges. For the plan to have succeeded, BIL and SIA would have had to pay 44 per cent more than the ruling share price to match the amount the business needed—far beyond what the New

Zealand's sovereignty rules allowed. By September 2001, Air NZ was worth just A$189 million, a mere fraction of what Ansett had cost.

Between January and October 2001, the cash bleed from Auckland to Ansett amounted to A$112 948 751 and a further $150 million was written off in a farewell settlement negotiated with the Ansett administrators. The debt-to-equity ratio stood at a high 87 per cent. John Waller, the senior PriceWaterhouseCoopers partner hired by Air New Zealand to investigate its finances, warned that most airlines were geared within the 50- to 80-per-cent range. Waller, in advice he gave to the Air NZ board, noted: 'Those close to 80 per cent are considered highly leveraged.'[2] Waller's findings tolled the death knell for the ailing carrier that was then in the final phase of a terminal illness. The parent company needed quick solutions. Voluntary administration or liquidation of Ansett remained the only alternatives.

By a curious set of circumstances, Waller's sister firm, Price-WaterhouseCoopers (PWC), Sydney, was handed the job. But the PWC administration lasted only as long as it took the Australian Council of Trade Unions and its myriad Ansett-based member unions to learn of the work Waller did for the parent company. Claiming conflict of interest, they used their combined industrial muscle to have PWC replaced by a new insolvency team from Andersen Accounting.

What News Limited chairman Lachlan Murdoch described as a 'win, win, win situation' for News, Air New Zealand and Ansett when the sale was announced 21 months earlier had soured after senior Ansett executives were purged and the former Air NZ directors disappeared from the Ansett board. Matters were not helped by the Clark Government's delayed response to offers by SIA, BIL and Qantas to inject capital and restructure the airline. SIA and BIL were prepared to inject $150 million. Qantas offered cash and would have separately bought the scrip held by SIA and BIL.

The story of how things turned bad begins when nine of the airline's top ten executive general managers were fired or quit after the new Kiwi managers attempted to stamp the Australian operation with their brand of leadership. Auckland head office went into the Ansett deal expecting to save a total of $462 million—$154 million (NZ$188 million) a year—over three years. Savings would be obtained by consolidating the administrative and operational activities for both airlines into a central office. Tapping the lucrative Australian market and the further earnings that Ansett would generate from the Star Alliance network was expected to lift revenue by $161 million (NZ$200 million) a year. But when the expected synergies did not mesh and benefits failed to happen Air NZ was left to service the A$616 million (NZ$770 million)[3] chalked up when buying Ansett.

A report by PA Consulting Group correctly identified that 'a lack of focused leadership' in the first months after the takeover—between June 2000 and the appointment of a new executive team in January 2001—had delayed the integration process. Air NZ had in place the right management team with a strong track record in airline turnarounds, PA told the New Zealand Government in July 2001, two months before the company crashed. PA noted that, without outside assistance, there was not enough time, sufficient capital, or enough leverage to generate the necessary level of benefits needed from the cross-Tasman carrier alliance.

The departures of key Ansett executives and the switch to Air NZ's different style of customer philosophy distanced its troubled Australian subsidiary from the movers and shakers in charge of corporate travel. Winning them would make Ansett 'a great airline, great business,' Ansett chief Rod Eddington declared, in a reference to his earlier diagnosis when charting his recovery course in October 1999. Eddington handpicked his executive team through the three entire levels of management. Maintaining a link with corporate clients was the key driver of his business strategy: 'we are identifying those customers who are our most frequent flyers and responding to their particular needs,' he announced in his 1999 annual review. Managers were told to focus on the business market first, then on leisure travellers. Business travellers provided eighty per cent of Ansett's core profits. Each year some 870 000 Australian companies booked airline travel and 94 000 individuals chalked up $5.5 billion in sales of tickets. Ansett received just under half that sum, with sales revenue amounting to about $2 billion a year. Management acknowledged that about $1 billion was earned from major corporate contracts while small to medium-sized businesses contributed about $780 million and leisure travel topped up the rest.

Sales managers complained they were overloaded with mandatory processes that did nothing to improve productivity. In addition, as well as being overly process driven, in the absence of real or measurable goals people were judged on how well they followed a process, not on the results they achieved. Said one manager: 'The problem was exacerbated because many of the processes were manual and paper based, meaning a long and cumbersome sales cycle.' Qantas struck back using its size, network strength and lower cost base and mounted an aggressive challenge to win over corporate business. The managers claimed that Qantas began to rebate cash (to travel agents) and discount (fares) at levels that could not be sustained by Ansett. Several large accounts were given rebates in excess of 40 per cent while others, to the tune of $5 million a year, were averaging a 30 per cent rebate. Qantas knew that its yields would fall to just 20 cents in the dollar in a price war. Keeping 60 cents in the dollar was far more attractive, managers claimed. Ansett had to cut prices to retain clients and compete—a dangerous precedent considering the high cost base Ansett had in running its ageing fleet.

Qantas also operated a bundled rebate program, whereby travel agency and contract clients received a sales commission from the carrier based on the combined volumes of their domestic, regional and international travel spending. In many instances Ansett had to exceed the Qantas offer just to compensate the corporate client for the bonus they would lose for not reaching the tickets target set by Qantas. At the same time, and with Ansett in trouble, Qantas stripped restrictions from its top discount fare deals.

By the following April, Eddington was gone. Craig Wallace, who had been executive general manager commercial planning before succeeding Eddington for a brief period, went to the private train and tram operator National Express as chief executive and Gary Kingshott, who had been in charge of sales and distribution, shifted to Ansett International. As one Ansett source said: 'With that group gone the corporates walked across the road to Qantas.' Air NZ appointed its own team to replace the trio. This proved disastrous because the incoming New Zealanders had few contacts and little knowledge of the local market. Sales strategies of one-off fare deals that bettered those of Ansett's rivals might have been successfully trialled in New Zealand but they were shot to bits in the air wars with Qantas. 'They simply undercut us every time,' noted one manager. 'They could afford to lose. Ansett couldn't.'

Eddington's handpicked team was eventually reduced to two: executive general manager operations Trevor Jensen and regional airlines boss Ron Rosalsky. Jensen, who held the vital Air Operator's Certificate and the right for Ansett to fly as domestic and international passenger carrier, was not easy to move. Rosalsky had been shifted to run the regional air services. But those who left fared much better. Lyell Strambi, whom Eddington appointed executive general manager in charge of business recovery, was snapped up by Virgin Atlantic (VA) and was made chief operating officer of the UK carrier. VA, controlled by Singapore Airlines and with colourful entrepreneur Richard Branson as founder and the minority stakeholder, pioneered the successful no-frills travel concept that Branson again employed in launching his Virgin Blue start-up in Australia. By mid 2001, Air NZ executives and their top economic advisers were focused on a plan to wipe out the Branson rival that had trimmed fifteen per cent off the operating yield of Ansett. It is no insult to Lyell Strambi that, like his former boss, his considerable skills and talents were overlooked in that first Air NZ shake-up at Ansett.

Other members of the A-level executive general management team— Pamela Catty (PR and government relations), Paul Birch (human resources), David Irvine (finance) and John Vincent (engineering)— quickly found other posts. Catty, who had control of a $3-million budget and managed a direct staff of thirty-six, shifted to a 'big four' bank then, in 2002, to Coles Myer; Paul Birch went to electronics maker Siemens Australia; and David Irvine became chief financial officer of Boral. John Vincent holds a respected senior engineering post at Qantas. Jensen remained with Ansett until it folded into administration and left amid negotiations to sell what remained of the shell to the Fox–Lew syndicate. He succumbed to an offer made by Qantas CEO Geoff Dixon during a chance encounter at the University Cafe in Melbourne's Lygon Street.

Over the next year Air NZ replaced Ansett's top 250 commercial, marketing and sales managers. They got rid of people operating in the commercial Australian market at a time when new competition was beginning to burgeon. 'Little wonder the corporates crossed the road to Qantas,' exclaimed a former executive. Former chief pilot Mark Rindfleish expressed the same view, arguing strongly that the problems were compounded by the peremptory removal of most of the frontline Ansett management team and noting the significant fact that the airline lost the commercial and marketing expertise of professionals who maintained strong relationships with the business travel market.[4]

From 1994, and through the Eddington era, Australian travel agents judged Ansett the best airline, despite its ageing fleet and dwindling market share in the battle to compete with Qantas. The Ansett skies were friendly skies and frequent travellers considered the service superior. But all of that changed under the stewardship of Air NZ.

Aviation strategists suggest that the Kiwis made the cardinal mistake of believing that revenues would not change if operating costs were slashed by putting the carriers together. What they forgot was that running a successful airline involves making serious attempts to maintain personal contact with customers. A homespun example of this theory at work was the 1960s fallout between Ansett Airlines and Carlton and United Breweries. Former general manager Graeme McMahon related the story of one of his predecessors, Frank Pascoe, who dealt with the threat that the brewery's travel account was to go to his TAA rival:

> Frank received a letter from the boss of Carlton and United Breweries, Lew Mangan, informing him that because of continuing stuff-ups, his company would no longer be using Ansett's services; he was moving the account. Frank replied: 'Dear Lew, I regret very much your decision to cease using the services of my company. For what it's worth, I will continue to drink yours'. Lew wrote back: 'Frank, You have got me, again'.[5]

The Ansett 'spaceship' in Olympics livery.

Running an airline business might have become more sophisticated in the new age of networking and, as the Eddington strategy proposed, a 'great business looks after the minders'.

Ansett spent huge sums on corporate clients. Its 2000 Olympic commitment, as the designated official carrier, was spread over the budgets of several years and is said to have totalled upwards of $70 million. The Sydney Games spending listed in Air NZ's December 2000 half-year accounts amounted to $21.7 million. The Games deal was done pre-Eddington and the spend was initially fixed at around $50 million. It is believed that, among the Games budget items, was $1 million earmarked for related public relations activities. Ansett picked up the tab. Insiders say that Air NZ, at the best, put in $5 million and won Games traffic from overseas. 'I still wonder what all the money did to generate business,' said one informant, adding: 'A year on, I looked and could not see any identifiable gain, not one ticket extra.'

With the Games over, Eddington and Wallace gone, and McCrae having similarly disappeared from the top post across the Tasman, the combined group was handed to Selwyn Cushing to run. Cushing, who had previously run a medium-sized business, had been befriended by Ron Brierley who installed him as chairman of BIL and later catapulted him into the position of influence as chairman of the country's national airline.

In what can be only be regarded as an unfortunate act of fate, Selwyn Cushing found himself with day-to-day responsibility for the affairs of an enterprise for which too much had been paid when the $500 million SIA offer to News Limited was outbid the previous year. Air NZ was well aware at that time that Ansett had to be re-equipped with new aircraft, which would involve raising a $5 billion debt to buy them. Blind Freddy could see that the merged Air NZ–Ansett Group could not survive without a benevolent shareholder. But winning government backing to change the share structure to accommodate a debt-for-equity deal would not be easy. The ultimate control of Air NZ at that time rested with the single Kiwi share held by the national government. The appointed representative of the government had the right to use that share to veto issues perceived not to be in the national interest.

The initial plan was to raise capital from overseas markets, as amounts of the required size could not be sourced from investors in a nation as small as New Zealand. But an act of parliament restricted foreign investment in the airline to no more than 25 per cent by any single overseas airline and to 35 per cent by all airlines. Having been rebuffed in its attempt to buy fifty per cent of Ansett, SIA turned its sights on the Kiwi parent and snapped up the maximum 25 per cent stake allowed in the first months of 2001. The SIA partnership would offer hope and the promise later that year of a lifeline, but in those first months of 2001 government approval was needed to tap equity markets offshore. The ultimate problem for the Clark Government, though, was that any deal with overseas lenders could result in losing control of the company that carried the country's flag to destinations abroad. The political risks were huge: the government could offend Kiwi ideals of national sovereignty and allow a controlling stake to be sold to foreign interests, or it could allow the airline's shares to slump and put at risk the savings of several thousands of 'mum and dad' investors. A third option, whereby the government itself made a substantial injection of taxpayers' cash, was also canvassed.

The subsequent collapse of the Air NZ–Ansett group proved that all such options should have been canvassed at the outset, not patched together in a hurried fix-it operation when one of the carriers had gone belly-up and the other was financially vulnerable. The New Zealand Government and the directors of Air NZ waited too long to effect the rescue. 'This need not have happened,' said Mark Rindfleish. 'If Singapore Airlines' proposal to buy half of Ansett during Rod Eddington's days had gone through, Ansett would still be flying.'[6] Rindfleish was well placed to observe what was happening: he had held various executive pilot roles in his twenty-eight years with the company, including (at the end) the top post of executive general manager operations and (before that) head of flying operations and chief pilot for Air New Zealand. Rindfleish argued that Air NZ scarcely understood the complexities of the Australian business market:

> It was a good regional airline that tried to impose its culture on Ansett and that was never going to work. It was in real trouble from the start. They took so long to get going with the consolidation of the two airlines. They appointed more consultants to see how the whole thing should be structured; they took more than six months to appoint a new CEO; they dallied with the offer from Singapore to buy 50 per cent of the business. And all the time the operations were bleeding to death—everyone felt cheated and greatly disappointed when the Singapore proposal didn't come off.

9
BIG MAN, BIG PLANS

AIR NEW ZEALAND appointed a big man with big ambitions to run the Air NZ–Ansett conglomerate as a big league airline. Gary Toomey had jumped from Qantas where he had been deputy chief executive and former chief financial officer. Toomey, then aged forty-five, had a long and impeccable record in airline management but he had been passed over for the top job with the Australian carrier in favour of the shrewd marketer Geoff Dixon. The opening at Air NZ provided an opportunity to move on and demonstrate his ability to build a cross-Tasman rival for Qantas.

Toomey's credentials seemed a perfect fit for the small New Zealand airline wanting to tap new profits from its purchase of the bigger but troubled Australian operator Ansett. He could also lay claim to valuable hands-on experience in the Australian domestic market in his past life as a senior executive with the Qantas domestic forerunner, Australian Airlines. He was seen as the right turnaround specialist to restructure the finances and fleets of both carriers and was well capable of the task of uniting the skies over the Tasman.

Toomey would not face the challenge alone. He arrived in Auckland in January 2001 with his 'red team', dubbed so by Ansett staffers because of their former roles at Qantas. Adam Maroney, who had been Toomey's former deputy in Sydney, shifted across and became chief financial officer of the Air NZ–Ansett Group; Kevin Turnbull, former Qantas general manager accounting and performance and group general manager operation services, became Air NZ's senior vice president business performance; Andrew Pondekas, formerly general manager Qantas flight catering, became senior vice-president ventures. Peter Harris, vice president government/international affairs, was recruited from CASA in Australia. Trevor Jensen, the only surviving member of the old Ansett team, was made executive general manager operations and inflight services for both airlines.

But Toomey was barred from taking a hands-on role until December 2000, eight months after Rod Eddington left Ansett and six months after Jim McCrae's sudden and unexpected departure. His Qantas contract forced him to take four months 'gardening leave' after his appointment, which left the chief executive's spot at Air NZ vacant for too long and the airline group rudderless during those vital few months when every resource was being tested by the make-or-break challenge brought about by the merger.

Gary Toomey was a different man to different people. He commanded respect, was easily upset and was finicky. He changed the company culture, calling himself president and those nearest to him senior vice presidents. He told staff: 'We're going to be successful and grow the business.' He spoke of building a fleet, opening new routes and promoting the airline. 'We've got to earn the right to grow and that means being efficient, using all our existing resources to best effect.' What he suggested was not unlike the strategy that had been previously invoked by Eddington. Customer service was a priority. 'I'm not going to take prisoners on compromising that. I won't tolerate people who treat customers badly.'

The new CEO walked into a problem that was not of his making. With the Air NZ balance sheet severely hit by the Ansett purchase and a serious capital injection needed, Toomey's brief from chairman Selwyn Cushing and SIA's C.K. Cheong was to grow the airline, improve on time performance and attract high yield business clients. That goal would not be achieved without new planes, Toomey told the New Zealand Government, and foreign investors would want a bigger say in running things. Toomey was about projecting an image and when he came to Ansett he did not like what he saw: threadbare carpets and worn chairs in the Golden Wings lounges, and old planes that were run to the nth hour of maintenance cycles, so that they needed to spend months out of service or be replaced.

At the September 2001 results announcement Toomey said:

The fundamental legacy we found when we came aboard in January was that it was not just about trading losses, there were also significant problems with financial systems. There were losses in travel agencies and we needed to replace aircraft. We found that aircraft had been run out to maximum hours. During the coming year, instead of having three aircraft in heavy maintenance, we would have had up to ten to twelve aircraft in heavy maintenance throughout the year. We would have had to arrange for those aircraft to be sent offshore, and that would have resulted in a decrease in capacity which is directly correlated to market share.[2]

Gary Toomey, former AirNZ–Ansett CEO

Gary Toomey sought to project an upmarket, on-time image for Air NZ and Ansett. He wanted seamless travel for high-yield business customers, which would have enabled them to fly into Australia and New Zealand and move about either country with the same airline group. But building the upmarket image meant having to start again and replace the basics, like the carpets in the Melbourne terminal at Tullamarine.

On his first official visit to Melbourne, Toomey was met by staff who stood awkwardly spaced about the terminal foyer. They had been told: 'stand on the chewing gum spots and cigarette burns so he doesn't see them'. Toomey was determined to make changes that would instil a customer focus within the operations area—'to make pilots, ground handlers and check-in attendants consider the customer first'.

> **Toomey was met by staff who stood awkwardly spaced about the terminal foyer. They had been told: 'stand on the chewing gum spots and cigarette burns so he doesn't see them'.**

He built a reputation as a frenetic worker, running the company with a mobile phone seemingly glued to one ear. One executive in Melbourne was issued with a second mobile just to receive his calls. Incoming calls frequently disrupted meetings, frustrating staff, who were made to sit and wait for as long as the conversations lasted. Typical was a key strategy meeting at the reception centre at Werribee Zoo, which was stopped for half an hour until Toomey's conversation with a caller ended. Melbourne-based executives told how their strategy meeting to find a way to down-size the company and shed 3000 staff was disrupted by a call from Gary; the airline might have been falling apart, but after a flight to Perth the boss was asking: 'Why have we got peanuts on those planes?' Minutes later, he was on the line again: 'I've been talking over here to people about hold-ups delaying flights out of Melbourne ...' Said one source: 'I remem-ber once when we had the whole team there and he said, "I'm the most important person in this company. I'm the most expensive person, so what I want takes precedence over everything else." '3

By all accounts, Toomey was obsessive about his personal security. The head of safety and security, Peter Keating, was dispatched from Melbourne to oversee the installation of a $35 000 home security system at his Auckland residence. When the alarm went off unexpectedly a few days later, an agitated Toomey rang the Melbourne office, not someone in Auckland, demanding a replacement. Keating was sent back to fix the sys-tem, only to discover that a next-door neighbour with the same security code in his garage door remote controller would be setting off the alarm in the Toomey household each time he pressed the button. The story made the rounds of Ansett offices and brightened the workday drudge of many. But Gary Toomey cannot be held responsible in any way for the death of Ansett and the subsequent financial collapse of the parent company. His team was handed a situation not of their making; decisions had already been taken when they arrived. The accounting and manage-ment systems of both carriers had already been merged. The Auckland head office was serving both carriers from a single treasury and backroom accounting system.

Only weeks after Toomey arrived, Selwyn Cushing had to face share-holders and announce a 97-per-cent half-year profit downturn to just A$3.8 million for the six months to December 1999. Matters got worse from that point. Toomey's 'red team' was engulfed by events not of its making—events which, over the coming year, would concentrate the attention of two national governments and the carrier's board.

The storm began only days before the Christmas 2000 peak travel period, when two Ansett Boeing 767-200 aircraft, among the oldest flying anywhere in the world, were officially grounded after Boeing service bulletins that warned of the need to check tail fins for cracks were mislaid. It was later learned that an employee attending a course in the United States sparked the alarm after being shown the bulletins during a routine computer demonstration. The situation worsened the following April when it was revealed that Ansett had missed by more than six months a Boeing deadline for maintenance checks on the wing engine pylons.

The horror story then turned into a nightmare when the Australian air safety regulator CASA grounded all ten of Ansett's 767s after discovering that one aircraft had flown for more than a day with none of its emergency slides in the operating position. The findings were the last straw for CASA, which had the nation's internationally acclaimed air safety record to protect. These events marked the beginning of the end for Ansett. The airline never recovered from that damaging assault on its reputation for safety. Only a year before, Ansett had been recognised as the world's second safest airline—behind Air Canada and ahead of Qantas. Ansett's engineering and maintenance managers had become distracted, busily re-applying for their own jobs and unsure of their future after a decision was made to merge the Ansett and Air New Zealand service divisions into a single stand-alone unit known as Ansett–Air New Zealand Engineering Services (AANZES).

> **What began as a gentle glide into insolvency that April became a near vertical death dive by August.**

The Christmas and Easter groundings drew a blaze of headlines and occupied prime time news bulletins. A survey of passenger intentions showed that only one in four travellers intended to re-book for further travel. Toomey spent days doing the rounds of television and radio stations apologising to travellers. Requests for interviews by newspaper journalists were not refused. Re-booking intentions lifted to 58 per cent, and that win was the catalyst for the $20 million '*ABSOLUTELY* Ansett' advertising campaign that featured a close-up of Toomey's face, and the faces of a series of high-profile sports and entertainment stars, posted on bill-boards and in full-page newspaper ads. But in promising '*ABSOLUTELY*' the best on-time airline and inflight service, Toomey was forever branded as the unfortunate face of the troubled airline—far from the ideal image that any chief executive of a major company would want to portray. Toomey is known to regret becoming the face of '*ABSOLUTELY* Ansett'; and equally regretful executives said that the lift Ansett got from Toomey's efforts that Easter convinced them that 'Gary had to be the face of the company'. Ansett was all but finished from then on. What began as a gentle glide into insolvency that April became a near vertical death dive by August. Official New Zealand government Cabinet papers and numerous airline documents released on 11 April 2002[4] show that neither the directors nor the management of Air NZ were aware of a looming financial crisis in those first months of 2001.

The carrier's newly appointed CEO was anxious to begin restructuring finances. When he wrote to Prime Minister Helen Clark on 19 March 2001, he told her: 'In order to survive and develop internationally, the Air NZ–Ansett Group requires access to a larger home base … Air NZ has no alternative to achieving access to significant additional equity'. He warned that to 'do nothing' would cause the rapid and inexorable decline of a major New Zealand strategic asset.

Qantas and Singapore Airlines would, within weeks, begin a bidding war for stakes in the Kiwi carrier. Qantas wanted a partnership arrangement, initially offering to buy the existing 25-per-cent stake held by SIA and to acquire and repatriate to New Zealand a significantly larger holding owned by Brierley Investments. SIA, in turn, would be handed Ansett and gain seamless access for its Star Alliance international services to a domestic carrier in Australia. But SIA was not a seller and argued that its interests would be better served by part of a revived SIA–Air NZ–Ansett triumvirate. It would make a capital injection of $150 million and, with necessary government approval, lift its stake to 49 per cent. The New

Zealand Government was being asked to umpire a decision that would protect New Zealand interests and preserve national pride despite its existing legislation allowing a single foreign airline to hold no more than 25 per cent of the flag carrier.

Qantas turned its attentions to the New Zealand Government. CEO Geoff Dixon played the NZ national interest, saying the traditional Maori Koru symbol would not disappear from the tail fin of Air NZ aircraft. Dixon wanted a genuine partnership to grow two operations 'that had the economic and financial scale to compete in world market.' He told Finance Minister Michael Cullen in a letter dated 25 June: 'As you know from our various meetings and telephone conversations, our aim would be to replace Singapore Airlines as the cornerstone investor in Air New Zealand.'[5] Singapore Airlines would acquire Air New Zealand's stakes in Ansett and Ansett International, resulting 'in two strong and viable carrier groupings, of comparable size, better positioned to compete against the background of increasing globalisation and pressures for consolidation'.

The Australian Government stood firmly behind the Qantas bid. A meeting of the Cabinet in Canberra on 31 July dismissed the views of two senior ministers—Deputy Prime Minister and Minister for Transport John Anderson and Treasurer Peter Costello—who favoured the SIA plan to recapitalise Ansett. It was argued by Air NZ's Jim Farmer and Gary Toomey that Canberra's support for the Qantas plan sparked further indecision by New Zealand Government. Soon afterwards Anderson had to travel to Wellington and convey the Australian Government's position supporting Qantas. Anderson, though, remains adamant that the New Zealand Government was 'as frustrated and angry as I was about the Air NZ board's incompetence and intransigence'. Farmer later accused the Australian Government of interfering in the New Zealand Government's decision making. He claimed that Australia's support for a rigorous examination of both proposals had 'distracted' the New Zealand Government.

Some months later, after Ansett collapsed, Australian Prime Minister John Howard explained his support for the Qantas proposal in a speech to parliament on 18 September:[6] 'The government did unashamedly have a preference for what was called the Qantas option for quite some time. Quite unashamedly because we took the view that if you are going to have two airlines it would be a good idea if one of them was Australian owned.'

The Australian Government claims that it was not aware of how desperate Air NZ–Ansett's finances were by the 31 July Cabinet meeting. John Anderson maintains that the full picture did not emerge until 14 August when Farmer flagged the situation in a letter to John Howard, whereas both Farmer and Toomey claim that Canberra had been alerted as early as May that the airline group had serious financial troubles. The evidence supports the Anderson line that Air NZ insisted till mid-August that it was not in trouble. Gary Toomey, in a speech in Sydney on 11 June, chided the financial press and some 'ill-informed commentators' for their 'gloom and doom' scenarios of Ansett's projected full-year loss. 'They haven't suddenly ballooned and they will be nowhere near the $400 million figure bandied about this week,' he told an audience of aviation writers at a lunch at the NRMA Club.[7]

By early September Ansett was in a death spiral, with Air NZ stocks having fallen to the 20c price range. The share price collapse caused SIA and BIL to withdraw from an arrangement that would have seen each inject $150 million in new capital. The amount was to have been matched with a NZ$550 million loan from the New Zealand Government that was initially earmarked to save Ansett. This initial fix was to have been followed by an NZ$800 million market capital raising in 2002.

Reports[8] show that the New Zealand Government was aware in June that Air NZ had access to just A$642.4 million (NZ$803 million) cash and a further A$305.6 million (NZ$382 million) left in an undrawn, unsecured facility. Secret talks were then begun to buy Virgin Blue and thus remove Ansett's cut-price, no-frills competition in Australia. The takeover talks lasted from May until August when, on a visit to Melbourne, Branson ripped up a mocked-up Air NZ cheque for A$250 million. Bidding had begun at US$80 million and the deal became a drawn-out three-way wrangle with Branson demanding US$120 million, Air NZ prepared to offer US$100 million and SIA holding firm that Air NZ was not to go beyond US$80 million. The airline board remained publicly resolute that the problems would be overcome by winning backing for the SIA–BIL plan to inject new capital. But as matters worsened, New Zealand Finance Minister Cullen was told on 29 August that the airline would need between A$800 million (NZ$1 billion) and A$1.2 billion (NZ$1.5 billion) to recapitalise and acquire Virgin Blue from Branson.[9] A memo sent to the minister by the government-appointed intermediary to the Air New Zealand board reported: 'Our assessment is that management will conclude that Virgin Blue is critical.'

The Virgin Blue strategy turned out to be the last card Air NZ had in its Ansett recovery pack. Virgin executives, who had steeled themselves for a price-cutting onslaught from Ansett after Branson announced in September that he would not sell to Air NZ, were startled by the lack of response. They got their answers ten days later when Ansett was cut adrift by its owners and the first team of administrators from PriceWaterhouseCoopers walked in.

Not until the final weeks was Air NZ or its directors prepared to acknowledge the seriousness of their company's plight. Throughout the preceding months, the mood they displayed had been upbeat, typified by Toomey's 11 June speech in Sydney that:

> Our group is not asset poor or strapped for cash. We're confident that we'll have a billion dollars to call on as we go into the next financial year—more than enough to meet our operating requirements.

Toomey has since said that the group had the billion to call on, but his speech made no mention that the carrier had almost fully exhausted its source of unsecured funds.

The 'billion in the bank remark' became the smoking gun that determined Australian attitudes. The Howard Government in Canberra resurrected and reminded Australians of the comment when Farmer claimed that Air NZ–Ansett was let down by Canberra in its pleas for help. Jim Farmer and Gary Toomey had spoken to John Anderson in Canberra at a meeting on 27 June, just seven weeks before the formal advice to the Australian Government of the seriousness of the carrier's plight. Nothing emerged from their talks that caused the Australian transport minister any real concern. Farmer and Toomey conveyed the view that Ansett had serious operating difficulties but both appeared confident that the airline, under Air NZ management, would find a way out of its problem. A new yield-management system was being introduced to measure the cost of the seat against the operating charges of running the airline and Ansett was overcoming maintenance problems that had grounded the airline the previous Christmas and Easter. At the same meeting Toomey was said to have repeated the comments he made in his speech on 11 June. Anderson recalled: 'Absolutely, oh absolutely. That's exactly what he said: that they had a billion dollars in reserves.'[10] Farmer and Toomey were said to have tabled graphs, but took their documents with them on leaving the meeting. Anderson believed afterwards that Air NZ was hurting but still basically sound. Neither Farmer nor Toomey had asked for help; they left Anderson and his staff with the impression that they had simply extended the courtesy of briefing the government on the position they were in and where they were going. With a 'billion' to call on and capital promised from 25-per-cent shareholder Singapore Airlines, the Air NZ–Ansett group would fly through its financial storm.

Both Farmer and Toomey would later claim in television interviews that the Australian Government knew very well of the parlous financial position of Ansett and did nothing about it. An incensed Anderson strenuously denied the accusation, claiming it was 'another example of blame shifting by Dr Farmer and Mr Toomey. Their assertion [that they kept the Australian Government informed of Ansett's financial position] is simply untrue.' Anderson said the media and the New Zealand Stock Exchange were told by the airline only that Air NZ needed recapitalising. In an interview with the *Brisbane Courier-Mail* on 27 June, the day he met with Anderson, Toomey is reported as having said: 'There is no threat to the funding of Ansett or the Air New Zealand group at least over the next year or so.' On 10 August Toomey was again in Canberra for a meeting with Transport Department Secretary Ken Matthews. He reiterated the need for Air NZ to recapitalise, but Toomey's other comments were consistent with his previous assurances to the Government. The airline, he said, was not in immediate difficulties and needed the funding for its medium- and long-term expansion.

Air NZ's determination to see through a deal with SIA opened a rift with the authorities in Canberra. In an exclusive report published on 18 August, *Brisbane Courier-Mail* journalist Fleur Anderson offered a clue to how bitter that became. The reporter had been travelling with Toomey and was at a breakfast meeting that day where the airline CEO had sought to sell corporate travel deals to government decision makers. Among those in the audience that morning was John Howard's department head, Max Moore-Wilton. Fleur Anderson noted that Gary Toomey was angry and appeared shaken after a brief conversation with Moore-Wilton. The *Australian Financial Review* followed up the *Courier-Mail* story and later reported that Ansett executives confirmed what Moore-Wilton had told Toomey that morning: 'he didn't give a shit about Ansett', that the government was doing everything it could to protect Qantas because it was the only truly Australian airline.[11] Fleur Anderson's report had said: 'Speculation quickly spread through the airline industry [that] Moore-Wilton had warned that the Federal Government would rather see Ansett fail than have Qantas at risk from Air NZ–Singapore Airlines.'

In his 14 August letter Jim Farmer warned the Australian prime minister that Air NZ was in a difficult financial position. The letter said, in part, that the group's financial results included 'very serious losses at Ansett', which:

> are being sustained only with the support of the wider group. This situation has emerged ... in part due to the lack of sufficient attention in the past to costs and investment within Ansett's operations. I particularly wish to advise you that my board has considered, and will consider again before the results are announced on September 4, whether the group's liquidity is sufficient to enable it to meet its obligations as they fall due. While we are naturally investigating all potential avenues for maintaining the group's short term and medium term liability, we remain deeply concerned that without early resolution of the equity situation and recapitalisation of the group there may be breaches of loan covenants triggering a right for lenders to demand immediate repayment of loans.[12]

Clearly the position was parlous but Farmer's comments only confirmed in the minds of the Australian authorities that Ansett would be saved. Farmer had further postulated that 'the fortunes of Ansett and Air NZ were now deeply tied together by the debt levels entered into to acquire Ansett' and that the two businesses 'are now deeply enmeshed'. He continued: 'The investment required for Ansett to operate on its own, and the time and leadership essential to address CASA's concerns, mean that no practical separation can occur.' Farmer concluded that 'an early recapitalisation of the Group with assistance from SIA remains the preferred position adopted unanimously by the Group's directors.'

At no stage did Jim Farmer seek Australian government financial assistance; only its support in allowing SIA to increase its holding in Air NZ. Anderson and his advisers felt confident, from Farmer's letter, that if 'no practical separation can occur' then Ansett would remain an integral part of Air NZ. Selectively leaked parts of the letter alluding to the serious financial problems that faced Air NZ over Ansett were designed to embarrass the Australian Government but all they achieved was to polarise the government view that Ansett was a commercial problem requiring a commercial solution. Anderson was not going to be bullied or cajoled into a position that would possibly expose the Australian community to an unnecessary financial commitment. By 12 September, when the airline's annual accounts were released, Air NZ reported an operating loss of $230 million and wrote off its $1.2 billion investment in Ansett.

Anderson continues to be amazed that SIA, which has a reputation for being tightly run and ruthless in business and which also had three members on the Air NZ board, could not have been aware of what was happening to Air NZ's finances. Similarly why were Air NZ directors of Ansett not aware of the carrier's inherent and developing problems at the time of the takeover in June 2000? Senior New Zealand government ministers told Anderson that they developed less and less confidence about what they were hearing from the Air NZ directors about the future viability of the airline. Finance Minister Cullen was, at the outset, not particularly concerned whether SIA or Qantas bought into Air NZ; his aim was to secure a future for the carrier. The New Zealand Government finally bailed out the Kiwi carrier on 27 November 2001 after the SIA and BIL offers had fallen through. The New Zealand Government spent A$735 million (NZ$850 million) acquiring an 82 per cent stake that wiped out all but 9 per cent of the combined BIL–SIA interest. SIA had lost not only the best part of A$250 million but considerable face for its own government-controlled administration.

Three years earlier, Air NZ had stopped Rod Eddington from selling Ansett's ageing Boeing 767s, then ten years old, to buy later models. Selwyn Cushing and Jim McCrae argued that group funds had to be applied to buying planes for Air NZ. When Eddington regularly suggested that Ansett International should fly to Los Angeles, he was again blocked because it might have taken business from Air NZ. The Kiwis did not consider that Australians might want to travel to LA the shorter way, without island hops to Auckland and Honolulu. A former top executive has since said:

> They would not spend any money to re-equip because when Eddington first turned up, the case was put forward to get us some new 767s and get rid of the old ones, and of course it was knocked back.[13]

The simple fact was that during his reign the planes got older. They went from proper block maintenance to a fix-up arrangement in which they were run to the absolute maximum time allowed between checks. Eventually their on-time performance fell to pieces and delays began to occur.

After the Ansett collapse, Jim Farmer, the man who stepped into Selwyn Cushing's job as acting Air NZ chairman,[14] sought to blame News Limited for selling the airline a sick and troubled company. He claimed in an affidavit to the Australian Federal Court on 9 October that proper due diligence was not allowed.[15] What he didn't say was that, as CEO of Air NZ, Jim McCrae had worked with Rod Eddington to develop and implement the Ansett business recovery program. McCrae, as an experienced engineer, backed plans to curb servicing costs for both carriers. Both McCrae and Eddington had planned the stand-alone company Ansett–Air

New Zealand Engineering Services that eventually would have been floated and operated as an independent business billing each of the carriers separately for maintenance. The same company would also seek to service contracts from Star Alliance partners. It is believed that, before the sale, Air NZ inspectors checked the books and clambered all over plant and equipment at Tullamarine. 'They went right through the place,' said one source.

During a media conference with Australian journalists on 13 September 2001, Gary Toomey took a shot at News and TNT, claiming that when 'we came aboard in January, we found that the previous owners of the airline had not been investing in the aircraft or product for many years … Air NZ would have had to continue to put cash into the airline to keep it flying.' This drew predictable fire from Robert Gottliebsen, economics commentator for the News Limited-owned publication the *Australian*. Gottliebsen would not accept the Toomey line and his immediate response cut to the heart of the matter: 'In fairness to the previous owners, they knew that and sold it to an airline that could have fixed it.' By contrast, Toomey's response appeared lame: 'I could not comment on that, I wasn't here when the decision was taken.'

News certainly believed that a sale to Air NZ would achieve the best long-term outcome; that is made obvious by the decision the publisher took to accept scrip based on the future value of the carrier. By retaining a small equity stake rather than pressing for extra cash, the company reckoned on reaping dividends from the $100 million it agreed to leave in the airline and was to recoup two years after the sale. Addressing his shareholders a month after the Ansett collapse, News chairman Rupert Murdoch said that attempts to grow the airline under the joint Air NZ–News partnership were blocked by Air New Zealand. 'We knew very well that it had to expand, it had to expand overseas and have US dollar earnings and foreign currency earnings,' he told shareholders. 'We had ambitions to take it on routes that we were entitled to take on, which certainly would have been profitable. At every point in that, Air New Zealand—as a 50 per cent shareholder—blocked us.' News was 'very proud', he said, 'of our association with Ansett and what we did for

Ansett'. As to the prospect of recovering the final payment owed under the Ansett sale agreement: 'Whatever that alleged 100 million [shares] is in our books at, I can assure you there is a write-off coming. You can say we got $580 million rather than $680 million, which was pretty good.'

The company's chief operating officer, Peter Macourt, further described Ansett at the time of its sale to Air NZ 'as a business in very good shape run by a first class management team led by Rod Eddington'. He went on: 'It won't wash to apportion blame to previous owners when it is clear the problems confronting Ansett arose during Air New Zealand's time at the

> 'It is clear the problems confronting Ansett arose during Air New Zealand's time at the helm.'

helm.'[16] Figures he produced showed that, from 1993 until News sold its interest in June 2000, Ansett had an operating cash flow of $3.6 billion. Capital expenditure on fleet and facilities improvements amounted to $1.6 billion. Ansett's net debt was reduced from $2 billion to $817 million. News had drawn dividends amounting to just $15 million between 1993 and when Eddington arrived in 1997. All entitlements after that were ploughed into reducing debt. Macourt rejected claims that Air NZ's due diligence was flawed and that it was somehow duped into buying the airline. 'In the first instance, Air New Zealand management had access to all levels of the Ansett business following their acquisition of their first 50 per cent interest,' Macourt said. 'They were deeply involved in the business recovery programme instituted by Rod Eddington. Secondly, Singapore Airlines conducted due diligence on Ansett and offered to acquire News Limited's 50 per cent shareholding for $500 million. No one has suggested that Singapore Airlines failed to do its homework.'

Toomey was at least right in one aspect of the speech he made that previous June: we're actually living through one of the most interesting and challenging periods in world airline history. The changes we're seeing in our region are probably the starkest, most dramatic and dynamic to be seen anywhere in the airline industry today.

Also not lost was the irony of another of his lines: 'our industry is going through a savage shakeout. It's a time when the tough get going … and some hard calls have to be made'.

Toomey resigned that October, 2001, having been miscast as the scapegoat for sins he did not commit. 'In the end, and after all that he and his team did, nobody can identify what he did wrong or what he could have done better,' a friend and senior colleague said. 'Gary worked hard and put plans in place that would have achieved $450 million in savings in 2002.'

10
A WAR ON TWO FRONTS

JOHN ANDERSON'S HOPES of escaping the workday grist of Canberra ended with the trans-Tasman phone call to his central New South Wales wheat and cattle spread that Sunday. At 8.30 a.m. on 9 September 2001, Australia's Deputy Prime Minister was told that the Air

NZ–Ansett marriage was over. The divorce would become absolute after the release of the Air NZ accounts the following Wednesday. The news conveyed by Jim Farmer and Gary Toomey caught Anderson off guard. Nobody within his portfolio Department of Transport expected Air New Zealand to disengage from Ansett. He later recalled: 'It was like a bolt from the blue to be told that they intended to let Ansett go down.'[1]

Anderson's view was coloured by arguments the Kiwis had put to the Australian Government over several months that the Air NZ–Ansett union was needed to tap a lucrative flow of tourists from Australia to grow their airline and by what Farmer had told the Australian Prime Minister John Howard on 14 August: that the Ansett–Air NZ operation was 'deeply enmeshed' and that no 'practical separation can occur'. The New Zealand Stock Exchange was advised on 6 September, three days before the Farmer–Toomey telephone call, that Air NZ's future capital requirements were simply driven by its need to make a substantial re-investment in equipment. The failed bid for Virgin was not a problem, the exchange was told. But further questioning by the New Zealand Exchange's Market Surveillance Panel extracted an admission the following day that the capital raising was incomplete, and SIA would not make an equity injection at the previously agreed price of $1.49 a share.

Anderson's spirits lifted after the stock exchange announcement. He suggested at a specially called press conference that there was hope yet for Ansett. As he prepared to leave Canberra for that weekend at Newstead, near Mullaley, Anderson learned that Toomey wanted to talk. Annoyed that he had been left red-faced by the airline's conflicting statements, Anderson insisted that Farmer and Toomey call him together. He wanted to hear one message from the most senior board member and the airline CEO, not opinions that could be countermanded by either party. In his view there had been too many mixed messages coming from New Zealand.

That Sunday phone call began a tumultuous week for John Anderson and seven days that will be remembered forever in world history. On one front the Australian transport minister had the Ansett crisis to deal with and on another the fallout from the 11 September terrorist attacks on New York and Washington. John Howard was stranded in the United

States as a result of all aircraft groundings and John Anderson held the reins of power over the whole nation.

On that Sunday, Anderson woke after a restless night. He got up early and spent the next hour in his 1959 restored Land Rover inspecting the farm. Returning to the homestead, he learned the worst. Advisers and officials from myriad departments were called and told to bring a change of clothes and prepare for a long night back in Canberra. Little did they know just how long that evening would become. But the first hurdle faced by Anderson, who that weekend found himself wearing John Howard's boots as Acting Prime Minister, was to get to Canberra. The RAAF did not have a VIP aircraft available, and holding down the nation's top job meant that he could fly only in a plane manned by two pilots. Getting a two-crew charter at short notice took time to arrange.

Arriving in Canberra, Anderson booked in to the Embassy motel before joining his team: department chief Ken Matthews, office chief-of-staff Peter Langhorne, media adviser Paul Chamberlin, and aviation adviser Bill McKinley. The aim that Sunday was to piece together a true picture of Air NZ's finances. Official Australian thinking to that point was that the Air NZ–Ansett group would be kept intact and that there was no way the New Zealand Government would allow the operation to go down. Throughout the rest of the day and into the evening Anderson and his advisers worked through everything they knew and could learn of Air NZ's arrangements to establish whether, legally and financially, the two carriers could be separated.

John Howard was told the news upon his arrival in Washington. Anderson was asked to get further legal advice on a possible separation of Ansett. Howard was adamant that a way must be found to stop the divorce. Anderson's team was by then convinced that a break-up could not be stopped; Howard wanted all legal opinions checked and re-checked and checked again. Staffers were dragged from their beds at midnight to restart the process. By early Monday, 10 September, the government had internal and outside opinions from Queen's Counsel that the Kiwis could legally cut Ansett adrift.

Anderson saw the need to limit Australian taxpayers' exposure. Ansett was a commercial insolvency for which government had limited responsibility. He took the view that commercial realities would fill the void—taxpayers' funds would not be used to rescue the entire operation. Ansett had to be kept flying as long as possible and the wind-down had to be done as well as possible, in the interests of the travelling public. Qantas and Virgin Blue executives were called and told only that they needed to help the government with a contingency plan to uplift and return home a lot of people. Information packages were drafted, hotlines were set up and other issues were put in place to minimise the impact on stranded travellers.

The minister and his team worked almost round the clock that Sunday and Monday and until late on Tuesday. People with special skills were co-opted and by Tuesday the heads around the table included John Howard's chief-of-staff, Arthur Sinodinos; Treasurer Costello's chief-of-staff, Phil Gaetjens; Roger Fisher, from Finance, who was later to join Transport; David Borthwick, from the Office of Prime Minister and Cabinet; and other officers from the Attorney-General's and Workplace Relations Departments. The latter pieced together the financials to establish how much the airline was losing.

The initial plan was to inject up to $70 million to keep the airline flying for two to three months, courtesy of the taxpayer. The aim of this was to allow for an orderly wind-down and, perhaps, provide the time needed for a new operator to take over the airline. Canberra was not prepared to buy or operate an airline, but in the national interest the government was prepared to help an administrator manage things in an orderly way. Anderson's ministerial team worked for the next six months reporting to a group of ministers on issues that would normally have been handled more slowly through the Cabinet process. Events dictated that quick decision-making was needed. The meetings took place via e-mail, teleconferencing and phone links from different ends of the country.

Qantas was asked that Monday to conduct a scoping study of the Ansett books amid hopes that Ansett might be bought and some jobs rescued. But, after the Qantas team went to Auckland, the carrier's CEO Geoff Dixon declared: 'There was just too much in there, too many debts, lack of productivity. We may well have been able to do that, but I was afraid that our management would have been tied up for quite some time, possibly years, trying to integrate the two operations. It surprised us, I must say, that they were losing that much.'[2]

Anderson was convinced by 12 September that Air NZ was not competent to manage the crisis. He confided to staff that options had to be explored on how the Australian Government could get Ansett transferred into the hands of an independent manager. The catalyst was a letter he got from Farmer suggesting the Australian Government underwrite Ansett losses while Air NZ restructured the carrier into a no-frills, Virgin Blue type operation. Air NZ had already had more than a year to restructure Ansett and had not made a start. The Australian Government took the view that Air NZ management had shown they could not manage the company with their own money. Why should Australian taxpayers' money go into an operation on which shareholders' funds had already been wasted?

Anderson actively canvassed the scenarios of continued operation, voluntary administration and liquidation of Ansett in a further phone call with Toomey. He told him: 'What I am hearing is ridiculous. I have to tell you we've lost confidence in your capacity to keep Ansett flying while we work it out.'[3] Toomey agreed that the best chance was to put Ansett in the hands of administrators and suggested PriceWaterhouseCoopers (PWC), whose Auckland office had worked for Air NZ on previous occasions. Anderson replied: 'All right, we'll run with that.' Clearly the Australian Government, not the board of Air NZ or the New Zealand Government, was in charge. Members of the Anderson team say PWC was 'very enthusiastic, like a couple of puppy dogs furiously wagging their tails'. Ansett would be the largest insolvency project tackled in Australian history and far more difficult and complex, and with more assets to deal with, than the recent debacle with HIH Insurance.

PWC moved quickly and discovered that Ansett losses had escalated at an alarming rate. They were not $1.5 to $3 million a day as first thought. PWC told the Government that $180 million was needed to keep the airline going for just a couple of days. 'It was just extraordinary,' Anderson remembers. 'Every time we peeled back another layer, we found a whole new canvas of horrors that nobody had known about.'[4]

Transport Department secretary Ken Matthews pressed PWC for figures on what it would cost to keep Ansett in the air. Matthews was given a fast-changing picture. The figures went up by tens of millions of dollars in the course of a few hours. Fuel and leasing charges and catering expenses were owed all over the place. Creditors were coming out of the woodwork. At one point an aircraft was being blocked from leaving Canberra Airport over unpaid landing dues. Matthews' department had to intervene to get the aircraft released.

'Every time we peeled back another layer, we found a whole new canvas of horrors that nobody had known about.'

The Government was prepared to draw up $10 million from the Treasury to prevent panic and keep the airline flying that Wednesday to get people home. A senior Transport bureaucrat was on standby that night with a mobile phone and the taxpayers' cheque book. Matthews took responsibility and briefed the public servant to spend what was necessary to stop any asset seizures. Anderson and the team were eating late at the Deep Dish restaurant at Manuka that Monday when yet another ringing phone tolled more bad news. The PWC team calculated that $300 million was needed to meet the immediate bills. They wanted the Australian Government to put in half but had neither the guarantee that Air NZ would foot the rest nor that this would be the last such call on the taxpayer. Still, after long days and early mornings, the Ansett jigsaw was coming together. Nobody was under any illusions about the difficulty of the task ahead.

Anderson, in his dual roles at that time of Acting Prime Minister and Minister for Transport, was struck by the enormity of the twin disasters of the Ansett collapse and the events of 11 September in the United States. He had returned to his hotel about 11 p.m. that Tuesday 11 September. He went to bed immediately and had been asleep about twenty minutes when his mobile phone rang. On the line was media adviser Paul Chamberlin who had said to his own wife: 'I have to tell the Minister that the United States is under terrorist attack.' Chamberlin told his boss to switch on his television. The remote control wouldn't work and minutes were lost trying to get the receiver to find a channel.

Anderson, like millions everywhere, was immediately dumbstruck by the killings and the devastation in New York and Washington. His first call was to Defence Minister Peter Reith. They covered the ground in a few words and spoke about how the defence arrangements would trip into place. The next call was to Foreign Minister Alexander Downer. Again the conversation was short. Downer said the relevant security agencies would be calling. Anderson then spoke to chief of staff Peter Langhorne and asked him to set up a number of briefings for 7 o'clock the following morning. The first priority was to contact John Howard in Washington, then to make arrangements to reassure Australians that the nation was safe.

At one point, and to Anderson's total and absolute amazement, he was told to ring a five-digit number on his mobile phone. Anderson dialled and was put straight through to the Australian Prime Minister in Washington. The two had what Anderson described as a 'very sober' conversation and one 'far less emotional' than had taken place earlier that evening about Ansett.

A group of intelligence operatives briefed Anderson to stay in his hotel room, that Parliament House was off bounds, and that security was being arranged for his wife and children at home. Families of other high-placed VIPs were being located and placed under the protection. The various agencies swarmed over the national capital and other sites across the country placing them under full protection. The Cabinet was to be gathered together and ministers who were not in Canberra would be contacted by telephone. Anderson got back to bed at 2.30 a.m., knowing that he would need to look fit and calm the next morning when he addressed an anxious nation on television.

When Anderson did get to his parliamentary offices, waiting for him at the lift well with a camera crew was none other than Channel 9's tenacious Laurie Oakes, one of Canberra's most respected and knowledgeable commentators. While the presence of Oakes did not surprise Anderson, he gave him credit for beating the usual press gallery pack. He gave Oakes a brief appraisal of the situation before preparing himself for a more detailed television address to the nation from the Prime Minister's office to try to reassure people amid a world in chaos.

At the time neither Anderson nor his advisers knew what might or might not follow the events in the United States. There were no security briefings that assured them that something else might not occur. And the crisis did not pass without a touch of farce. A terrorist false alarm was raised on a Sydney-bound jet diverted to Brisbane. The pilot sent a private alert after a young passenger was noticed playing a terrorist-based computer game, a fear that was overcome when all passengers alighted without incident in Brisbane.

Anderson noted to his advisers that night that Qantas chairperson Margaret Jackson and Chief Executive Geoff Dixon had mapped out strategies about the effects of the terrorist attack on the world aviation industry. In contrast, Air NZ did not foresee the potential consequences for days afterwards. The airline's then financial adviser, Roger France, who later became a director of the company, acknowledged:

> Over the next week, it became increasingly apparent that the terrorist attacks in the USA were going to have a dramatic effect on the profitability of airlines at least in the short to medium term, and that airlines which did not have a sound capital base had a very high probability of collapse.[5]

At one point Anderson told New Zealand Finance Minister Michael Cullen that Australia had gone from two to four airlines and had no desire to go back to two. Cullen replied that New Zealand had no desire to go from two to none. Cullen was said to have expressed the view that he wanted the group to survive and did not want to see it split.

That Wednesday night a team of fifty personnel from PWC moved in to Ansett headquarters in Melbourne. The airline was beyond hope, but heads were buried to the harsh realities of an insolvent icon. Nobody wanted to hear the worst: that Ansett was dead. Anderson would come under fire for writing off Ansett that week and likening the beleaguered company shell to a carcass. It was not the sort of news that worried staff and the unions wanted to hear, but he would eventually be proved right.

Earlier that day four Australian journalists grilled Farmer, Toomey and chief financial officer Adam Maroney in a trans-Tasman phone hook-up. Alan Kohler (*Australian Financial Review*), Robert Gottliebsen (the *Australian*), Leonie Wood (the *Age*) and Geoff Easdown (the *Herald Sun*) found the Air NZ group noticeably reticent and uncooperative at that press conference to announce the carrier's annual results. Maroney could not provide a current figure on how much Ansett was losing a day.

Kohler: How much is Ansett losing right now, this week, per day?

Maroney: I can't tell you right now, at the moment.

Kohler: Well, OK, last week. What is the extent of the cash flow from Ansett now?

Maroney: I can't tell you right now because in the airline system you don't collect the coupons for about a week, so typically it would be the Sunday before last.

Kohler: OK, that will do.

Maroney: I'd say cash flow neutral.

Kohler: Cash flow neutral last week?

Maroney: No, not last week. The week ending the Sunday before that.

Asked what that meant in terms of the New Zealand Government claim that Ansett was losing $1.3 million a day, Maroney confirmed that it was a book loss of some $12 to $15 million a week, far more than had been imagined.

The journalists then turned their attention to Farmer and a claim he had made that Air NZ was not obliged to meet the cost of Ansett staff redundancies because Air NZ was separate from Ansett as an entity. Before he could finish his reply, Kohler interjected with a curt: 'You don't believe that nonsense, do you?' Farmer then said: 'I will say this. Whatever legal obligations Air NZ has for Ansett, it will honour. That is all I will say.' Leonie Wood noted that the boards of Air NZ and Ansett Holdings were identical and that fiduciary duties existed. Farmer responded sarcastically: 'If you want to give me a lecture on law, I will be happy to hear it. I will pass it onto our lawyers.' The press were not finished with Farmer. He was then asked to elaborate on the refinancing proposal put to the Australian Government the previous day. The new Ansett was, Farmer said, to be a meaner, leaner example than the present high-cost airline. The Australian Government was asked to support it in the short to medium term.

When Easdown asked: 'Why would you expect the Australian tax-payer to bail you out of the problems you have with Ansett?' Toomey responded: 'The New Zealand Government and the Government of Australia regulate the industry very, very closely and, therefore, they have a responsibility for it.' It was a shallow response from a senior airline exec-utive well aware that, a decade before, Australia had ended the Two Airlines Policy and its outmoded system of taxpayer-funded subsidies. The Toomey line would not wash with the Howard Government and its com-mitment to a free-enterprise system of business competition.

11
THE FIRST ANSETT ADMINISTRATION

ON THE EVENING of Wednesday, 12 September, Peter Hedge, Greg Hall and Alan Watson found the cupboards bare and the tills empty after leading their team of 100 specialists into Ansett headquarters. The fate of thirty-five companies, 16 000 workers and their families, and untold assets worth tens of millions of dollars had been lumped on the three accountants from PriceWaterhouseCoopers. Ansett was not going to provide the short-term BandAid treatment they had been asked for by Air NZ; Ansett was the worst corporate disaster in Australian history.

Hedge, Hall and Watson had no cash, no credit and no means to buy fuel. They had to raise $170 million urgently to keep planes in the air and to pay the bills. Their chance of finding a generous benefactor disappeared the night before, as a result of the aircraft hijack attacks on New York and Washington. During talks that night Air NZ reluctantly agreed to cough up $20 million to fund that week's Ansett payroll. The only remaining lifeline was a letter of comfort that Air NZ directors had sent to three Ansett companies on 8 August. Hedge, Hall and Watson played a heavy hand and briefed lawyers to launch court proceedings to claim the outstanding $380 million.

Their chance of finding a generous benefactor disappeared the night before, as a result of the aircraft hijack attacks on New York and Washington.

The Ansett appointment was a plum job for any insolvency firm and the sort every turnaround specialist dreams of. It had the essential ingredients of size, scope, assets, and debts running into the billions. Only a big firm, such as PWC's own accounting practice, could muster the resources needed to recover debts, pay staff and creditors, and extract fees from the asset base. The PWC team would receive $1 084 180 in court-approved fees for just five days of work

Hedge, a softly spoken man with a discernibly gentle edge, sought to reassure the workers that their salaries, holiday pay and long service leave entitlements were safe. 'One of the benefits the law provides for employees is that they enjoy a priority over other creditors,' he told journalists at the first of two press conferences where confusion arose about the PWC role. Hedge, Hall and Watson were going to run the airline as any board of directors would. They spent that Wednesday night and most of the next day trawling governments, banks and institutions on both sides of the

Ansett workers' response to news of Ansett's demise.

Air NZ plane with Helen Clark on board, stranded by a union picket in Melbourne on the day Ansett was grounded.

Tasman for money. The best they could do was to squeeze $20 million from the Air NZ treasury to pay the wage bill at Ansett that week.

But all other efforts came to nothing and ended at 12.30 a.m. on Friday, 14 September. Ansett was officially grounded two hours later and the last planes landed before breakfast in Melbourne and Sydney after overnight flights from Perth. The airports became a mixture of emotional scenes and chaos. Ansett staff and intending passengers learned of the overnight decision only when they turned up to travel. The words on the departure screen at Melbourne Airport simply read: 'Regret all flights cancelled due to the suspension of Ansett operating.' When the Boeing 767 touched down at Melbourne with passengers from flight AN 218 aboard at

5.30 a.m., the passengers and flight crew learned what had happened after the aircraft door was opened. Similar scenes, with teary flight attendants, handkerchiefs at their noses, were played out at all major airports.

With the grounding came also a wave of Kiwi bashing at levels previously unknown in Australia. Among the victims was the New Zealand Prime Minister Helen Clark who suddenly found herself hostage at Melbourne Airport that morning in an Air NZ Boeing 767, which seething workers blocked off with parked aircraft tractors and heavy container hoists. Baggage and cargo handlers refused to touch the plane. 'It can sit there and rot for all I care,' said airport worker Ashley Williams whose partner Sarah Richards was the grand-daughter of Sir Reginald Ansett. An Ansett security worker arrived at the terminal declaring: 'Air New Zealand have absolutely screwed us and thousands of others like us. They bled the company dry and just ditched us.' His female co-worker, who heard the news on early morning radio, added: 'it's unbelievable we found out this way. When I left work last night we were told that everything would operate normally and I came in to work expecting that to happen.'

What began that morning as a major corporate disaster had boiled over into a serious diplomatic incident. The stranded prime minister had to be rescued by police and flown 200 kilometres by helicopter to a waiting military aircraft at East Sale RAAF base. The incident obviously left an unsettling impression on the New Zealand leader because over the following weeks she encouraged the directors of Air New Zealand to reach a financial settlement with the administrators of Ansett.

The Ansett crisis prompted action that day on many fronts. Angry workers were demonstrating at airports and in city streets. The Australian and New Zealand Governments were in crisis talks, and a group of Ansett unions and the Australian Council of Trade Unions were working behind the scenes to replace Hedge, Hall and Watson whose attentions were concentrated on the airline's books and seeking to get answers from an apparently indifferent parent company. Their initial task was to determine what had gone on and to talk with the people in New Zealand who had made the decision to abrogate responsibility for Ansett. When they came face to face for the first time with the Air NZ board in a teleconference hook-up between the airline offices in Melbourne and Auckland, on 14 September, their first impression was that Air NZ might be using their administration as an interim measure to quarantine Ansett and allow the parent company to generate funds and restore depleted cash. Hedge, Hall and Watson also noted that Gary Toomey had resigned as a director of Ansett Australia Ltd on 24 August. Their view was that directors do not normally offer their resignations unless they have serious misgivings about the affairs of the company or a major crisis looms. Their insolvency radar was beginning to beep. Toomey told reporters that his decision to resign from the boards of Ansett and Air NZ subsidiaries was based on his belief that his subordinates were better placed to fill the role.[1]

The trio posed a few key questions to the Air NZ directors: How much cash have we got? When are the wages due, and how much cash have we got to pay them? (The till was empty.) They then asked why Ansett was cut adrift, and why the board was given advice that voluntary administration was the correct route to take. Their aim was to establish a clear picture of what they were taking on without prejudging the issue. The response was not overly helpful. The directors were talking in terms of a temporary separation, not an absolute divorce. The teleconference call ended without an equitable settlement, leaving the three PWC partners no more the wiser and distinctly unimpressed. What they did recognise was that the Ansett administration was not a temporary measure but a final parting of the ways. Strategies had to be implemented in the context of stand-alone Ansett solutions for an airline operating in the Australian environment. The question they asked themselves was: What sort of airline, if there was to be one, should the new Ansett be?

PWC had no intentions of shutting Ansett down when it grounded all planes that Friday. The move was simply to save funds and preserve reserves of fuel. PWC had no way of knowing whether it could achieve the cash flow needed to pay for $1 million worth of aviation fuel. Staff were neither put on notice nor terminated. A clue to PWC's strategy was in the stand-down order the accountants got from the Industrial Court that allowed the firm to send the workers on unpaid indefinite leave. Making the staff redundant or issuing termination notices would have triggered entitlement claims of up to $600 million. The entire Ansett staff on that Friday was on full pay. All the administrators had, in effect, done was save the cost of fuel and operating aircraft for a day. The grounding of the fleet, done with the support of the unions, had a strategic significance in helping to disabuse what one insider referred to as 'a continued head-in-the-sand attitude that Ansett would never stop flying, that the money would come from somewhere'. Apart from the fact that putting staff on notice would have triggered a round of savage redundancy payouts, it was not part of the PWC strategy, as they had every expectation of being able to restructure the airline—to have Ansett back in the air. This was not some quaint notion, some flight of fancy, but a determination to present an alternative that would work.

Secondly, the PWC plan was that the airline would no longer be in the hands of Air NZ, an organisation whose ability to run Ansett had been found wanting and in which PWC had no confidence. The plan was for Air NZ to surrender its shares in Ansett and allow the airline to be returned to Australian hands, with staff owning 10 per cent, creditors 30 per cent and with media magnate Kerry Stokes holding the remaining 60 per cent. There would be jobs for a reduced workforce of about 10 000 working under new workplace agreements; it would not be the same sort of union shop that had existed in the past.

The plan was supposedly coming together when fate, the unions and another accounting firm intervened. Kerry Stokes withdrew what was to have been a $500 million offer, declaring that 'the airline lacked effective and competent management'. PWC staff were noticeably reluctant to discuss the composition of Stokes' syndicate using the veil of 'commercial in confidence'. PWC's successors claim they were never told that an offer was in the wings. The unions believed that PWC did not have a structured strategy for survival of the old Ansett and decided to flex their industrial muscle to bring about changes in the way the administration was being run. The unions represented the biggest group of creditors and won an order from the Federal Court on 17 September to represent the creditors' rights of all Ansett workers. For the unions it was an important victory and a ground-breaking precedent that could be useful, indeed, with other company collapses on future occasions.

ACTU secretary Greg Combet recalled that he was very concerned about the first administration's lack of direction and had become concerned for the employees as the priority creditor. Combet argued that what he saw was not a strategy for survival but what looked like the stage being set for liquidation. It was not a prospect that he would allow to happen until all other options were tested and tried.

Hedge and Hall had barely five days to implement their plan before they resigned in controversial circumstances amid claims of conflict of interest linked to the Auckland office of their firm. John Waller, the firm's most senior partner in New Zealand, had been providing advice to the Air NZ board. It was learned additionally that a recently retired New Zealand PWC partner Roger France was also giving advice to the airline. (France has since been appointed a director of the now New Zealand Government-controlled airline.) Melbourne-based partners of Andersen Accounting, Mark Korda and Mark Mentha, were asked by the unions to take the appointment after representatives of several firms of accounting professionals were paraded before a selection panel at ACTU House on 16 September, a Sunday.

The first move in the union ploy to oust Hedge, Hall and Watson had begun with a surprise phone call to Leon Zwier, a corporate insolvency specialist and senior partner with Arnold Bloch Leibler, at 8.30 a.m. the previous Friday. Issues raised in the call, made by the ACTU's legal advisers Maurice Blackburn, would occupy Zwier's every waking moment for at least the next six months. The firm of labour lawyers needed assistance and, in an odd twist, Zwier seemed the ideal choice. But Zwier was Chris Corrigan's lawyer and had acted for him (and therefore against the unions) during the waterfront dispute two years before. And here was the union movement asking for his assistance in another matter of major importance to its future. Zwier's skills had come to union notice again a few months earlier when he worked briefly for Visy Industries chairman Richard Pratt. On that occasion he was matched against Australian Workers' Union boss

Bill Shorten, who, like Combet, was one of the new breed of educated and articulate unionists. The verdict on Zwier was that he had been extraordinarily tough but fair. The union movement needed those attributes in what it saw as the current impasse with Ansett. Zwier accepted with alacrity.

At a three-hour briefing, Zwier told the unionists they should consider alternative firms to take on the administration. He reminded them that, while the staff were priority creditors, they were by no means the only creditors on the Ansett books. They should consider other major accounting firms, especially those who would be willing to make strategic commercial decisions. He told them to look at firms who could borrow $100 million to save a company worth $1 billion. There were insolvency practices that would tackle the problem head-on and others that would shy away, he warned. The unions needed the former if they wanted Ansett to survive. And, while the unions might well have believed that a change of administrator was needed, Zwier said significant issues must arise to warrant any change of administrator. It was not a *fait accompli* just because they might want it. The issues they had to consider included prior dealings, conflicts, relationships with Air NZ, strategies, and what any administrator would do to enhance creditor returns.

'Here I was, Chris Corrigan's lawyer, walking into the ACTU chambers,' Zwier said. 'It was a very unusual step by the organisation, and my being there clearly created a bit of tension.'[2] The more militant elements at the meeting advocated 'necking' PWC on the spot. Zwier had to be careful but he also had to be mindful of the responsibilities both he and any new administrator would bear. Many of those at the meeting did not understand the difference between liquidation and administration. They had to be told that it was imperative that they do nothing to impede the process, and that they must act like any other corporate client. Zwier was treading on eggshells but he had a strong ally in Combet, who indicated that what was being suggested was 'the only way forward if we are to have a viable, sustainable business'.

The meeting agreed that Zwier would represent them, the first time that one lawyer had acted for fifteen unions and probably the first time the union movement had been represented by other than labour lawyers. It was a measure of their commitment to the process and Zwier was heartened by their support. He rang PWC to say he was on his way to see them but they did not respond to his call. When he did get to see the administrators he quickly formed the view that they lacked strategy and an effective plan to extract money from Air NZ that would not see the carrier collapse. And he found that PWC had not attempted to work with the employees. Their objective, in Zwier's view, was to liquidate. He asked if they would support a representative order being made at the creditors' meeting to allow the unions to vote on behalf of all employees. 'They seemed unwilling to communicate with us and it seemed inevitable to me that we would need to seek to have them replaced,' Zwier said. He knew of the Andersen experts Mark Korda and Mark Mentha and knew they were 'blue chip' insolvency specialists. They would not have a bias towards either business or labour and they would remain focused on the task. Zwier knew that they had been at the cutting edge of some of the biggest administrations in the country, like Brash's, during which most of the law in relation to employee entitlements was championed.

That same evening Combet met Greg Hall and questioned why it had taken the accountant so long to see him when he represented the biggest block of creditor votes. Combet considered the outcome unsatisfactory and demanded an urgent meeting with all three members of the PWC team which would determine the fate of the airline and the old Ansett workforce. One token administrator sent to appease him was not good enough. 'We're not babes in the wood. We were the priority creditors and we wanted to know just where these administrators were heading,' he later said.[3] He had unanswered questions about the strategy that would be pursued, how it would be implemented and what provisions would be made to protect entitlements and salvage jobs. Earlier on the same day, soon after Ansett workers had learned of the grounding of Ansett, a mass meeting had been called outside the Victorian State Library in Swanston Street, 100 metres from ACTU headquarters and a block from the Ansett head office. It was, recalled Combet, attended by 'thousands and thousands of Ansett workers, spilling out from the library lawns onto the road.'

Combet outlined a strategy that called not only for the preservation of
worker entitlements but one that would see the airline back in business.
The crowd greeted his words of hope with wild enthusiasm. On the
hustings, Combet is a formidable force.

On Sunday, 16 September, Combet and his union colleagues again
met with Hall, but this time the other administrators attended as well as a
phalanx of advisers and lawyers 'in tow'. Combet had prepared a set of
questions, the key one of which was the union movement's apprehension
that PWC was advising the board of Air NZ on how to extricate itself from
the Ansett mess. Asked by Hall how he knew that PWC was working for
Air NZ, Combet simply responded:

> It's a small world, mate. We have been in contact with Air NZ in the lead-up
> to Ansett going into administration and in those immediate and following
> days I was in touch with the chief executive of Air NZ, asking what the hell
> was going on. I knew directly that PWC had been advising but there was a lot
> of gossip around the commercial world as well.

Combet wanted to know whether PWC in New Zealand was advising the
board of Air NZ and whether their advice included the options to take
with Ansett. His understanding was that they had suggested putting
Ansett into provisional liquidation. 'We believed that they were giving
advice on how to sever and insulate, sever the financial arrangements and
insulate Air NZ from the fallout.' He felt it inappropriate to have Ansett
in the hands of PWC in Australia while colleagues in New Zealand were
trying to dump the airline and insulate Air NZ from legal action. 'We just
thought it was an unacceptable conflict of interest, if not direct, then a
very strong perception of one.'

While this may have been serious enough to influence its thinking, the
ACTU was even more aggrieved when it was advised wrongly of the date
of the first creditors' meeting. Remembers Combet:

> It was a day earlier than what they said; well, I don't know how they could
> fuck that up. They say it was an innocent mistake but it was a significant

mistake because we were trying to organise proxy votes for all those workers around the country. That really crashed the confidence of the union officials in the administration.[4]

It was a loss of confidence compounded by the fact that the unions could not get a clear strategy from the administrators and, while it was 'early days, we had the view that as priority creditors wanting the airline resurrected, we wanted to see a strategy that looked to selling the airline as a going concern.'

> **'As priority creditors wanting the airline resurrected, we wanted to see a strategy that looked to selling the airline as a going concern.'**

What PWC did do was present Combet with a suggestion that Ansett wet-lease aircraft to Qantas and possibly Virgin to meet marketplace demand, a suggestion that had been put to him by Deputy Prime Minister John Anderson. 'I understood the rationale behind the strategy,' Combet recently commented, but:

> when you hear the same story from the Ansett administrators, you don't have to be a genius to work out that there has been dialogue going on between the Government and PWC. We were willing to contemplate wet-leasing arrangements to meet short-term emergency needs but we could not be certain, given our commitment to reviving the airline, of just how long the wet-leasing arrangement might last and how that might affect our plans. It was never enunciated.

The notion was just too uncertain and Combet saw it as an attempt to put Ansett at a competitive disadvantage in the event that it did recommence flying. Combet recognised that selling an airline that was no longer grounded would not only increase the value of the assets but provide a better return for creditors. His constituency was his primary concern and he was not about to start playing around with its welfare.

The door was now open for a change of administrator and, according to Combet, 'there was no shortage of interest from all levels of the accounting profession'. Contrary to popular belief, Korda and Mentha from Andersen were neither an automatic nor an exclusive choice. Combet explains:

> The fact is that a number of the unions knew them from the work they had done on other significant insolvencies. I knew their reputation but had never met them before that Sunday afternoon. We had canvassed a number of alternative administrators and took advice from our own lawyers, Arnold Bloch Liebler, as well as Maurice Blackburn and Slater and Gordon, and a number of others.

The various accountants were interviewed in the second-floor conference room of the ACTU headquarters with all unions present. It was a new experience for white-collar professionals used to dealing with the top end of town—the banks and other large financial institutions, the big corporates—to be facing a group of unionists whose key, indeed only, interests were the welfare of their members and maintaining at least the appearance of union power.

Korda and Mentha were seen to have done their homework about both Air NZ and Ansett. They had an understanding of the commercial realities and the problems faced by both airlines. But, more than anything, they put across the point that it was possible to develop and implement a strategy to sell Ansett as a going concern: back in the air with the prospect of a long-term future; not the same as before, they were quick to point out, but a business nevertheless, employing up to 4000 people. The audience heard what it wanted to hear and voted to begin proceedings to oppose the PWC appointment on the basis of a perceived conflict of interest. Sensing a drawn-out, unsavoury brawl over who would make money from the carcass of Ansett, PWC resigned the next day, opening the way for the unions to have Mark Korda and Mark Mentha nominated and appointed by Justice Alan Goldberg, the judge presiding over the Ansett case. But first Zwier also had to obtain a court clearance for the pair

Solicitor, Leon Zwier   *First administrators, Alan Watson and Peter Hedge*

because of their earlier role as business advisers to Ansett subsidiary Hazelton.

Zwier had deftly changed the dynamics of the corporate administration process. The unions could wield the muscle of employee votes and hold down positions of unprecedented power in future corporate insolvencies. Zwier would play a major role and, in the months that followed, two previously unknown accountants would become household names as 'the two Marks who were running Ansett'. The seventeenth-floor executive suite had barely been occupied by the PWC team before it packed and left, frustrated and bemused by both the speed and the nature of their departure. Hedge, more than his other partners, was bitterly upset: he broke down in tears and could not continue to read to reporters the resignation statement.

The replacement of PWC by Andersen became a continuing controversy within the accounting profession. PWC has said publicly that it believes to this day there was no conflict of interest arising from the fact that one of its New Zealand partners, John Waller, was advising the board of Air NZ while the firm's Sydney and Melbourne partners were seeking to come to terms with the debts of Ansett. John Waller is to New Zealand what David Crawford, former KPMG partner and one of the country's best known insolvency practitioners, is to Australia. PWC's view was that it was not wrong for a major company to ask Waller for second opinions on advice from strangers in Australia and that his role did not create a conflict of interest. How else would a company decide to hand itself over to external administrators without understanding what it all meant beforehand? Second opinions were necessary and Waller was not sitting in on meetings. Where was the conflict? For its part, Andersen was believed to have been providing advice to Ansett. This was denied by Andersen.

Research has revealed that, in the period when the Air NZ board was contemplating appointing a voluntary administrator to Ansett, Mark Mentha was actually in New Zealand hoping to be called to present his and Korda's Ansett recovery plan to the directors of Air NZ. The pair was later shocked to hear that a different firm got the appointment and they were not asked to present their plan. What they initially proposed, but which they did not get to outline, was an arrangement in which they would have organised outside funding to pay wages, fuel charges and leases. This was to have been done via a loan to the administrator. Liabilities, meanwhile, would be frozen and stakeholder issues resolved quickly. Andersen predicted that Ansett would be preserved as a going concern and as many jobs as possible saved.

Mentha had travelled to New Zealand and while there a lawyer friend, Nick Stretch, rang Mentha to ask him if he would be available to do the Ansett administration if asked. Stretch was a partner in the Melbourne legal firm Gadens, which gave advice to the Ansett board. Mentha was questioned by Stretch about the role Andersen had as auditors to Hazelton Airlines, an Ansett subsidiary. Mentha advised that, because of this, another administrator would need to be appointed to Hazelton. Similarly, he was confident that Andersen had ample resources to perform the task. Mentha's belief at the time was that PWC had a potential conflict of interest not so much over the involvement of John Waller but because the firm had worked with Air NZ for some time via the airline's banking syndicate. The possibility of a conflict had not concerned some Air NZ officials, whose only interest appeared to be in saving Air NZ, not about its dying offspring. Air NZ's concern centred on cutting its liability for ongoing Ansett losses. Mentha said:

They [PWC] had shut down the reservations system, the banks had closed down payroll, everything had just been closed down. The company had been pushed away from the dock without a rudder and no means of obtaining fuel to get anywhere. There was not one dollar in the bank.[5]

PWC can only be judged on what its team achieved during its limited period in charge of Ansett. Hedge, Hall and Watson extracted from Air NZ $20 million that the company's payroll needed during those five critical days. PWC was determined to press legal claims for the $380 million outstanding from the letter of comfort that Air NZ had given in August. Had the action been successful, the Ansett administration would have been a lot richer than it was in the months going forward. But Air NZ clearly no longer had that amount of money to shell out towards paying the claims of Ansett creditors. As it was, the Kiwi airline had to plead a case of pending insolvency to obtain from the New Zealand Government the $182 million required to settle the Ansett claim and provide a farewell payout to workers.

THE SECOND ANSETT ADMINISTRATION

THE COMPANY DOCTORS from Andersen Accounting arrived at ACTU headquarters that Sunday afternoon with the message the unions wanted to hear. They offered hope that the airline with the Southern Cross tail might fly again and a faint ray of sunshine for 15 000 stood-down workers. 'Korda and Mentha just blew them away. They were reasoned and blunt and they had no intention of pandering to the unions,'[1] said Zwier, who had been asked by Combet to sit and advise the union selection panel. The two accountants outlined options and strategies they believed could be used to revive the company and preserve jobs.

The ACTU and its affiliated Ansett unions needed a miracle. Their rank and file confronted sudden and unexpected redundancy. The bulk of the airline's 15 000 workforce was stood down without pay and the prospect of this legion of workers being able to return to their jobs looked decidedly grim. When the planes were grounded two days before, PWC administrator Peter Hedge had warned that he was hopeful of selling only the 'viable segments' of what had once been Australia's biggest domestic airline. Hedge left everyone who attended his late-afternoon press conference that Friday with the clear impression that any chance of Ansett returning to the skies in its own right had vanished. There had been some interest from potential buyers in the regional subsidiaries Hazelton and Kendell airlines. But the main-routes airline was at that time the orphan that nobody wanted. Hedge and his PWC promised only to obtain the best value for whatever was sold to improve the prospects of the workforce. What Hedge left unsaid was that an asset sale spelled job losses on an enormous scale, the likelihood of wide-scale welfare problems and an almost certain fall in union memberships.

Korda and Mentha were approached by Zwier at 8 a.m. that Saturday and told that the unions wanted a change of administrator. Were they willing to put their ideas to the meeting at ACTU House on Sunday? Not only would they do this, but they already had a valid plan to revive the brand and keep as many jobs as possible. Mentha, who knew the union bosses on first-name terms from past insolvency appointments, was confident their plan would win support and lead to an application to the court the following Monday. He left work that Friday determined to take a break, knowing that, should Sunday go well and court approval follow, neither he nor his partner would see much of their families over the coming months. A family man who married late and had two young sons, Mentha would spend the weekend with his wife Kerry and the boys at their Melbourne bayside beach house. Korda spent the weekend at home, fine-tuning the pair's plan and catching occasional glimpses of AFL football on television.

At about 6.30 on Saturday evening, Mark, Kerry and their children were at Big Joe's Pizzeria in Main Street, Sorrento, when Mark's mobile phone rang. With his favourite Small Capricciosa with Egg going cold, he chatted for a few minutes with a partner from a labour law firm who had heard that the pair had been short-listed for the Ansett job and that their firm was well qualified and equipped to handle some of the legal work that might follow. Mentha had grabbed the call hoping at first that it might have been good news about the likely decision at the following day's meeting. While it was not news on that front, it did highlight one thing: the word was out that their firm, Andersen Accounting, had a good chance of winning the appointment. Mentha went back to his pizza, content that he and Korda had done everything within their power to prepare for the next day, when they would tell the unions that they would not at that early stage set out to liquidate the company.

Waiting for Korda and Mentha at ACTU headquarters that Sunday were Greg Combet as well as representatives of the Australian Workers' Union, the Australian Services Union and the Electrical Trades Union. The pair were questioned about past insolvencies and what they might do at Ansett that would differ from the strategies already undertaken by PWC. They replied that they could not properly answer that until they had reviewed the books and the financials. They had a three-point plan to stabilise the business, develop a strategy and perform an investigative process, promoted as 'the Ansett solution'. They told the meeting they would stabilise—and minimise—the costs of the various Ansett business-es and then determine whether it was possible to resume operations. Next they would develop a solution that kept as much as possible of the Ansett group in existence while maximising returns to creditors. And finally they would perform the necessary investigations.

Asked at the meeting whether he would bend the rules to accommo-date an outcome, Korda replied: 'No. If it was the right thing, we would do it. If it was not the right thing, we would not do it.' He was blunt. Neither he nor his partner would be beholden to the unions; and the unions, pragmatically, recognised the fact. They were impressed and at the same time appeared delighted to have found professionals who would represent them as a creditor block—fairly and forcefully. Zwier went before Justice Alan Goldberg the next day and the rest is now history. Zwier also sought separate approval for the ACTU and the unions to represent all Ansett workers at the creditors' meeting the next day. Goldberg accepted that time had not allowed the unions to secure the necessary proxy votes to ensure that significant issues involving Ansett employees were approved by the meeting. Over the following months Justice Goldberg had a key role approving decisions taken by Korda and Mentha at hearings where a veritable phalanx of QCs and lesser legal lights presented their opinions.

Korda and Mentha's 'Ansett solution' required them to find the right management, provide a business plan and ensure that the business was properly capitalised. They flew to Singapore and recruited help from world-renowned carrier Singapore Airlines. Locally they won ACTU support and backing for this endeavour from the Federal and Victorian governments. Korda and Mentha believed the right business plan was to position the new Ansett somewhere between a full-service, Qantas-type carrier and the no-frills, Virgin Blue value service. There was much 'white space' between the two that a revitalised Ansett could fill. To succeed, they had to retain and maximise the value of the assets and the long-term viability of any new airline.

They were pitching to snare 20 per cent of the domestic market. Pre-administration Ansett had between 38 and 40 per cent of the market, having fallen from a situation in which it had a 55-per-cent market share in the early 1990s. 'Given the assets we have, given the cash we are looking to have, 20 per cent is not unrealistic,' Mentha noted in one of the many interviews he did in the first weeks of the assignment.[2] The third move was to investigate the company failure: who was to blame and who, if anyone, should be prosecuted?

Mentha and Korda operated for weeks on a four-hour sleep cycle described by Mentha in a press interview on 5 October as having 'at times … stretched us in terms of our biorhythms'. The challenges in managing all the issues, he said, were just incredible. The pair were running not just the Ansett administration; they also had charge of the affairs of thirty other troubled companies. Between his duties at 501 Swanston Street, Mentha would visit and speak to workers at the Bradmill textiles factory at Spotswood, addressing different work shifts. On one particular day, he addressed nightshift workers at 6.30 p.m. and the day shift at 7 a.m., going back that night, when the afternoon shift finished at 11.30 p.m., to address another team of workers. He spoke to them passionately and eloquently, destroying any myths that he was a dry, dull accountant interested only in the black ink at the bottom of the company bank statement.

The Bradmill problem, like the Ansett crash, was compounded by the events of 11 September. Finding a buyer for a top Australian mill and fashion label was not easy when the headquarters of the world's denim market had been in the New York World Trade Center. But Bradmill was sold soon afterwards to United States interests who guaranteed the future, at the Melbourne factory, of the plant and the four hundred workers who chose to stay; as well as full redundancy payments for those who opted to go.

Although Korda and Mentha owed their appointment to union support, they proved over the months that followed that they were no puppets. Fiercely independent, they renegotiated with the unions workplace agreements that substantially cut labour costs. Similarly they showed themselves prepared and ready to stand up to government. In one celebrated standoff with Federal Transport Minister John Anderson, the Minister claimed that the administrators had, that November, made an election-eve deal favourable to the Opposition Labor Party. Mentha replied: 'I answer to the *Corporations Act*, not the Electoral Act.'[3]

The unions, desperate to preserve jobs amid Ansett's teetering fortunes, had to be realistic and accepted the pragmatism of the arrangements. Sweetheart deals that operated under Ansett workplace agreements were set aside and most staff who did get work during the Korda–Mentha administration were paid on an hourly rate, not on the basis of their former forty-hour-week agreements. They virtually became permanent part-time staff in what was a groundbreaking and entirely sensible arrangement, considering the straitened circumstances confronting the airline. Pilots who worked for an hour were paid for an hour's operational duty. The same applied to flight attendants: hourly pay rates allowed them to job-share and gave larger numbers of staff a chance to work, albeit on a much lower income. Rules were changed that enabled flight crews to fly east coast–Perth return flights without the airline incurring the cost of overnight crew accommodation. The former arrangement required a layover in Perth before flying the return leg across the country.

Like Hedge, Hall and Watson the week before, Korda and Mentha arrived at Ansett headquarters at 501 Swanston Street late on Monday, 17 September knowing that they had to prepare for the first official creditors' meeting the following morning. With their own team of fifty specialists in tow they got down to work and stopped at 4 o'clock the next morning. They snatched a few hours' sleep and managed somehow still to look fresh for their meeting with staff and creditors that morning. Mentha recalled:[4]

Mark and I worked right through the night trying to understand what we had been appointed over. PWC briefed us until 11.00 p.m. Mark and I began to consider where we were at. We went home around 4 and were back at 6 a.m. I had to work out what I was going to say, develop the process of dealing with the issues and face those people who were owed so much.

At 10 a.m. Korda and Mentha faced 2000 employees and creditors in the ballroom of Crown Casino, where Mentha balanced the seriousness of the occasion with some lighter elements. He broke the tension in the opening moment, telling the crowd that under the television spotlights he was not sure whether he was Britney Spears or Michael Jackson. Over three hours Mentha juggled the official business of setting the legal arrangements with hearing tales of woe from employees. He was handed a catalogue of errors of corporate management that had led to the failure.

'Our number-one priority is to put food on the table and to get those planes back in the air,' he told the crowd, who succumbed to his laid-back style and uncomplicated delivery. What he said shocked: his team had arrived the previous night and found the financial cupboard bare, he told the audience. 'There was a complete lack of financial systems; there was no treasury function, no assets registry, no cash flow figures, no profit-and-loss accounts.' It was, he confided later, 'a bit like going away on holiday on your own and then coming back and asking your partner "Where has all the money gone?" ' Amid placards reading: 'ABSOLUTE FURY' (a twist on the Toomey ad campaign) and others with the blatant anti-Kiwi line 'AIR NEW ZEALAND—NOWHERE TO RUN. NOWHERE TO HIDE', Korda and Mentha left the ballroom to face the first of their many media conferences.

It is hard to imagine the enormity of the task handed to Korda and Mentha. Ansett had employed more than 15 000 people; had maintained, in the combined Ansett trunkline carrier and its subsidiary regional airlines Skywest, Kendell, Hazelton and Aeropelican, an operational fleet of 133 aircraft; had carried 14 million passengers in 2000; and had carried 111 147 tonnes of cargo in the 2001 financial year. Ansett and its subsidiary regionals served 111 bush towns and cities across Western Australia, the Northern Territory, New South Wales and Queensland and had generated, in the year to 30 June, revenue of $3.2 billion, recording a monumental loss of $378 million. The grounding cut services to 130 destinations and ended 900 daily flights across the network—a far, far bigger operation than Air New Zealand's principal business of loading tourists onto jumbo jets and flying them into and out of the country. Ansett also operated major travel agencies through its separate Traveland and Showgroup trading arms; leased somewhere in the vicinity of 350 different buildings and retail premises; dealt with Australia's federal and various State governments and their agencies; and, by September 2001, had to generate at least $200 million a month to break even.

Ansett was the Australian corporate basket case burdened with a $3.5 billion debt. Korda and Mentha knew that, to continue, they somehow had to liquidate cash from eighty-three aircraft and the previously lucrative space the airline had leased to retail traders at numerous airports. But in the days following the 11 September terrorist attacks nobody anywhere was interested in buying or investing in an airline, let alone one so troubled as Ansett. As Korda and Mentha explained in a letter sent some months later to creditors: 'With aircraft worth in the vicinity of $2 billion, even a shift [in value] of as little as a 10 per cent can drag down the values as much as $200 million.'[5] And at a time when every dollar counted, the events of 11 September struck a terrible blow to the chances of reviving the airline and finding an equitable solution for a workforce stood down without pay and without hope of finding alternative airline employment.

The *Corporations Act 2001* would, however, allow them time to stave off, for the moment, myriad claims from the finance dogs that had begun to bark. Korda and Mentha were treading a tightrope, held at one end by the hope of a future sale and rescue, and at the other by creditors hell bent on redeeming what cash they could from a liquidation and asset fire sale. Staff would remain stood down without pay until a deal could be cut with the Commonwealth Government. Declaring any of them redundant would have tipped the airline into terminal mode and triggered liquidation. The issue was made worse when, suddenly and without notice, key accounting staff seconded by Ansett from Air New Zealand packed their bags and left Melbourne for Auckland during the fateful second week in September.

The first challenge was to track the titles and establish ownership rights to aircraft and end the stream of repossession agents clamouring at Ansett's door. With an aircraft fleet 133 strong, numerous property and equipment leases, and matching documents held in repositories on both sides of the Tasman, establishing who owned what was not going to be easy. Coupled with that, and making the challenge more difficult, was an accepted airline practice of swapping engines and other expensive equipment between planes. Jet engines, auxiliary power units, expensive navigational aids and licensed computer software, some of which were worth millions of dollars and held under lease from different owners, had been swapped seemingly indiscriminately between aircraft.

A member of the Korda–Mentha team, Delma Thompson, explained to Federal Court judge Alan Goldberg on 28 September: 'I am informed by Ansett operational staff and believe that engines are often swapped between aircraft for various reasons to allow servicing of engines while the airframe of the aircraft remains in use ... Many of the aircraft may presently have engines which do not belong to the owner of the aircraft.'[6]

Thompson added that power units fitted to planes were held under separate title and were not the rightful property of the aircraft owner. Some onboard computer software also was licensed from third party suppliers.

When asked which companies and who owned 52 aircraft leased to Ansett, Thompson told Justice Goldberg at a hearing on 1 October, 'I think I am dealing with about 35 individual groups or syndicates, of which there would be something like 20 or 30 participants in some syndicates.' And, on the matter of leased properties, she said, 'My estimate is there are something like 40 or 50 lessors. On the computer side, there are five or six, and on several other items, there are presumably rental arrangements that we haven't got to yet, such as equipment hire companies.'

In the Federal Court on that Monday morning were arrayed the legal representatives of a veritable Who's Who of world aircraft leasing and the international banks: Simona Lessors, Gelco Corporation Inc, Trident Jet Australia, Credit Lyonnais, Deutsche Verkehrsbank AG, BNP Pacific (Australia), Nord Deutsche Landesbank, Girozentrale, Sumitomo International Finance Australia, Sanwa Bank, Mitsubishi Trust and Banking Corporation, HSBC Bank plc, National Australia Bank, IMG Lease (Ireland) BV, Expert Development Bank of Canada, De Nationalie Investerings Bank Asia, Commerzbank AG, CIT Financial Australia, Air Canada, and the ANZ Banking Group.

As a result of that 1 October hearing, Korda and Mentha were granted relief to put in place arrangements for the orderly, rather than forced, return of aircraft assets. Justice Goldberg's decision effectively silenced the baying dogs that wanted their assets returned first to avoid what was to become a long and time-consuming wait for the hand-over of planes with their full kit of official documents. But wait they had to, because as Thompson told the judge:

The aircraft cannot in any event be moved by the owners without the Ansett Group supplying to the owners the engineering and maintenance records. A pilot or first officer is not able to take possession of an aircraft without such documents without putting the pilot or first officer's own certification or licence at risk.

In the weeks that followed, a 120-strong team from Andersen Accounting pored over the accounts of forty-one separate Ansett companies, running for a time and selling some fourteen different, but related, Ansett businesses. Their investigations showed that Ansett itself was owed $100 million in unclaimed debts; that it owned or held property leases worth $300 million; and that equity amounting to a further $300 million existed in aircraft, engines, spare parts and engineering equipment.

On the opposite side of the ledger,[7] staff were owed some $730 million; the fuel bill totalled $20 million; hire car companies were owed $1.5 million; various financiers had claims exceeding $100 million; the telcos were owed $16 million; and miscellaneous claims, including Golden Wings members, trade suppliers, frequent flyers, and unused ticket holders were also pressing for in excess of $1.1 billion. Claims were uncovered from more than 7000 creditors, without taking into account debts owed in workplace entitlements to the 15 000 staff, 2.7 million frequent flyers and 130 000 Golden Wings members, and the $250–300 million that had to be refunded for unclaimed tickets. A committee of representatives from 32 major creditors who were owed a total of $798 865 607 oversaw the activities of Korda and Mentha and their team of 120 specialists. The tenets of the *Corporations Act* were observed and all major decisions were submitted for final approval to Justice Goldberg.

> **A committee of representatives from creditors owed a total of $798,865,607 oversaw the activities of Korda and Mentha and their team of 120 specialists.**

The insolvent airline presided over by the two Marks was soon dubbed 'Ansett Mark II' by the media as Korda and Mentha sought to revive the company and find a buyer. This play-on-words was dream stuff for sub editors and made for many a catchy headline. Over the next six months the two Marks would enjoy constant media presence and their regular commentaries kept workers well informed of their progress. They held

Mark Korda (left) and Mark Mentha at   *Partners, Korda and Mentha*
their first press conference.

daily media briefings for the first two weeks, initially in the seventeenth-floor Ansett boardroom, then when the crowds got too large, in the second-floor Ansett head-office cafeteria.

Of the two men themselves, they were more than just partners in a major accounting practice. They were good mates who enjoyed a near-inseparable twenty-year friendship. Mark Korda had driven Kerry Mentha to his best mate's wedding; and he was godfather to one of the Mentha children. After the controversial collapse of Andersen Accounting, the pair established their own consulting practice, Korda,Mentha and Colleagues. On the Ansett job they held no false hopes and at times their moods became quite sombre. Late one evening, two weeks out from the election, Mark Mentha admitted in a conversation with two journalists[8] his worst fear that, after the 10 November federal election, a re-elected Howard Government could seek to exercise its right as a major creditor and win support to overturn the administration and move to liquidate the airline. At that time Korda and Mentha were juggling prospective bids, one of which had come from controversial 'union buster' and Lang Corporation boss Chris Corrigan, a favoured son of the Howard Government over his labour reform on the waterfront who had temporarily joined forces with Virgin Blue and was offering jobs to 2000 staff stood down at Ansett.

As Korda and Mentha battled through competing proposals, the

Howard Government turned up the heat on the two Marks by delaying for weeks a decision on how it would underwrite the $195 million they needed to fund staff departure entitlements. While the issue dragged out, the pressure built for Korda and Mentha to find a buyer or abandon their three-point plan and liquidate assets. Hundreds of small businesses that supplied the Ansett–Air NZ group were themselves 'staring down the barrel of a gun'. The first to crash was Swissair-owned Gate Gourmet, principal supplier of in-flight meals and refreshments. A senior Canberra figure would confide later that the Howard Government had hoped for a sale to Corrigan because of the labour reforms that would flow through the aviation sector due to his involvement. As fate and a set of unfortunate circumstances decreed, Corrigan and the government largely got what they wanted.

But, in those first weeks of the Korda–Mentha administration, both partners remained tight-lipped about what bids they had on the table. The only detail they would openly discuss was what the bidders themselves had made public. Korda lectured:

> It is not fair to be building up the hopes of the workers in any administration. You just have to keep trying to make the very best of what you've got to work with, of what's left when you come in. To us the people are the most important part of any administration.[9]

Both were well experienced in high-profile insolvencies. They took charge of Budget Rent-a-Car after it went belly-up in 1989 while under the control of Reg Ansett's son Bob, who had taken a very successful private car rental group and floated it into a failed public company. The Budget crash was an insolvency that led to changes in the *Corporations Act* allowing for troubled enterprises to be placed under voluntary administration and beyond the control of former directors. Korda and Mentha also took charge of Collings Real Estate; Bradmill; and the home builder, Jennings Industries.

Not all of their current administrations were big projects. Throughout the Ansett administration, they also ran a foundry that provided work for forty-six people in the rural Victorian city of Horsham. Someone else might have shut it down but it was a key local industry and neither of the Marks wanted to deprive that small community in the Wimmera of any employer who handed out weekly pay packets.

Another incident involved them in a plea for help from the Cobram–Barooga Golf Club, across the Murray River from Mentha's home town of Cobram. Mentha, a single-handicap golfer, knew the club well and knew how much it was relied on as an employer and provider of leisure activities for the locals. A mate from his schooldays had called him on a Sunday morning with news that the club was about to fold and the creditors were gathering. Collecting Korda in his car, the pair drove north to the Murray, cleared the creditors from the room and white-boarded a solution over a couple of hours with the club's directors. The fix they instituted was not via extra poker machines or new up-market dining facilities; they simply hiked up membership and green fees. Cobram–Barooga Golf Club has thrived ever since, with strong membership and a profitable balance sheet. The debts that so troubled the members had been paid off within a year.

While Korda is Melbourne-born and raised, Mentha likes nothing better than to return to Cobram and fish for cod in the Murray. 'Red gum sap runs through my veins,' he likes to say. And he does like watching the lads of Cobram play football. The two mates have set up a bush-style 'corporate box' to which they delight in taking clients. Better, they believe, to spend a weekend playing golf and watching local footy than hobnobbing at the Melbourne Cricket Ground watching the big league. Says Mentha:

> [The clients] are staggered when we invite them to join us for the game in our corporate box and then pick them up in a bus for the trip to Cobram. It's not exactly what they thought it would be but invariably it's a lot of fun.[10]

They are indeed an odd couple, Korda and Mentha. The former is thickset, dark, swarthy and a deep thinker. The latter is tall, of slim build and sandy colouring, with a quick mind and a sharp wit to match. He likes to throw one-liners around the place. Neither was university educated. They gained their accounting tickets at what were once technical colleges:

Swinburne Institute and Royal Melbourne Institute of Technology. At the time of the Ansett administration both were in their forties and had enjoyed the status of accounting partners for more than a decade. Korda was made an Andersen partner at age thirty-one, and Mentha at twenty-nine. They think differently and complement each other. Mentha says of Korda: 'He has a steel-trap mind when it comes to segregating financial statements. I've never met anyone better at analysing, interrogating and linking things together to form a picture.' Mentha's strengths, on the other hand, are commercial. He hates confrontation and litigation, preferring to find a pragmatic solution to problems through negotiation and open dialogue. He sees himself as being strong on people skills. 'Bring the people in and make them part of the solution rather than alienate them'. It was very much the way they conducted the Ansett administration—Korda in charge of the sale of the business and Mentha in charge of dealing with employees, unions, the government, and the people side of the process. Said Mentha: 'I can't recall ever having an argument [with Mark]. If I've got a problem, he's the bouncing board and if he's got a problem I play the same role.' Korda describes himself as being the passionate one. 'Sometimes I explode and get called Mount Vesuvius.' Korda is well organised—he hates leaving the office without tidying his desk. Mentha on the other hand, is laid back, less conservative, less neat. Korda likes the odd bet at the casino while for Mentha, gambling has no appeal, calling his friend 'the Ayatollah of Cashollah'—a reference to his predilection for the punt or a game of craps. Both are family men. Mentha's leisure time is spent at his holiday house, Korda preferring his mobile home at Bonnie Doon and water-skiing with his wife Rhonda and three sons on Lake Eildon.

Korda has known what it is like to struggle. He worked as a truck jockey delivering garden sheds while studying at Swinburne. But he quickly tired of delivering them and set up his own business installing them. He kept this business going at the weekends after he went to work as an accountant. 'I used to make more money at the weekends than in a whole week in accounting.' Both have had interesting assignments. Korda was the director and sole shareholder of the Hospitality Management Company, which bought up to fifty Victorian pubs for New Zealand brewer

Lion Nathan. It was a 'very behind-the-scenes project', he says, with family and colleagues nominal owners to avoid starting a price war. He later set up a company known as the Epping Land Development Company to subdivide a large slab of outer Melbourne and establish a new suburb. With such diverse, hands-on backgrounds of their own, they bring experience and real interest to the administration process. The beauty of their current job, says Korda, 'is that every administration has its own peculiarities. No two are the same and the variety keeps us on our toes at all times.'

Despite being highly paid professionals, Mentha and Korda cut their charges on the Ansett project to an hourly rate that was 35 per cent below that normally charged by Andersen. During those first, at times frantic, three months, up to eighty to a hundred partners, directors, managers, support staff and contracted specialists worked on the account. They attracted total fees, approved by the Federal Court and the various creditors' committees, which exceeded $10.8 million from the time of their September appointment until 14 December 2001. This makes an interesting comparison with the $1 084 180 that PriceWaterhouseCoopers claimed and were paid for five days' work.

'In those first three months, we put over fifty man years into the administration of Ansett.'

The 35 per cent fee cut translated to a partner's charge-out rate of $359 per hour; the PWC charge was fixed at $420. The fee schedule was openly documented in the reports to creditors and was at all times subject to Creditor Committee and Federal Court approval. As this book went to production, the fees for the total administration were expected to reach $30 million, a figure that neither Korda nor Mentha resiles from.

We knew when we came into this administration that it would be very difficult, very complex and much bigger than anything we or any other administrator had ever come across. In those first three months, we put over fifty man years into the administration of Ansett.

The $4 billion collapse of HIH Insurance was in every sense a national disaster, but what happened to Ansett would in some way affect every Australian, not just airline workers and those in the aviation industry whose businesses had serviced the airline. Three generations had grown up with the Ansett name and at some stage in their lives had booked a seat and travelled with the airline. The Ansett plight was the biggest challenge undertaken by Korda and Mentha and their team from Andersen Accounting. Mark Korda said: 'HIH was about paperwork and lost millions. Ansett was about people, planes and lots of infrastructure. What happens to Ansett is about a very large slice of the Australian workforce'.

13
THE POKER GAME

POKER IS NOT a game for the faint hearted. It
calls for nerves of steel and a capacity for dupli-
city, or bluff as it is officially known. According to
Hoyle, the bible in such matters, the basic principle of poker is to build 'structures' consisting of
'two or more cards of a kind ... sequences of

cards … hands composed of the same suit'. Interestingly there are no official laws of poker and every game reserves the right to make its own rules. The ultimate object, of course, is to win the pot, whether by actually holding the best hand or by inducing other players to drop and leave the pot to be taken uncontested by a single player still willing to bet.

Mark Korda and Mark Mentha got into the biggest poker games of their lives when they took on the administration of Ansett and, having made a quick review of the situation in which they found themselves, determined to claw back some of the outstanding debts from its parent, Air New Zealand, the trans-Tasman minnow that had swallowed and then regurgitated the pride of Australian aviation. The problem was that Air NZ itself was in diabolical strife and threatened by the same black hole that had engulfed Ansett. The game would be a tricky one, calling for guile, patience, tough negotiating skills tempered with a recognition that there was not much meat left on the bone, and a willingness to compromise when it is the last thing on the players' minds.

As the two administrators considered their options in dealing with Air NZ, they may have recalled the words of country and western singer Kenny Rogers singing 'The Gambler', the chorus of which goes:

> You got to know when to hold 'em, know when to fold 'em
> Know when to walk away and know when to run
> You never count your money, when you're sittin' at the table
> There'll be time enough for countin', when the dealin's done [1]

This was Korda and Mentha's play: a high-stakes poker game with a battered and bruised opponent—but an opponent nevertheless determined not to play its hand. This was bluff and counter-bluff at its best, Air New Zealand playing 'draw poker' throughout, discarding original cards in the hope of receiving a better hand, while Korda and Mentha and the indefatigable Leon Zwier were prepared to 'stand pat' until the Kiwis might be forced to show their hand. All the elements of high drama were there—trans-Tasman phone conversations, secret meetings arranged with the emphasis on security, drawn-out negotiations around a boardroom table followed by breakout meetings of the chief protagonists and their advisers, a final offer before the cards were turned face-up and the administrators were able to scoop up 'the pot' (in this case $150 million, the largest settlement in an insolvency case in Australia's corporate history).

The game started barely 24 hours after the administrators were appointed, when Mentha picked up the phone to call long-time friend and fellow St Kilda football team supporter, Nick Stretch. Stretch, who was acting for the former Ansett board as a partner with the law firm Gadens, was told that the administrators needed to talk urgently with Air NZ and the former directors of Ansett. After listening to their rationale for such a meeting, Stretch was able to engineer talks with ANZ Banking chief Charles Goode, who had resigned his directorship of Air NZ only weeks before. While Korda and Mentha were eventually to walk away with the prize they sought, right then they were shuffling the discards, and they had a useless hand. All they could do was refer back to a letter of comfort that Air New Zealand wrote on 8 August 2001 to the directors of Ansett Holdings Limited, Ansett International Limited and Ansett Australia Limited as the ultimate parent company, to confirm that the wholly owned subsidiaries of the three Ansett companies were able to meet their debts as they fell due. The letter also said that Air New Zealand would make available 'on request in writing from time to time' advances for the sole purpose of enabling the three Ansett companies to pay working capital liabilities incurred by them in the ordinary course of business. The letter included a statement that the maximum amount of all such advances could not exceed A$400 million. Just over a month later, the directors of the Ansett group decided that the companies were insolvent or likely to become insolvent and that an administrator of each company should be appointed. That was when the first administrators, from PriceWaterhouseCoopers, were appointed and, in their wisdom, decided to ground the airline and stand down all employees.

Critical though these steps were, the other part of their initial strategy—to sue Air New Zealand—would have been disastrous if implemented. PWC instructed solicitors to make a demand on Air New Zealand to pay further advances of the balance of the A$400 million over and above the $20 million they had already received to cover wages bills. If the demand was not met, legal proceedings against Air New Zealand would begin. The threat seems to have been a knee-jerk reaction—an attempt to get cash into the operations at any cost—rather than a considered and logical assessment of the real position. They had discarded their original hand in the hope of being dealt a full house!

What followed was the real game of 'brinkmanship poker', featuring the corporate doctors Korda and Mentha on one side of the table and Air New Zealand, worried at the state of play but willing to participate in the game, on the other. Korda and Mentha were concerned about pursuing a course of litigation against Air New Zealand, judging, reasonably, that it would be a long and messy affair with no satisfactory outcome. Still, it was an option. First, though, they asked their Andersen colleagues in New Zealand to provide a general financial picture of the airline. As a result of those inquiries and the rapidly falling price of its shares following Air NZ's $1.2 billion write-off of its Ansett investment, the administrators decided that the legal proceedings route would be counterproductive.

Clearly Air New Zealand was in a financial hole—just how much they did not then know—and any pursuit of the outstanding hundreds of millions from the letter of comfort could lead to Air NZ itself being placed in insolvency administration. That scenario would have left the pot empty. There would have been no winners, only losers. At the same time, the Ansett administrators believed that Air NZ could survive only if it could 'disentangle' itself from Ansett quickly and with as little fuss as possible. They recognised two important and related alternatives. If Ansett was to resume flying, with a concomitant longer term survival strategy being implemented, they required cash, which a speedy commercial settlement of the claims would satisfy. Or, in a worst case scenario, should the airline not survive, they required sufficient cash to at least maximise returns to creditors. A strategy for the game was beginning to take shape and Korda and Mentha were desperate to start. While the game would be played in the best traditions of poker, giving a little to take back a little more, relinquishing ground to consolidate further down the track, exercising options but sticking to a game plan, it was not to be acrimonious. Indeed, in an interview with the Melbourne *Herald Sun*, Mentha said: 'It is sometimes better to ask for something nicely than wait and pay for a court hearing. We prefer to ring direct.'[2]

> 'It is sometimes better to ask for something nicely than wait and pay for a court hearing. We prefer to ring direct.'

The administrators' overall concerns were compounded by the lack of information on Ansett available in Australia. There were no books, no consolidated accounts, no financial statements, no executive management. Everything and everyone was located in New Zealand. 'Like we had pieces of the jigsaw but no box lid to see what the end picture was like,' Mentha used to say to describe the situation. 'We needed help and we needed access quickly if we were to meet our objectives.'

> There were no books, no consolidated accounts, no financial statements, no executive management. Everything and everyone was located in New Zealand.

Following the intervention of Nick Stretch and Charles Goode, Mentha took a phone call from Dr Jim Farmer, Air New Zealand's acting chairman, on 22 September in which it was suggested that it might be useful for the administrators to meet with some of the Air NZ board to discuss 'a number of pressing issues'. Mentha acceded immediately, suggesting a meeting on the following Sunday. Farmer wanted the meeting to be kept a secret, ostensibly for security reasons. He did not want it to attract media attention and potential disputation. Again this was honoured, although the NSW-based law newsletter the *Justinian* did run a fascinating profile on Farmer just two days after the clandestine Melbourne meeting of Air NZ, their advisers and the administrators along with Leon Zwier in the boardroom of Arnold Bloch Leibler in the heart of Melbourne's central business district. The *Justinian* said that many at the

Sydney Bar would recall Dr J.A. Farmer, QC, the New Zealander who turned up on these shores to ply his trade in the early 1980s. Referring to the Ansett crisis, it went on to say:

It is not the first crisis in which the mighty silk has been enmeshed. In fact, he seemed to spend much of his time when he practised in Australia distracted by a fight with the Irish down at the Department of Customs over his importation of a Porsche motor vehicle.[3]

With Farmer at the Melbourne meeting were John Waller of PWC, an adviser to Air New Zealand, the airline's legal adviser Allan Galbraith, QC, its financial adviser Roger France, and Mark Swee Wah, an observer from Singapore Airlines, part owner of Air New Zealand. As they faced each other at the 'without prejudice' meeting, Korda proposed a ten-point agenda that included reaching a full and final settlement, obtaining a clearer picture of the Air New Zealand situation and the position of the Australian corporate regulator, the Australian Securities and Investment Commission. It was to be an all-day and into-the-night meeting during which the administrators were to be apprised not only of the stunning decline of Ansett but, equally, of the parlous position in which Air NZ found itself. Farmer was no longer the arrogant airline chief who wanted to walk away from Ansett on 13 September without paying a cent in redundancies to its 15 000-strong workforce. He was now a man desperate to do a deal that would disentangle the two airlines and give each a chance of surviving. Like Korda and Mentha, he was a man with a mission.

The administrators were to learn that the Ansett group had been losing money at the startling rate of A$1.3 million a day before the administration and that this, quite reasonably, was jeopardising the financial security and viability of Air NZ. No explanation was tendered for how this devastating situation arose, except that Farmer appeared anxious to deny on a number of occasions throughout the day that the board of Air NZ had ever acted dishonestly, recklessly or other than with a reasonable degree of care and diligence. Clearly any apportionment of blame would need to look beyond the board and the role of individual directors. There was no way any of the directors could be held responsible for the astonishing mess that was now Ansett.

The meeting was told that Air NZ's debt-to-equity ratio was at eighty-seven per cent and going up and it could not survive without a capital injection, which it could not expect without a resolution of the position with Ansett. At the time, Air New Zealand had NZ$500 million on deposit but with its financial obligations and budgeted losses this would be entirely eroded. It was a glum picture which was not improved by the veiled threat that, if the airline could not make significant progress to settle its disputes with Ansett by 3.00 p.m. that day, the directors of Air NZ would apply to their government to appoint a statutory manager. The administrators were well aware that, if the airline went into statutory management, there would be no money at all from the letter of comfort. It was time for the game to reach its zenith.

> There was no way any of the directors could be held responsible for the astonishing mess that was now Ansett.

Shortly after lunch, France and Waller began working on the Air NZ offer, reiterating unnecessarily that the airline was in serious financial trouble. Waller stressed that the letter of comfort was neither intended as a letter of credit, nor could it be construed as such, given that A$400 million was the maximum sum available. At the same time, any consideration of what was to be paid needed to take account of A$184 million that had already been allocated for wages, tax liabilities on aircraft, landing slots at Japan's Narita airport, spare parts and debts due by Ansett to Air New Zealand. The maximum amount due, therefore, was A$216 million, although this amount was not offered. Around 7 p.m., France, confident and at ease that a deal was ready to be struck, came into the meeting room and laid his cards on the table—a cash component of A$150 million and not a cent more. The Air New Zealand banking syndicate would not allow a greater sum to be paid to the Ansett group. Moreover, if there was a push for more money, the Air NZ group would collapse.

Bluff or not, it was time to bring the game to a head. If the administrators were shocked or dismayed, they didn't show it. It was the nature of the game. They kept a straight face before withdrawing to discuss the proposal in detail—'know when to hold 'em, know when to fold 'em'. Their deliberations did not take long. At 7.30 p.m., the administrators and Zwier emerged to play out one last bluff. They would accept the offer provided the New Zealand Government granted them an indemnity absolving them of any attempt to claw back the $150 million if Air New Zealand's finances worsened and liquidation was ordered. There were further trans-Tasman phone calls between the Air New Zealand contingent and the New Zealand Government. Agreement followed and a Memorandum of Understanding was prepared forthwith.[5] The last cards were played. While it may not have been the level of financial support they hoped for, it was also something that would never have happened if they had forced Air New Zealand into statutory management. And it was enough to see realised the first part of their vision for Ansett: the limited return of the airline to the Australian skies. As Mentha commented at the time:

> The settlement was the first step. It is the biggest thing that has happened so far in the administration. The real high, though, will come when we can announce that there are over 10 000 people back at work and that the employees and unsecured creditors are to receive 100 cents in the dollar or at least more than they would in a liquidation.[6]

They had sat at the poker table and stared down the Air New Zealand contingent, coming away with a major stake. Three days later they would begin putting their winnings to good use.

14
GETTING BACK INTO THE AIR

THE LAST SATURDAY in September is arguably the most important day in the Australian sporting calendar. It is when a 100 000-strong crowd of sports-mad supporters fill the Melbourne Cricket Ground for the Australian Football League Grand Final. But football was far from the minds of Korda and Mentha when the Essendon Bombers and the upstart Brisbane Lions clashed in the last match of the year on 29 September 2001 to decide that year's premiership. That day, two weeks after the fleet had been so unceremoniously grounded, Korda and Mentha were putting Ansett back into the air. The first Ansett flight, an Airbus A320, left Melbourne at 9 a.m. for Sydney, passing another that was heading in the opposite direction towards Melbourne airport. The Melbourne terminal, so ominously empty after the 14 September shutdown, was filled with beaming smiles and a brass band that *oom-pah-pah*ed away for the occasion. The first passengers to fly were welcomed by flight attendants in a guard of honour.

Mentha was talking up the occasion and told the crowd that Ansett Mark II was the first new airline to begin operations since 11 September. Flying Ansett in its own right, and not leasing planes to Qantas, was the gamble Korda had devised to offset losses that would occur if the carrier remained grounded. Korda knew that he and Mentha, if dealt the right cards, could avoid an asset fire sale and would have a bigger pot to share with creditors. All they needed was to be dealt that hand.

The key to the Korda–Mentha strategy was to win back passenger confidence. Nobody was going to book seats with an airline that might go belly-up within days. Travellers who flew with the new Ansett would require a copper-bottom, money-back guarantee that their fares were safe. 'What we needed was a kangaroo and an emu,' quipped Mentha,[1] later explaining how the pair persuaded the Federal Government to lend its support to a fares guarantee.

But all of that was weeks down the track when the pair hatched their plan to generate revenue by getting planes airborne. The story of how Ansett was relaunched begins the morning after the Korda–Mentha appointment on 18 September. An hour before facing creditors at Melbourne's Crown Casino, Korda was on the phone to the 'enemy' headquarters: Qantas in Sydney.

He told Geoff Dixon that he and Mentha would like to have an open dialogue with the nation's flagship carrier and further discuss the wet-lease deal their predecessor PWC had arranged to rebuild and restore passenger air services. But wet leasing was not viewed by the two Marks as being in the airline's best long-term interests. Korda said little to Dixon other than to exchange formalities and to add that they would speak again that evening. Dixon indicated that he wanted to lock in the arranged ninety-day lease deal arranged with Korda and Mentha's predecessors for 12 Ansett A320 aircraft. School holidays and the grand finals in the AFL and Sydney Rugby League competitions were two weeks off and neither Qantas nor Virgin Blue could meet the demand for aircraft. Korda rang off, promising to call Dixon back at 5 o'clock that evening. Dixon had sought to screw Korda down, ever so gently. The national interest must be considered—now; Ansett's long-term future could be considered later. If Dixon expected an immediate response, he was sadly disappointed. The two Marks would make up their own minds how the planes would be used.

A surprise call from Dixon at 2 p.m. left Korda stunned. The four-hour creditors' meeting had not long ended, followed by a press conference in which he and Mentha were heavily probed. Neither wanted to talk deals. The pressures of the previous 24 hours and a night without sleep left neither in any mood for talking deals with Qantas. Korda rang off, repeating that he would get back to Dixon after five that evening. National interest or no national interest, they were not about to kow-tow to Qantas, its all-powerful chief executive or the Federal Government. Why tie up planes for short-term gain and long-term disadvantage? The A320 fleet was the most cost-effective aircraft Ansett had and would be needed for any scaled-back operation if the carrier was to resume flying.

Dixon was told that night the deal was off. Korda later noted that he rang-off, seemingly surprised that, when strapped for cash, they would reject an offer that represented guaranteed income.[2] But neither Dixon nor the Federal Government was prepared to accept the no-deal decision as a final answer.

Korda and Mentha were being driven back to Ansett headquarters the following afternoon when Korda's mobile phone rang. Calling just after 3 p.m. was John Anderson from Canberra:

Can you get re-engaged with Qantas on wet leasing? I am asking you this in the national interest. School holidays are starting in Victoria this weekend. The footy grand finals are coming, so can you please work with Qantas and see if you can find a solution for the wet-lease deal.

Korda recalled:

We spent a lot of time on the Thursday and Friday on the Qantas deal, having already said No on the Tuesday night. But we respected the fact that the Federal Government was a key stakeholder, having made statements that an entitlements scheme would be put in place to help Ansett workers. When the deputy prime minister rings, you respond. We spent long hours and worked into the night with Qantas, finishing at 2 a.m. on the Thursday and then continued into Friday.

Everyone was trying to work in good faith. They wanted to take eleven planes. We came to an agreement about price. The aircraft were to be flown by Ansett pilots, with Ansett crew and Ansett ground-handling, baggage and the like. We continued the discussions right through until the following Tuesday and then put out a joint announcement. Qantas would pay a charter fee for each plane of $6250 an hour.[3]

But matters were complicated by the commercial realities of hiring out aircraft owned by leasing companies, of a world insurance industry in chaos post 11 September, and with the standard $2 billion public liability cover for acts of terrorism suddenly slashed to $50 million. Any chance of a deal ended faster than it had begun. Korda was to add:

We went to bed thinking we had a deal and would wake up next morning without one. We changed the deal from a wet lease to one where we got around the legal technicalities to an agreement where we would carry some Qantas passengers. We just could not overcome the hurdles.

But the Marks learned much from the experience and a lot about what was involved in starting an airline. The events of 11 September in the

United States devastated the airline industry. Ansett, if it was to fly, had to renegotiate insurance arrangements, gain regulatory approvals, make agreements with airport operators and come to a settlement with finance companies that leased aircraft. Nobody doubted that the so-called 'Ansett kick start' would lose money and this had to be weighed against the responsibilities of running a company administration. The administrators felt justified with their plan to relaunch the carrier. Part 5.3A of the *Corporations Act* required that they maximise the chance of Ansett remaining in business, or if that could not be done, that they get the best return on a sale of assets. Korda and Mentha believed the airline had to fly to provide a return to creditors.

But finding a buyer meant going operational. With a $22 million-a-month bill for the IT system, and with leases on aircraft and terminals, it wasn't going to be too much of an added burden to put planes into the air.

At 6 p.m. on 24 September, five days into their appointment, Korda and Mentha walked into the Air NZ–Ansett office in Melbourne. 'What does it take to fly this airline?' Korda asked. Trevor Jensen, executive general manager, operations and inflight services, and Reg Smith, industrial relations chief, both looked up, realising suddenly that the Marks were serious. The gloom of airline executives flying nowhere lifted as the news swept the executive floor. Andrew Miller, who had charge of operational strategy and the aircraft fleet, joined the group as Korda and Mentha began to probe for answers. The team moved from Jensen's office, then to Smith's, calling in others—corporate partners and legal partners. In a matter of minutes, the team would grow to thirty. The big question that had to be answered was how to persuade fare-paying passengers to buy tickets and have faith in a troubled airline.

'People have faith in a government guarantee,' said Mentha, having just stated his need for 'a kangaroo and an emu'. 'We needed that backing. People would not understand that we could put up the assets of the airline to guarantee their fares.' That afternoon the pair flew to Canberra for meetings with John Anderson, Treasurer Peter Costello and later talks with John Howard and his advisers. A ticket guarantee deal was worked out during two hours of talks with the deputy prime minister's advisers.

Anderson came and went from the meeting, which broke up at 4 p.m. before moving into a dining room within the prime minister's office where further talks involving John Howard, Peter Costello and John Anderson and their chiefs of staff lasted a further ninety minutes.

The talks were businesslike, at times tense, and the government appeared to suspect that the two Marks were mere union puppets on the make for a government handout. They arrived at Parliament House only two days after John Anderson had created further uncertainty for the worried and stood-down workforce with his insensitive description of Ansett as a carcass. (Melbourne *Herald Sun* economics commentator Terry McCrann was similarly critical, noting in his 15 September column that Ansett was dead. 'There is no way it can be revived. It sure ain't going to walk—far less fly—again on the third day.' Although both would ultimately be proved right, at the time they sparked an outrage.) Korda and Mentha believed their strategy was correct and that they had every right to expect government support for their initiative. That the Government agreed readily both surprised and delighted them; in the space of two days the Government appeared to have swung full circle. Mentha's lasting impression of that Parliament House meeting was of the intellectual skills of John Howard.

> Once we explained the ticket guarantee, John Howard's ability to get over the issue and to understand the detail was just stunning. It was incredible. With all the bureaucrats there giving advice, he was stunning. You have just got to sit back and say, wow … This guy has a mind like a steel trap.[4]

The first twenty minutes of that meeting were not so cordial. Neither Korda, Mentha nor Zwier was given an opportunity to speak. Howard, Costello, and Anderson were hyped from Question Time. The atmosphere was tense. Costello raised concerns about Zwier's role and whether the advice he had given the unions and his appointment as legal counsel to the administrators amounted to a conflict of interest. The Marks, too, had not realised that their $150 million 'poker winnings' from Air New Zealand had crossed Australia–New Zealand bilateral relations. That same morning, the New Zealand Finance Minister had phoned Costello explaining that the Kiwi Government would underwrite the $150 million advance. New Zealand was anxious to avoid the further embarrassment that might arise if its national airline also went into administration and a liquidator tried to claw back funds sent across the Tasman.

Drawing on interrogatory skills honed in his former career at the Victorian Bar, Costello came at the trio about what other deals they might have been doing and why they were wanting help from Canberra when they had drawn cash from Air New Zealand and had been to Asia the previous weekend for talks with Singapore Airlines. 'And what deals are you also doing elsewhere?' Costello quizzed. Then came Howard's turn: had they cut a deal with Air New Zealand that fettered the ability of the Australian companies watchdog, the Australian Securities and Investments Commission, to probe the activities of the former group of Ansett companies to see whether they had operated legally prior to their collapse?[5]

Zwier returned the volley. He knew Costello from their university days at Monash in Melboune and his oratorical skills equalled those of the Treasurer. No, he had no conflict of interest because of the advice he had given the ACTU and the unions about Ansett; he could not be branded a labour lawyer. His clients included Chris Corrigan's Patrick Corporation and O'Connor's, the Victorian-based meat processing and export corporation that was involved in a drawn-out and costly union fight. John Howard also raised points that Costello appeared to feed from. Zwier responded in forceful tones that the administrators had not and would not attempt to confine or impede the activities of the companies watchdog; nor had they, and neither would they, seek to pervert the course of justice. Said Mentha later, 'Mark and I just sat back and watched … And, wow!'[6]

The talks settled down and covered the Qantas wet lease talks and why they had failed. John Howard asked whether Virgin Blue had discussed wet leasing. If so, what was the administrators' position and and what were they doing? The Marks replied that Virgin had put forward a plan to use Ansett planes to fly the North Queensland tourist routes—Brisbane, Cairns, Townsville and Hamilton Island. 'But when we got down to the detail, they were concentrating on Melbourne–Sydney and were making sure we didn't fly,' Mentha said.

Korda and Mentha then explained that unless Ansett was able to fly, other businesses—such as the travel agencies, the engineering facilities, its engine shop, cargo business and its various regional subsidiary carriers—would not be able to be sold as going concerns and thousands of jobs would be threatened. The debt from employee entitlement would multiply and the superannuation funds would have a $300-million shortfall, given that stock markets had plummeted in the wake of the 11 September terrorist attacks. The message the pair delivered to the ministers and the team of up to twenty advisers sitting across the large dining room table was that, to restore consumer confidence in the airline, they needed a kangaroo and an emu on the front of the ticket in terms of a money-back guarantee.

Korda and Mentha explained that the Government would not be favouring one carrier over another. Neither Qantas nor Virgin Blue would miss out. Ansett at that time had asset backing of around $700 million. What they were seeking was for the Government to underwrite for a limited period a $25 million ticket guarantee. Said Mentha:

> What we were looking for at any one time was a maximum guarantee of $25 million, so what we were saying was, it was really a loan advanced to the administrators. We were giving them a $25 million mortgage on a $700 million house.

Howard, Costello and Anderson left the room and talked with their own commissioned insolvency advisers David Crawford and Steve Parbury. They returned twenty minutes later, saying: 'We'll do it. When can you fly? Can you fly Grand Final day?' Mentha later recalled:

We really needed time to arrange bookings and to get things set. But we agreed to do it. The costs of flying were not great. We had some costs for crew and fuel, but we also had huge fixed costs and assets we had to protect, such as the equity in the planes, the equity in the terminals. We still had to pay the rent and the lease costs. We had only to add fuel, the people to fly and attend the planes and, without adding food service and the alcohol, it was a cheap operation flying the busiest routes. It was a marginal cost exercise for us.

That night, Korda, Mentha and Zwier found themselves stranded in Canberra. The deal having been done with the Government, they had to wait around until near 11 p.m. for the legal paperwork to be completed. Without so much as a change of clothes, a razor or a toothbrush between them, they arranged a hotel booking and left for Melbourne on a Qantas flight at 7 a.m. the next day.

As well as the fares deal, the Australian Government also agreed later to arrangements in which 8600 workers who were stood down on 14 September without pay would be made redundant and share $195 million in a taxpayer-funded advance to give them their long-service leave pay and four weeks' wages in lieu of notice. But the advance was to become a polit-ical football, with government demanding repayment from subsequent asset sales. Korda and Mentha along with the unions argued unsuccess-fully with Canberra that the advance should be treated as an unsecured credit line, with the Commonwealth waiting its turn with other creditors. It was an argument that didn't wash, but it dragged on for weeks, leaving hundreds of families near penniless and dependent on friends and family.

On that first trip to Canberra, Korda and Mentha argued that they wanted a government imprimatur on a straight commercial deal. The tax-payer would be given a $25 million mortgage over Ansett assets in exchange for underwriting a twelve-week, money-back, tickets guarantee. Ansett planes would fly again under their plan and travellers would have their travel and fares guaranteed. When Korda and Mentha emerged from the Canberra meetings they were able to announce that their 'Ansett solution' was under implementation: by that coming Saturday Ansett would operate flights on the main Melbourne–Sydney trunk route.

Mentha would later muse: 'When we came in here we had a couple of hundred thousand cash and a wages bill of $12 million to pay on the second day. We got some dough from Air New Zealand and we still faced challenges.'

One of the challenges was to get the green light from the Civil Aviation Safety Authority (CASA) to fly that Saturday. In contrast with the Epsom salts treatment of the previous Christmas and Easter groundings, the planes sailed through their maintenance checks and CASA gave approval to fly that Friday. Call centres were re-opened, an Internet booking system was fired up and, with very little notice, Ansett put 3500 seats on the market for weekend travel. The hard part was to fill them and to maintain scheduling as routes were extended to other states. Every plane in the air equalled 110 Ansett jobs.

> **Every plane in the air equalled 110 Ansett jobs.**

Given the airline's long history of strong brand loyalty, the Marks believed that, armed with their tickets guarantee and a determination to keep operating, they would revive the carrier and win public support. But it was clear from the beginning that Ansett needed more than old-fashioned customer loyalty to win back custom. Travellers who had been caught by the previous Christmas and Easter groundings were not going to be inconvenienced again. Business travellers wanted more bang for their buck: inflight meals, comfy airport lounges and frequent flyer points to take the spouse and the kids on a once-a-year holiday. Bottled water on Ansett Mark II could not compete with a relaxing drink, a lunch box and a cup of tea 30 000 feet above the country. Korda and Mentha's kick start gamble is said to have lost $25 million between 29 September 2001 and February 2002. Korda acknowledged to creditors on 29 January 2002 that continuing to keep the planes aloft was expected to strip a further $6 million a week from their dwindling resources.

Nevertheless, the administrators argued, the losses were justified to sell the trunkline and separate subsidiary regional carriers. Preserving the goodwill in keeping the airline flying would retain value in the Ansett name and reputation. They believed, too, that the value of aircraft and terminal leases would be seriously diminished in any fire sale if the planes were grounded. Other Ansett businesses, such as the engineering centre in Melbourne and the regional airlines, would be made more saleable if the mainline carrier was sold as a going concern. Selling the airline in an operational state would also avoid the need to terminate up to 3000 employees and save creditors more than $200 million. Alas, as circum-stances and entrepreneurial whim dictated, this was not to be.

When Korda and Mentha arrived at Tullamarine around 8.00 a.m. on the launch date, they were swamped by ecstatic Ansett employees. Moving to the Chairman's Lounge for a pre-flight media conference, they felt vindicated, adding that it was a new beginning. 'It was very, very sat-isfying being out at Ansett,' said Mentha. Three days earlier the pair had walked through a near-empty terminal on their return from Canberra. 'It was dead, it was black and all the lights were turned off and there were papers in the terminal and it looked like a ghost town,' Mentha said, going on to reflect:

> To see that, it's no wonder people were talking about Ansett as a carcass because it was very tragic ... 'there was this little army of people in the Golden Wings lounge who were still keeping the spirit alive. They were ecstatic that people were going to be flying again. We knew there was a spir-it and heart at Ansett. We always knew it at head office but when you're out at the airport and you see it in the eyes of these people maintaining a daily vigil, keeping the dream alive. It encouraged us to press ahead with our plans.

With planes in the skies the possibilities of finding a buyer had become a priority and they firmly believed the chances of achieving that would improve markedly. But keeping the planes flying meant they needed a structured business plan put together by skilled airline managers. Korda and Mentha were company doctors, turnaround specialists who knew how to break down a balance sheet but knew precious little about running an airline. By settling the $150 million compensation deal with Air NZ they had access to the Ansett books, which the Kiwi carrier had removed from Melbourne.

'We started to get information about route profitability, fleet management and all the other things you need to run an airline,' Mentha remembers.

We had the pieces of the jigsaw but someone had taken away the lid and we couldn't see what the picture was. Can you give us the consolidated picture? Can you give us access to your people? They were helpful and over the course of the week we started to get information about route profitability, fleet management, what was owed and what were the liabilities.

We didn't have that information at first because it was in New Zealand and Ansett had been cut adrift with an uncertain destination. Mark and I spoke to Gary Toomey, to Adam Maroney, their chief financial officer, and to Jim Farmer to establish what their difficulties were and where they were trying to position Ansett.[7]

> **By settling the $150 million compensation deal with Air NZ, Korda and Mentha had access to the Ansett books, which the Kiwi carrier had removed from Melbourne.**

With diplomatic and corporate links restored across the Tasman, the two Marks were able to look for help from Air NZ's major airline partner. They turned their sights on Singapore Airlines, hoping that any rapport they developed might draw an equity involvement. Mentha and SIA chief C.K. Cheong (colloquially known as C.K.) would regularly chat into the small hours of the morning about the directions the Marks were taking with Ansett. On one occasion Mentha hung up at 3 a.m. after lengthy discussions with C.K. in which they planned a secret meeting between Mentha, Korda, Zwier, and C.K. and his team in Singapore over the weekend of 5 September. Mentha noted:

We were talking with Dr Cheong direct because he was clearly concerned about the plight of Air NZ. We also knew that the long-term prosperity of Air

NZ was very dependent on the right 'Ansett solution'. Air NZ had originally proposed that its major shareholders Singapore Airlines and Brierley inject $150 million each into the airline, which was to be matched with a loan of $550 million by the New Zealand Government. Nobody was going to put any money in while a claim was outstanding from Ansett. Air NZ's future was dependent on the view Mark and I took which was another obligation Mark and I had over and above the public interest one asked of us by the Australian deputy prime minister.[8]

By taking the action they did, the two Marks were able to persuade C.K. Cheong to send a team to Melbourne to help guide the 'Ansett solution'. SIA was interested in acquiring a piece of Ansett, but had been severely burned in the collapse of Air NZ. It had also accrued substantial losses in seeking to gain a toehold in domestic airline operations in India. When the shareholding of Air NZ was restructured on 4 October 2002 after the Clark Government injected NZ$885 million into the accounts of the carrier, SIA's previous 25 per cent stake had been diluted to about 4 per cent, costing the Singaporeans NZ$A250 million and much loss of face. SIA and BIL, which held a combined 43 per cent share of Air NZ before the bailout, had to sit back and watch as their scrip was reduced to a minority 9 per cent stake.

The government bailout involved rearrangement of appointments to the Air New Zealand board that saw the departure of Selwyn Cushing and BIL (formerly Brierley's) chief executive Greg Terry. The Australian born Terry and BIL's then Chief Financial Officer Andrew Shepherd resigned from BIL sixteen days later, on 20 March, after the company's half-year results announcement. BIL was said to have the equivalent of A$400 million in unrealised losses due to its holdings in Singapore International Airlines and Air NZ. The Bloomberg financial wire service reported that Terry had admitted that BIL's major shareholders were not impressed with the company's investment performance.

But Selwyn Cushing suffered the opprobrium of Kiwi investors over the collapse of Ansett and the near bankruptcy of the nation's own flag carrier. The country's Finance Minister told the parliament on 11 October that Cushing was the individual most responsible for the airline's near collapse. Earlier that day Cushing had claimed that 'prevarications' by the New Zealand and Australian governments had killed a plan for Singapore Airlines to inject capital into Air New Zealand and lift its shareholding to 49 per cent. Responding in parliament, Dr Cullen said: 'I think Sir Selwyn is the person who is singly most responsible for the loss of shareholder value in both BIL (Brierley Investments) and Air New Zealand.' Dr Cullen added that it was 'due to the incompetence of the Air New Zealand board under Sir Selwyn Cushing's chairmanship' that Air New Zealand bought the second half of Ansett Australia 'without due diligence'.

Cushing told the *Australian* newspaper that none of the blame for Ansett's collapse should rest on him as chairman of the Air NZ–Ansett group.[9] He said the decision to proceed with the purchase of Ansett was unanimous. 'The decisions were made by the board in conjunction with management consultants.' Announcing the New Zealand taxpayer-funded bailout of Air NZ after the Ansett collapse, Dr Cullen said: 'Air New Zealand has suffered from factional and dysfunctional leadership at the board level over a very considerable period.'[10]

Cushing, who was sixty-four, had a long corporate history in New Zealand, through Hawke's Bay boutique broker Esam Cushing, various roles at Brierley's and his chairmanship of the state-owned electricity commission ECNZ. He had been chairman of Brierley's since 1998 after taking over from former NZ government minister Sir Roger Douglas. While at Brierley's he oversaw the process of slimming down more than sixty investments into three key companies: Air New Zealand, Britain's Thistle hotel chain, and James Hardie Industries in Australia. Brierley received $700 million from the sale of its 28 per cent stake in James Hardie in May 2001, but the funds are believed to have gone straight to the company's bankers.

Having left the Air New Zealand and BIL boards, Cushing remained a director of the New Zealand rural services group Williams and Kettle. His only consolation amid the gloom from BIL and Air New Zealand was that Williams and Kettle enjoyed a bumper year and was predicting even better things to come when it announced a 20 per cent lift in first-quarter trading on 26 November 2001. Cushing, who was Williams and Kettle's main shareholder, had been a director of the company for twenty-three years. At that November meeting he was re-elected to the board unopposed. He also continued to hold down his appointment as chairman of the New Zealand Symphony Orchestra.

Cushing's role at Air New Zealand had not impressed his predecessor Bob Matthew. New Zealand's *Dominion* newspaper reported on 26 September 2001[11] that Air New Zealand knew before buying Ansett that the job of preparing Ansett for competition was not done, two years after the Kiwi carrier had bought Australia's number two airline. Matthew, who vacated the chairman's seat in 1998, had sat on the Ansett board with Air New Zealand managing director Jim McCrae. He told the newspaper that the Australian carrier had a lot of problems, and a lot of changes were needed:

> We were active, energetic directors. It was not a dog—that's nonsense. We bought a business that required significant changes to it, and we set up a process to do that. But it is true to say, when I left, the job had not been done.

Adding that Ansett had needed new aircraft, he said the Ansett board in December 1999 stalled a plan to buy new planes. Uncertainty over ownership was the reason cited. 'It [Ansett] had a very proud history and not so long ago had more market share than Qantas.'

15
BIDS FROM LEFT FIELD

ACCORDING TO HIS own correspondence
and that from his Australian 'agents', Horst
Hamm is a German industrialist living in Beirut.
Soon after Ansett went into administration,
Hamm, through intermediaries based in
Queensland, contacted the administration team

with an extraordinary offer. He was ready to take a 75 per cent stake in the airline in return for some US$2 billion of Russian jet fuel, to which he indicated he had access and which he could provide at discounted rates. He would, of course, require a letter of credit from the administrators to cover the cost of the fuel.

Hamm attested that he owned 40 per cent of a Russian refinery, named Balt Port. He also had a 50 per cent stake in a company called Avangard Drilling and Trading and ownership of a company named Wimco-Erica Shipping and Trading. He confirmed that his interests were ready, willing and able to complete the transaction immediately—within, in fact, a mere five working days. Little due diligence would be required. To the administrators, the offer may well have seemed too good to be true. In the event it probably was.

Offers such as that from Horst Hamm are part and parcel of the administration process. There is, it seems, a certain romantic notion about resurrecting a company. Or maybe it's about picking up something on the cheap. In the case of Ansett, of course, there was certainly a lot of the romantic. It was a big company with a big reputation. Its attempted revival was the biggest corporate recovery effort in Australia's history to date. It had all the ingredients to bring a variety of putatively cash-rich, eager and committed suitors out of the woodwork. And out of the woodwork they came, not only in the form of Hamm but from a variety of potential buyers ranging from the Principality of Caledonia, operating from a suite in the Melbourne suburb of South Yarra, to Sir Gregory Hardie's Knights Templar and the Fairbairn Hall Foundation. All had one thing in common: enormous amounts of money, more indeed than might be deemed decent. And they travelled in style to the four corners of the globe, snapping up investment opportunities! At least that's the image they projected.

In the early days of the administration, Horst Hamm's futile bid became something of a *cause célèbre*, bringing into its ambit the dubious influence of one of the country's most listened-to radio broadcasters, Sydney's Alan Jones, otherwise known as 'The Parrot'. For a time, 'shock jock' Jones took up the Hamm cause with a vengeance.

Jones interviewed a retired lawyer from Queensland's Sunshine Coast,

John Rivett. In his introduction he claimed to know Rivett and described him as 'a highly credible person, not given to irrational and inaccurate observations'. Rivett had, according to Jones, significant contacts, in a business sense, with a New Zealand businessman Dugal Harcourt and through that association had met Hamm. Jones went on to postulate that, 'from my investigation', Hamm was quite an extraordinary bloke, who did not believe in debt, had none and worked off his own capital. Fortuitously Rivett had personally witnessed certificates of deposit for Hamm to the tune of one billion dollars.

Jones's view was that someone with one billion in cash and two billion dollars worth of Russian jet fuel ready to exchange for a controlling interest in the failed airline should certainly be given a good hearing, no matter the evidence that might be available suggesting that all was not as it might seem. It was as if money was the overriding ingredient in any attempt to resurrect Ansett. Now, for the record, Hamm's bid, along with others, was given due consideration. Some bids, of course, were just too ridiculous to contemplate. In the case of the Hamm bid, there was such a barrage of communication, including use of the media, that, for a while, it developed a life of its own.

For example, Dugal Harcourt, designated as an agent for Wimco-Erica, in a letter to Mark Menthor (*sic*), said Hamm's interest was in purchasing the entire business, assuming responsibility for staff entitlements, creditors, including the fees of the administration and the upgrading of the fleet. He saw it as a fairly simple transaction with little need for any extended due diligence period. Other correspondence came from Queensland resident Maurice Shepherd. There were simply too many people becoming involved and none seemed to have a clear idea of just who or what Horst Hamm was.

A chronology prepared by the administrators revealed that Mr Harcourt—an ex-New Zealand farmer living in Queensland—had made contact numerous times each day for a month following the administration, ringing the Andersen switchboard, the Ansett switchboard and the Ansett sale contact line, as well as any Ansett and Andersen staff by indiscriminately dialling phone numbers. Hamm's interests provided a one-page offer that was complex and involved reinsuring standby letters of credit secured against Russian-based jet fuel.

Background checks were run, revealing that Hamm's major vehicle, Wimco-Erica, was not a trading company and that further dealing with the mysterious bidder would need to be cautiously embraced. It was suggested at this time to Mr Harcourt that, given that his client was not known to the administrators, the most expedient means of pursuing his interest in Ansett would be to engage a reputable investment bank or Big 5 accounting firm. Harcourt indicated that they were linking with the bid from former Ansett employees—the ANstaff bid—and were therefore being represented by Deloittes. Overseas—specifically in the Middle East—checks were made of Hamm, Wimco-Erica, and another associate, Mr Hassan Harb of the Lebanese United Insurance and Reinsurance Company, who provided evidence of Hamm's bona fides. A German export consultant, Mr Norbert Herrmann, wrote a letter to confirm Hamm's financial capacity to complete the deal but the letter itself raised doubts.

Hamm's bid was by no means the only one to be considered too good to be true. But it was certainly the most persistent and had the dubious benefit of bringing media pressure to bear on the bidding process. In the event this neither deterred nor influenced the administrators, who were interested in action rather than words no matter how well intentioned. They wanted to see a business plan, not a one-page letter that amounted to an expression of interest.

At the second meeting of creditors on 29 January 2002, a Mr Brian Best took the opportunity to present his case on behalf of a group called Buying Back Australia. Best first established his right to be at the meeting by professing to be a Frequent Flyer points holder owed about $2000 in credits. He then went on to tell the meeting that his group currently had an offer on the table with Andersen for the sum of $5 billion to support and buy Ansett. As CEO of Buying Back Australia he was concerned that Ansett was going into liquidation and that there had been no response to the offer which had been in force since 18 November.

Best wanted to let all creditors know that the offer would return them more than 30 cents in the dollar and provide employment for 6000 workers. Again, like all things that appear too good to be true, it probably was. The fact is that administrators and their teams are, from solid experience and training, skilled in assessing the legitimacy or otherwise of bids for companies under their care. All bids must establish their credentials by means of a credible business plan, have acceptable corporate advisory support and be able to withstand significant forensic scrutiny.

The Knights Templar's Sir Gregory Hardie later offered a three-paragraph expression of interest suggesting that his organisation had devised a program where all 'previous relative' Ansett staff would retain a position in the new company. Moreover they were capable of providing an amount to satisfy creditors and purchase all ground assets. No planes would be required as suitable financing arrangements had been made for the purchase of new aircraft. All the Knights Templar required was the purchase figure. Once it was known, all financials would be immediately forwarded. A simple notification of receipt of the letter by phone or fax was sought.

The Knights Templar sat there in left field along with other 'bids' from the edge, bids that failed to attract serious interest from the administrators in their quest to revive an airline, provide employment for as many Ansett workers as possible and secure a return for creditors. These elements, given their obligations under the *Corporations Act*, remained their unequivocal objective.

A Mr David Wood, Chairman of the Fairbairn Hall Foundation, professed to being a long supporter of Ansett 'reaching back to the days when the late Sir Peter Abeles treated the said airline as his personal fiefdom'. He went on to say that he had already put his hand up for Ansett's 'babies' including regional airline subsidiaries Kendell, Skywest and Aeropelican, as well as other groups. He had, he said, put together a war chest of some $5 billion for the acquisition, a figure that he could comfortably provide from family resources. He proposed retaining all staff and 'rather than cutting down on services, would have the passionate desire to see the services and staff ramped up and in so doing covering the costs of all back entitlements and underwriting such entitlements for the future in advance'. In short, he said 'we are in an acquisitive mode and have the "bickies" at our disposal to so acquire.'

Wood and his wife, it was indicated, travel extensively across Australia and internationally in the interests of their many commercial enterprises, 'usually in one of our own executive jets when travelling offshore'. Mr Wood himself was head of the trans-generational global umbrella organisation Fairbairn Hall Foundation, 'which organisation has no status in Australia'. As one would expect it had currency in both Europe and the Caribbean and it operated in the time-honoured English manner on the basis that 'old money is quiet money'.

Of the 197 000 people supposedly employed by this organisation, forty-six were known as divisional heads. No fewer than eighteen divisional heads were women and, of those, eight earned in excess of US$10 million in bonuses in calendar 2000. Each divisional head, moreover, had at their disposal an executive jet with trans-continental capacities and reach. As with all bids, that of Fairbairn Hall Foundation received due consideration.

Like Fairbairn Hall, the Principality of Caledonia or, more accurately the State of Sherwood, a province of the Principality, wanted to re-employ 100 per cent of Ansett's 17 000 employees as well as considering a 100 per cent payment of all valid unpaid amounts due to creditors. Not only did the Principality have sufficient funds available to purchase the entire Ansett Airlines group but it was in a financial position to consider the simultaneous purchase of Air New Zealand, Singapore Airlines, Virgin Blue and Qantas, if necessary. Here indeed was a bottomless pit of money. After approaching the Ansett Pilots Federation with details of its total purchase proposal, His Excellency, the Governor of the State of Sherwood, operating out of serviced offices in the elite Melbourne suburb of South Yarra, expressed disappointment, indeed annoyance, that the Federation had not got back to him. He suggested that there was a hidden agenda—'the possible pre-planned bankruptcy of Ansett Airlines and the other secret pre-arrangements as to how it will be sold off to the privileged few, these well known few who seem to never negotiate deals via lawful channels.'

And then there was Laurence Lilley, from the Port Macquarie Project, who advised that there was a 'buy back the farm' movement underway in Australia. Mr Lilley had been very much part of this movement, from the time 'when the nation began to go sour more than 30 years ago'. He really began to make his move just fifteen years ago, building up a project intended to reverse what was happening in country areas. Stage One was going to cost around $10 billion. A series of interviews with local bankers, lawyers and accountants in every town from Coffs Harbour to Taree elicited only that there was 'not a clue among them' on raising this sort of money. A Sydney 'pub crawl' of about 100 banks, merchant banks and finance experts resulted in them telling him that he was trying to work up a scam—all except one, a German lady working with Chase Manhattan, whose advice led him to visit banks and institutions in Hong Kong, London, Antwerp, Luxembourg, Geneva, Zurich, Toronto, New York, Houston and a few other spots. As a result he had discovered how to raise very large amounts of money for projects. Calling on the administrators to 'pay attention', Mr Lilley concluded his 'bid' by saying:

> Remember this—the incredible mess this nation is in has been produced— alone and unaided—by a collection of ignorami with business, economic, accountancy and law degrees. Decisions based on local financial expediency, while ignoring the ramifications of those decisions, will no longer be tolerated.

At the end of the day the administrators had to judge each bid on its merits.

16
THE TESNA BID

BY THE FIRST week of November, Korda and
Mentha were facing mounting pressure to find a
buyer for Ansett without further delay. The normal routine for troubled companies was for the
company doctor to arrive, stitch-up a fix for the

accounts and management, and move on to the next project. The creditors knew that Ansett was cash poor and asset rich and they were beginning to press for a handout. Most of the 8600 staff who were stood down and earmarked for redundancy had not been paid during the two months since their predecessor PWC ordered the planes grounded.

The two Marks hoped to attract a major international airline to buy Ansett outright or cough up enough cash to take a substantial equity position. A deal with Singapore Airlines would be a perfect fit and they had focused their sights on clinching such a deal with the island nation by opening negotiations with airline chairman C.K. Cheong in the first weeks of their appointment. SIA nibbled at the bait but in the end decided to tread carefully by agreeing only to develop a business plan for the two administrators. This decision followed a clandestine trip to Singapore on the weekend of 5 October by Korda, Mentha and Zwier, a meeting of critical importance but one that also had its lighter moments.

While ostensibly seeking a consultancy or management role for SIA, the priority task of the trio was to solicit the airline's undertaking to invest in Ansett. The trip itself was supposed to have been conducted in the utmost secrecy, a condition imposed by SIA. So clandestine was it that the three did not even tell the partners in their respective firms of their plans. They flew out at 1.00 a.m. on the Saturday and, even before they were airborne, their cover was blown. Zwier recalled:

> We were sure that we had not been noticed and that no one, apart from a few people in Singapore, knew we were coming. So it was a great surprise when we were about to land and a flight attendant noticed that I had not put on my seat belt. She gently chided me with the comment that Dr Cheong would not be happy. That broke us up.[1]

The issue of secrecy was compounded once the trio arrived in Singapore. On visiting an Internet site they were greeted by front page stories out of Australia on their visit and speculation about the possible reasons for it. In Singapore, before adjourning for lunch on their first day, the trio met with an Andersen partner who was a specialist on SIA.

Discussions continued into the afternoon. Before the Singapore trip Mentha and Zwier, in particular, had been working on a strategy that would see SIA a key stakeholder in Ansett Mark II. SIA equity involvement, in fact, was their number-one play. Still, the meetings were regarded as a success and even though they confessed to being 'dog tired' the Australian trio happily accepted an invitation to dinner from Dr Cheong. It was during the dinner that Korda, finally feeling relaxed, asked Dr Cheong how many planes were in the SIA fleet. The reply was that there were in excess of ninety. 'Interesting,' said Korda. 'At Ansett, you know, we have over 130.'

The airline industry was in disarray, with planes empty amid widespread cancellations. Nobody wanted to fly.

'Yes,' replied Dr Cheong, with a wry smile, 'but ours are modern, new and they operate profitably.'[2]

The key to the two Marks' strategy was to ensure that sufficient employees crossed to the new airline. This was critical because the greater the number of staff transferring to the new organisation, the less Korda and Mentha would need to find to fund employee redundancy entitlements. But their efforts and strategies were hamstrung by 11 September in the United States. Finding a buyer for Ansett might have been difficult beforehand; post 11 September, it became an almost impossible task. The airline industry was in disarray, with planes empty amid widespread cancellations. Nobody wanted to fly.

Airline operators who might have been potential buyers of the Ansett business were looking inwards to their own operational problems and, in not a few cases, to their very financial survival. They had enough on their plates without worrying about a sick, indeed defunct, industry player in the small, regional Australian market. Apart from the 11 September difficulties, Korda and Mentha had a limited time to sell the airline. They had taken a shutdown and grounded carrier, relaunched the operation with limited funding and urgently needed a buyer for what was still a big loss maker.

The marketing strategy called for reviewing and, if necessary, pursuing expressions of interest received as a result of the massive publicity that followed Ansett's collapse. The flood of interest created its own problems, familiar to most administrations, with some bids, as demonstrated, not worth the paper they were written on. While considerable interest surfaced from myriad groups wanting to cherry pick, the Marks were still not running a fire sale and liquidating cheap assets for cash. There appeared to be four obvious contenders. Two of them—Singapore Airlines and Lang Corporation (the Chris Corrigan company now renamed Patrick)—were, at best, peripheral to the process.

SIA, which—as one of the world's best equipped operators—lacks neither the resources nor the infrastructure to begin a start-up quality operation to keep alive the Star Alliance connection now missing from Australia, may well have used Ansett to test the waters here for future involvement in Australia's domestic aviation market. When this book went to production, SIA representatives were checking marketing strategies developed at Ansett while the airline was flying under the banner of the two Marks. One of the documents that SIA received and that was handed to the authors was a blueprint of how a revived Ansett might have been successful. The document stated:

> The key message is that the market wanted a business airline, not a budget carrier. Virgin did well in the small to medium enterprise market, but the premium traveller went to Qantas. It was a major challenge to get them to fly with Ansett under administration, as they were worried about the longevity, despite the government underwriting, and more importantly, they were pressured by Qantas and told that 'if they didn't come on board now, don't bother coming back for a deal when Ansett falls over again'. We managed to convince $620 million of the $780 million of pre-administration Ansett accounts not to sign long term deals with Qantas until we were in a position to bid for their business.[3]

The corporate insider who prepared the document noted:

Interestingly those who did sign with Qantas did so on a volume basis and not on a market share basis, allowing them to walk away from the Qantas deal at any time if a new deal from Ansett stacked up financially. The strategy represented a return to basics—give the customers what they actually want—and it worked well. For accounts worth $200 000 and above, distribution was only via travel managers. This had the effect of removing the conflict between the Ansett sales force and the trade and resulted in them working more closely together than ever before.

Under its consultancy arrangement, Singapore engaged a large team to review the due diligence material and work with Ansett staff in preparing the business plan, but there was no formal offer and no indication that equity might be taken. Singapore, with its investment exposure to the problems of both Virgin Atlantic and Air NZ, was unlikely to bid for an airline that continued to sustain heavy losses and would do so into the future. Not surprisingly, they walked away in the end without submitting an offer. The Asian carrier kept its word to the two Marks and went no further than providing a consultancy service for the Ansett administration.

Lang Corporation, on the other hand, indicated its interest in the mainline airline in a one-page letter in which Lang proposed acquiring Ansett's terminal leases in Sydney, Melbourne, Adelaide, Brisbane and Perth as well as other aviation assets. The company was not, however, interested in the name 'Ansett'. Two thousand former Ansett staff would be employed and Lang would assume responsibility for their entitlements. The administrators did not regard the proposal as capable of acceptance and did not believe it satisfied their obligations under the *Corporations Act* to either see the Ansett business continue or maximise returns to creditors. Chris Corrigan, moreover, was seen as a cherry picker, interested primarily in the Sydney airport terminal, the biggest single asset and the 'jewel in the Ansett crown'. The Sydney airport terminal was Korda and Mentha's greatest drawcard and they were not going to surrender it lightly.

The Lang bid was also not likely to get very far with the priority creditors—the unions—whose collective bitterness over Lang Corp's role as a waterfront 'union buster' remained an indelible memory. The view of the unions, who were the principal block of creditors, was that Corrigan was not an acceptable risk, given his successful program to drive through waterfront reform. The unions believed that Lang Corp would again exercise its powers in another industry sector known for the strength of union influence, one that the company might regard as ripe for its terms of engagement. The thought frightened the unions and they would not abide any proposal from Lang.

In the end, the chasm between the cash that ANstaff could raise and the cash that it lacked appeared to widen.

The only two bids capable of acceptance were from Lindsay Fox and Solomon Lew's consortium Tesna— 'ANSETT' spelt backwards—and from ANstaff, a potentially strong but cash-starved grouping of former Ansett employees, mainly pilots. ANstaff prepared what was regarded as a formidable operational business plan, lacking the one essential ingredient: post 11 September it couldn't raise the cash, as a world search for backers fell apart.

ANstaff made every effort to become a force in the sale process but, in the end, the chasm between the cash that it could raise and the cash that it lacked appeared to widen. When its bid faltered and finally collapsed, ANstaff threw its support behind the Fox–Lew consortium. It was a move that drew praise from Korda and Mentha, who regarded the action as a clear sign of the strong internal support for their strategy and a measure of the co-operation they could expect from the Ansett workforce once they had completed the sale.

Fox and Lew made it perfectly clear from the beginning they were not only the *best* chance of reviving Ansett but that they were the *only* chance. But Greg Combet warned them, before any deal was signed 'not to go around kicking fucking tyres':

> We were not interested in people testing the tyre pressures and wanting to be pop stars a few months. They reacted by pressing ahead to get a sale agreement, with KPMG, Clayton Utz and a raft of other advisers all in on the act.

They used every pressure point to get the sale agreement and that was a good sign and gave us some confidence. After they got the sale agreement they continued putting in a lot of hard work and, of course, once you're in that process, expectations start to rise.[4]

The pair went into the deal with the full support of the Victorian Labor Government. In a finely tuned public relations exercise three weeks before they were crowned as the successful bidders and eight days out from a federal election, they had an A320 Airbus specially flown out to the Fox-owned Avalon airport, near Melbourne.

This media extravaganza featured political and union heavyweights, including the Deputy Prime Minister John Anderson and his Labor shadow Martin Ferguson. Anderson turned up despite anxious office warnings from his campaign office that his presence might be improperly interpreted as a sign of partisanship, supportive of the Fox–Lew proposal. Howard Government election strategists went into damage control: having learned of his decision to attend the function, campaign headquarters in Canberra communicated its view that this would be inappropriate and potentially embarrassing when other bids were purportedly still on the table. Anderson ignored the ministerial note, attended the display, and told reporters that he was not favouring any one proposal. He left early after being summoned home unexpectedly as a result of a family crisis.

The Avalon affair placed enormous pressure on the administrators to make up their minds. At that point, any other bidders in the wings might well have thought that they should give up, pack up their proposals and retreat. A photo opportunity with Lindsay and Solly at the controls of the aircraft gave the appearance of a one-horse race: Fox and Lew would make their formal bid and it would be accepted. Surprise and dismay accompanied this powerfully orchestrated performance. Fox and Lew had done their homework.

The capacity of Fox and Lew to gather high-level bi-partisan support was a coup but one that was totally dismantled and discredited by an incident occurring the day of the bid decision by Korda and Mentha. What happened on that occasion earned Fox and Lew the enmity of the Federal

Government. The Avalon affair was a pre-emptive strike, an unequivocal alert to the administrators and anyone else with any interest in Ansett that Fox and Lew would brook no interference. The press conference turned into a Labor Party election affair that exposed the political naivety of the two individuals who in the weeks to come would confront the embarrassment of having to do business with a different party in government.

Korda and Mentha had gambled to revive the airline and had their buyer. When Fox and Lew emerged, Ansett Mark II was profusely bleeding cash. Load factors were well down and, in the short time given them, the two Marks were unable to instil sufficient confidence and win business from sceptical travellers. For Korda and Mentha this was the most difficult task they had ever faced and they admitted on more than one occasion that they had been thrown into the position of having not only to learn the business but also to run the airline as joint CEOs.

For two days before a final agreement was reached on the morning of 8 November, Mentha strolled the seventeenth-floor offices of Ansett confident that 'today could be the day when we have some good news to tell'. He repeated his mantra on the morning of the eighth but it sounded no more convincing than previous utterances. The business of the administration proceeded as before, with no indication that today indeed was the day. At around 1.00 p.m. the administrators and Leon Zwier, their legal counsel, broke from a meeting to call in the media advisers from Jarvis Communications. A deal had finally been struck with Tesna and a media conference needed to be called for 4.00 p.m. A statement would be drafted and approved before the briefing. The floor became a veritable hive of activity.

Under the terms of the agreement, the Fox–Lew consortium would acquire the mainline assets of Ansett and assume responsibility for the continuing employment of some 4000 employees. The total value of the acquisition and the cash injection would be more than $1 billion. Add to that figure the alleged acquisition and financing of a new fleet of twenty-nine Airbus aircraft with a value of $2.5 billion, and the two Melbourne businessmen were said at the time to be spending upwards of $3.5 billion, an extraordinary figure even given their personal wealth. But Tesna would, in fact, be required to raise only $240 million in actual cash to sat-

Lew and Fox in T-shirts, reading, 'I HELPED GET ANSETT AUSTRALIA BACK IN OUR SKIES'.

Workers celebrating the Tesna sale

isfy the administrators. Details of the deal provided to creditors six weeks later showed that the Fox–Lew group would assume responsibility for $244 million worth of Ansett employee entitlements after the takeover. But these would have to be paid in full by Fox and Lew only if their venture went belly-up. The deal also came with a number of 'conditions precedent', namely the right to transfer airport terminal leases and other leveraged equipment. None were considered unattainable. Lang Corporation lodged a more detailed proposal later but it was too late because the Tesna offer by then was accepted.

If Avalon was a PR triumph for Fox and Lew, then the formal announcement of their successful bid bordered on a PR catastrophe. Fox and Lew, accompanied by Greg Combet, Australian Workers' Union boss Bill Shorten, and the Victorian Premier Steve Bracks, arrived at 3.30 p.m. Also hovering nearby was Michael McLeod, former chief-of-staff to the deputy leader of the Federal Opposition Labor Party, Simon Crean, and by then working for the Lew organisation. And there, smiling benignly and bringing up the rear, was McLeod's old boss, Simon Crean himself. Crean's appearance, sitting in a front-row media conference seat just two days out from the federal election, was guaranteed to stir Federal Government anger. John Anderson exploded, later disputing that any sale had taken place. John Howard noted the deal would be reviewed once the election was over. Mentha's practical view on the episode was to say: 'I answer to the *Corporations Act*, not the Electoral Act.'

Fox and Lew hijacked the occasion, donning T-shirts boldly exclaiming: 'I HELPED GET ANSETT AUS-

John Howard's government was not about to kick-start the airline ownership careers of two of Australia's wealthiest individuals.

TRALIA BACK IN OUR SKIES.' The following week they confronted a chill wind from Canberra after the Howard Government was unexpectedly returned for a third term. At a meeting that week they pressed their claim for a major financial commitment from the Federal Government to ensure that they would lose nothing in reviving the airline. While the Federal Government had considered a small and temporary cash injection to keep Ansett on its feet, John Howard's government was not about to kick-start the airline ownership careers of two of Australia's wealthiest individuals.

Fox and Lew later claimed they had not sought cash from the Government, but government correspondence confirmed concessions sought by Fox and Lew that would have amounted to more than $1 billion a year in subsidies.[5] These included generous tax concessions, seat revenue guarantees under which the Government would make up any shortfall incurred if load factors fell below sixty-five per cent, and a five year break from funding staff entitlements.[6] The seat deal alone would have led to underwriting costs of up to $800 million a year. It was a request that the Government, quite properly, rejected.

Captain Trevor Jensen, Ansett's Executive General Manager, Operations and Inflight Services, was dispirited by what he saw of the

Tesna plan and the actions taken by some of the syndicate's advisers. He came to the view they could not differentiate between 'running an airline and running a travel agency'[7]. The Air Operating Certificate (AOC), issued by the Federal Department of Transport, is effectively the licence to fly an airline. In Ansett's case it was held on behalf of the airline by Jensen, who had been appointed to his former job in the new airline structure. Jensen was the company's officer accountable and responsible for the AOC. He said recently:

> The company had held the AOC for more than 65 years. We were managing it day in and day out, ensuring that the airline complied in every way with the myriad regulations governing its operations. But not once did [Tesna] come to us to find out if a procedure was in order or what might need to be done in relation to an operating issue. And yet the accountability and the responsibility for running the airline rested with me. They never asked me what I thought of the operation. There was never a SWOT analysis done involving any of us.[8]

Indeed, when the Tesna advisers from KPMG wanted to develop an organisation chart for the new structure, they sought advice from the third rung on the Ansett executive ladder—the managers—bypassing any input from the general managers and the executive general managers. It was as if these two most senior levels were to be kept in the dark about how the airline was to be structured.

There was a widely held belief among senior staff that Fox and Lew would have bought the airline one day and sold the AOC the next.

Jensen came to believe that the Fox–Lew bid was nothing more than a bid for the terminals. He also knew that the much-promised videos and in-flight phones were a problem. He remarked:

> Promises must be able to be delivered or, to put it another way, if it is fitted it must work. The maintenance associated with ensuring that in-seat videos

are serviceable is both time consuming, and that means potential delays, and costly. The telephone system on the Airbus aircraft we believed we were going to introduce was simply not compatible with the Australian network. The suggestion that videos and phones be available in the back of each seat was an outlandish statement.

Jensen believed that the time frame in which the aircraft introduction was going to be made, while it could have been met, would have put incredible pressure on the company. 'It begged the question that it didn't really matter if it screwed up because it was never going to happen. In the end they would have the properties.' There was a widely held belief among senior staff that Fox and Lew would have bought the airline one day and sold the AOC the next.

Under the Tesna proposal for the airline, simulators, normally regarded by an airline as a cost centre, were to be set up as a separate business, but that was not legally allowed under federal aviation rules. This was because every simulator is linked to a flight training system where pilot reports have to be channelled through the responsible AOC executive, which in Ansett's case was Jensen. 'They were told that if they tried to run the simulator as a profit centre in the way they had it structured, it would not be approved by the regulators.' Jensen advised the business accounting team advising Tesna, but said his comments appeared to 'fall on deaf ears'. CASA's Melbourne office intervened, telling the Tesna people that their plan for the simulators was flawed. Added Jensen: 'I tried my best but they weren't listening.'

Similar concerns existed about Tesna's choice of engines for the planes it intended to acquire from Airbus. Jensen said he and other technical staff preferred those built by General Electric which were used on Ansett's Airbus and Boeing fleets. He described them as far superior to the International Aero Engines (IAE) V2500 engines—a development of a consortium part-owned by engine makers Rolls-Royce and Pratt & Whitney. He said Fox wanted the V2500 engine, which was costlier to maintain than his preferred CFM56 engine built by the GE/SNECMA joint venture. Jensen said that, while a typical engine shop visit for a

V2500 was less, at around US$1.4 million, the $1.8 million CFM service did not have to be done until 12,000 hours. The Fox-favoured V2500 had a shorter working life between shop visits and came off-the-wing at 8000 hours, making the average maintenance cost of the CFM considerably less. The comparisons had been clearly established in technical analysis during previous aircraft evaluations projects. According to Jensen, Fox was always reluctant to enter into serious discussion about the Boeing or GE options. Exasperated, Jensen even went to the extent of sending Fox some specialist magazine features comparing the two but said Fox ignored him. Jensen said that Fox told the GE representative in Australia, Jack Lutze, that his engines were no good. This staggered Jensen:

> Fox may know something about trucks but he knows bugger-all about running an airline. The facts are that, while the IAE engines perform well in our environment, their cost of operation is terrible. Fox just did not seem to appreciate nor want to know about significant cost factors. There was just no argument as to the better engine but that was never a consideration.

Jensen's sudden and unexpected departure from Ansett on 23 January occurred six days before the second mass meeting of creditors called to approve the sale of the trunkline carrier to Tesna. He did not make public his concerns and left quietly to accept what he believed was a more stimulating and responsible job with Qantas. The truth was that Jensen and Qantas CEO Geoff Dixon had talked, on and off over several months, about his possibly joining the national carrier to fill a new post in Sydney.

Jensen's departure and the reason for it was not raised at the creditors' meeting, but should have been addressed by the 1200 creditors who attended the 29 January gathering that voted overwhelmingly in favour of the Fox–Lew Tesna bid. That nobody thought that the resignation of the carrier's most senior operations executive had anything to do with his perception of how Tesna intended to run the airline says much about the misplaced hopes of Ansett staff and creditors and how blinded they were at that time to their dreams of having someone revive the airline as a real competitor for Qantas.

In a detailed report that Korda and Mentha prepared before the meeting, the two accountants laid bare their findings and the action they had taken in the months since their 17 September appointment. Creditors were told that the Ansett Group's overhead structure was intended to manage a business with a turnover of more than $3 billion a year, 15 000 employees, several hundred properties and a complex information technology system. They told how they had had undertaken considerable efforts to minimise costs, by vacating properties, cutting the IT bill from $20 million a month to $5 million, by establishing an Internet-based and simpler-to-maintain booking system, and how they had consolidated call centre operations, closed Ansett-owned and operated travel stores, and had used only the cheaper to operate A320 Airbus planes in their attempt to revive the carrier through their Ansett kickstart program. Aircraft leases had been cancelled and some fifty-three different aeroplanes were to be returned to owners overseas. Eight thousand staff had been made redundant. The departure of many key employees had made the task of closing the books more difficult, they reported, adding: 'it is taking considerable time and resources to reconstruct the financial position of the Ansett Group as at 12 September 2001'. Over the preceding months, they had to re-open and establish bank accounts. Aircraft that were not used in the scaled-down kick-start arrangement had been stored at airports and in engineering workshops in Australia and New Zealand and one A320 was in Canada where it had been stripped down and was undergoing heavy maintenance.

The two Marks reported that, in the first few weeks after their appointment, significant uncertainty existed about the number of aircraft that were owned, owned but financed and not owned but subject to operating leases. They spent considerable time seeking to establish title arrangements for many aircraft. By 26 September, notices had been issued to lessors, owners and financiers of fifty-two aircraft that their planes were no longer required. A further notice was sent to the financier of one further aircraft shortly afterwards. New arrangements were also made to continue the leases on two planes used by Kendell Airlines. Coupled with having to hand back and sell fully owned aircraft was the need to locate and properly audit all log books and service documents. Aircraft that were to be sold or handed back had to be stripped of engines and equipment owned by other parties, and re-fitted and restored with original equipment. Australian and overseas licensing authorities stipulated that full airworthiness surveys were required to be undertaken before aircraft were returned or sold to new owners, irrespective of whether they would again fly as passenger carriers within Australian airspace. More than 10 million spare parts, ranging from jet engines worth millions of dollars to simple onboard food trolleys and crockery embossed with the Ansett crest for first class passengers, had to be separately itemised and checked before being put on sale, creditors were told.

None of this attracted a great deal of interest. Creditors were more focused on whether the Fox–Lew deal would conclude. Korda and Mentha had advised that 'the interests of creditors are best served by approving the sale of the mainline business to Tesna'. They argued that it provided the best possible return to creditors, maximised the chance of Ansett continuing, gave a large number of employees the chance of having work, cut redundancy costs and increased the ability of the regional airlines and other Ansett businesses to trade and find buyers.

On that afternoon of 29 January, when creditors gathered at Melbourne's Vodafone Arena, the debate centred on keeping Ansett flying, retaining jobs and getting fair value for frequent flyers' reward points that were owed for unclaimed travel. The points-versus-jobs issue split the audience into opposing camps, on one side

The delay would add $6 million a week to the cost of keeping Ansett alive.

of the closed auditorium sat one group and on the other sat workers bussed in to the gathering by the unions. Most came expecting to vote on a deal that would rubber stamp the sale process. But only hours before, the administrators learned that the deal had struck unexpected turbulence in a mountain of unfinished legal paperwork that was going to delay for up to thirty days any hope of the sale being completed. Korda and Mentha told the audience they were drawing a line in the sand: they wanted the sale approved, but subject to a completion limit of no more than thirty days. The audience heard that the delay would add $6 million a week to the cost of keeping Ansett alive. It involved a trading loss of $2.5 million per week and added 'info-tech' charges of $3.5 million a week, increasing Ansett's trading losses by a further $24 million if the sale process took the full month to be concluded. 'It is a difficult decision but we have come too far,' Korda told the audience. 'We need creditors to understand the risk. It will cost us some money to get there, but it has cost us money to get here.'

The sale vote was carried on a show of hands by about 900 of the 1200 creditors at the two-hour meeting. The administrators told the protesting frequent flyers that their 67 billion Global Rewards points were virtually worthless. Some of the heat was taken out of the meeting when a Diners Club representative with 5000 frequent flyer proxy votes was offered a place on the creditors' committee. AWU federal secretary Bill Shorten summed up the feelings of Ansett staff, arguing that frequent flyer concerns mattered little when it came to saving jobs. 'Saving a job far exceeds the value of any frequent flyer point ever accrued in the history of an airline,' he told the meeting. 'When it comes to frequent flyer points, I have never seen a situation where you can exchange your frequent flyer points for school fees, for food, for mortgages [and] for all sorts of essentials.'

Neither Lindsay Fox nor Solomon Lew attended the meeting. Their absence denied any creditor the opportunity to test their commitment to proceeding with the sale in a public forum. While Fox addressed staff on a public relations tour of various Ansett workplaces, neither he nor Lew allowed themselves to be questioned by creditors or skilled business analysts. Apart from tame interviews with selected cronies, they spoke to the news media only on two occasions and kept secret the business plan that

> **Neither Fox nor Lew allowed themselves to be questioned by creditors or skilled business analysts ... and [they] kept secret the business plan that they had put together with their advisers.**

they had put together with their advisers.

Then, in the first weeks of February, Fox and Lew went off on a secret mission to Europe without telling Korda or Mentha. Their absence from the country first surfaced when John Anderson called Fox on his mobile phone and learned, much to his surprise, that he was speaking to him at Singapore Airport. What Fox chose not to add was that he and Lew were headed to England, where they had arranged a meeting with Virgin Blue's Richard Branson. When their absence was publicised, their spokesman sought to cover up their mission as an inspection of Airbus operations in Toulouse to firm up details of their order for twenty-nine new planes. The pair did cross to France and visit the Airbus factory, which issued a press release to Australian newspapers saying the two businessmen had signed a memorandum of understanding to acquire twenty-nine new planes. A subsequent phone call to the factory revealed that the order was not binding and that no cash was exchanged.

The real purpose for the trip was to talk with the flamboyant and entrepreneurial Branson, whose Virgin Blue stood in the way of their plans to snare thirty per cent of the Australian domestic airline travel. A bemused Branson listened as the two novices outlined their plan that various experts say would have lost them $100 million in the first year of operations. They wanted to do a deal but various newspaper reports indicated that Branson told them that if they wanted control of Virgin they should buy Ansett and then come back and talk again. Branson was reported to have made it clear that it would be his show, a situation neither Fox nor Lew would entertain; they could be equity participants but it was going to be controlled by him and it would be a Virgin airline. Branson's bluntness and clear understanding of their dilemma took Fox and Lew by surprise. Further talks between representatives of both groups had a similar demise. Fox and Lew's plan for a full-service operation would not fit the Virgin no-frills mould.

Fox and Lew were under pressure either to challenge Virgin Blue head-on or walk away from their Tesna plan to take over Ansett. Having been handed a lesson in reality in the airline business, they had to decide whether to put their own cash at risk or to walk away.

17
THE LAST SUPPER

NOTHING ON THE morning of Tuesday, 26 February 2002 prepared the two Marks and the rest of their team for the events that would unfold that day. It was a day like most others that had passed in the weeks since Fox and Lew had put their names on the Ansett sale documents.

With two days left until closure, an optimistic mood was growing among the occupants of the seventeenth-floor executive suite. The frantic activity that had filled the early months of the administration had passed, and long gone were the 120 'suits' and their assistants who had made the floor a hive of frenetic energy the previous September. By 26 February, only a few core operators remained and the atmosphere seemed a little more laid back than before. Not even the low patronage of the fifteen A320 aircraft then in service detracted from the occasion.

Little remained to be done, and the two Marks and their reduced staff were totally confident that the deal would be completed without a hitch. They could not identify anything likely, in those last hours, to wipe out the long days of toiling to keep on track a sale of the trunk route carrier to the Tesna syndicate. The administration group was proud of what had been achieved, each member anticipating the satisfaction of knowing that their key strategy of relaunching Ansett and selling the airline as a going concern had worked in spite of massive losses. Some 3000 jobs would be created, some permanent and many part time, when the deal was ultimately settled in forty-eight hours' time. The unsecured creditors, with their hands out for the A$1.9 billion they were owed, would get five cents in the dollar. It was a pittance, but at least they would get something.

Korda and Mentha had been looking forward to sitting back a little. They still had heaps of assets to offload, but they would soon be free of their biggest task, having offloaded the airline to Tesna. But both were cautious not to get carried away and celebrate their achievement too early. Throughout their months of dealing with the media, each of them had repeatedly warned that nobody should take anything for granted; it was often in the last hours, at the wire, that deals fell over. They might have ruefully reflected on that fact around midnight that Tuesday when, just a few hours earlier, everything had appeared to be moving inexorably towards deal completion by the midnight deadline in two days' time.

Fox and Lew were themselves jovial and appeared totally committed to the deal. Only the previous day Mentha greeted Lew in his office and asked pointedly and deliberately: 'Do you have the money?' to which Lew responded: 'I've got it in spades' and they then got down to some last-minute deal making. No hint of anything insurmountable appeared on the horizon.

Fox and Lew had lined up a formidable team of advisers to deal with their bid. Around 9 a.m. David Dunn, from KPMG, corporate advisers to Tesna, and Antony Cohen, another KPMG operative, arrived for a meeting with the administrators and their legal adviser Leon Zwier of Arnold Bloch Leibler. Dunn, a lawyer-cum-merchant banker, was highly regarded on both sides of the table. He was a consummate professional, strong intellectually and on top of his strategy. The meeting was to thrash out the final bits and pieces of the contract and was regarded as a mere formality. It followed a predictable pattern, concluding with an understanding that both parties had reached their final positions, that finalisation of the deal could be reached, probably that day.

At one stage during the meeting there was a suggestion that Fox and Lew were conducting a risk analysis on going forward with the transaction, after which they would get back to the administrators. This—a risk analysis on going forward with just two days to go!—should have rung alarm bells. That it didn't can be attributed to the administrators' continuing confidence in the deal completion, a confidence based largely on the fact that Tesna had already devoted to the deal resources estimated at some $40 million, not including the plan to acquire up to twenty-nine new Airbus A320 aircraft to bring the new Ansett to full strength. Not even the mooting of a last-minute risk analysis could tarnish the shine on the demonstrated Fox–Lew bona fides. The meeting lasted about ninety minutes and the syndicate left, with no indication of what was to follow.

Around 5 p.m., Fox and Lew, relaxed and friendly, returned to the seventeenth-floor suite of Ansett's executive offices, with their conspicuous Bentleys parked in reserved spots in the basement car park. The two men were accompanied by Max Casen, of Clayton Utz, who constantly accompanied them to such meetings. Lew, in particular, was beaming and friendly, approaching numerous staffers with a smile and a word of encouragement. This had been his modus operandi since 8 November. Always immaculately dressed, he exuded a sense of wellbeing and bonhomie. There was not a hint from him, even when he emerged from Mark

Mentha's office at one stage during the meeting, that the deal was about to be, or had already been, dealt a blow from which it would not recover. Outside the offices of Mentha and Korda, Lew had a few words with the administrators' media adviser. 'What are we doing,' he remarked jocularly, 'writing a book on the rescue of Ansett?' What, in fact, was being written was one of two media releases that needed to be prepared—one that the deal had gone through, the other that it had collapsed. At that moment, ironically, it was the former that was being written, for it was the deal completion that everyone was still hoping for. Lew gave nothing away—not then and not at any time during the protracted negotiations aimed at selling the airline.

It was during that late-afternoon meeting that the first signs of emerging problems began to surface. It was then that Fox, Lew and Casen indicated there were real difficulties in completing the transaction. There was risk and they wanted to minimise that risk, a not-unusual position given the nature of the transaction. The impression was that they were still considering their position and that a final decision had not yet been made. It would be an understatement to say that this sent shock waves through the administrators—shock waves that quickly became incredulity as the administrators tried to digest the true meaning of the position Fox and Lew were now adopting. Mentha emerged briefly from the unfinished meeting with his right arm extended and the thumb wiggling downwards. 'It's not looking good,' he said, his face drawn and his complexion, naturally fair, more pallid than normal.

The deal breaker was identified as the Sydney domestic terminal transfer, a surprising admission given that a Tesna media release issued eleven days earlier had indicated that all issues with the Sydney Airports Corporation Limited (SACL) had been resolved. The release, dated 15 February, said, in part, that 'an agreement had been reached with Sydney Airports Corporation Ltd (SACL) in relation to all outstanding commercial issues necessary for the formal assignment of the Ansett Domestic Terminal lease'. The agreement followed an evening meeting the day before involving Fox and Lew, SACL's chairman David Mortimer and CEO Tony Stuart. In their Tesna press release of 15 February, Fox and Lew stated:

the agreement represents a key milestone as Tesna moves towards completion of the sale agreement with the Ansett administrators. We will work closely with SACL and the administrators to finalise the formal documentation as expeditiously as possible.

Now, suddenly, 'the jewel in the crown' had become the major obstacle. The administrators offered two possible solutions—one a court direction and the other a creative terminal leasing agreement that would not require their immediate transfer to Tesna.

When the meeting concluded at around 6 p.m., and all parties for the consortium had left the building, a series of urgent phone calls ensued, all focused on having SACL confirm that the DTL lease would be transferred. Zwier sought an urgent communication to that effect from the corporation's lawyer, Linda Abernethy. SACL, recognising the urgency of the situation, said it would be done within fifteen minutes. The parties were falling over each other to be compliant and ensure that the deal could be completed in time. Still the question remained—why was it taking so long to complete the transfer? Who was at fault? Zwier then rang Mallesons, SACL's legal advisers, and was assured that there was nothing to worry about with respect to the transfer of the lease. Zwier accepted the assurance but wanted an immediate e-mail confirmation. Time was of the essence and Zwier was under intense pressure to resolve the issue.

> **The parties were falling over each other to be compliant and ensure that the deal could be completed in time.**

The e-mail's arrival coincided with a call from Casen to Zwier, a call he took privately in a nearby office. Zwier was ebullient that the terminal question had been resolved and he could not contain his delight in his conversation with Casen. The impassive and matter-of-fact Casen interpolated that they had now considered the two solutions offered at the meeting and that, fundamentally, his team did not like the idea of litigation. Zwier responded without hesitation that his concerns were unnecessary as all the issues had been dealt with. The e-mail documenting the transfer of lease to Tesna had arrived. 'Your happy days are here again,' he told Casen.

In a later interview, Zwier said that the remark had been tongue in cheek.

> I wanted to make it as difficult as possible for Casen and to demonstrate to him and his clients that the grounds for their withdrawal were disingenuous.
>
> At the 5 p.m. meeting I realised that the deal was off. Lew, in particular, was smiling broadly and was very relaxed. There was absolutely no pressure on him ... To me the deal was as good as dead.[1]

To confirm his suspicions, Zwier put what he regarded as a very simple question to the man who would buy Ansett: 'Do you want to do this deal?' to which Lew responded obliquely with a question of his own: 'What sort of question is that?' It was not the response Zwier wanted, but it was the one he expected.

Zwier, with his strong strategic mind and keen intellect as well as an extraordinary knowledge of corporations law as it applies to insolvencies, had been a tireless worker behind the scenes to get the deal over the line. The moment when the deal could proceed to a conclusion was the one he had been eagerly awaiting. Without acknowledging what Zwier was saying, Casen told Zwier he was faxing a letter to the administrators. Minutes later the truth dawned that Fox and Lew had indeed pulled out of the deal. With the impact of the Tesna fax now sinking in, Korda and Mentha made one last attempt to retrieve the situation, making a late-evening visit to Lew's salubrious Collins Street offices. It did not work. With the protection of 'based on legal advice we do not believe we can complete the transaction', Lew brought to an end the Tesna commitment to what would have been one of the greatest corporate recoveries in Australia's history. He would not now have to make a massive personal financial commitment. Fox, meanwhile, could leave on a European skiing holiday, a trip he had booked around noon on the Tuesday, hours *before* the moment at which he and his co-chairman were seen to pull the plug irrevocably.

When Korda and Mentha returned to the Ansett boardroom late on Tuesday, they were, understandably, dispirited not only by the failure of the deal on which they had pinned much of their reputation but also on behalf of their team of Andersen staffers who had spent the bulk of the previous six months trying to turn the vision into reality. The mood, though did not last long. Indeed, it lasted only as long as it took to open a few bottles of soft drink and the neatly packaged boxes of Chinese take-away ordered and paid for by Leon Zwier.

Not just ordinary Chinese, it must be said, but exquisite offerings from the high altar of Australian cuisine: an exclusive Little Bourke Street restaurant. The banquet included dim sum with scallops and fresh prawns, Peking duck, Cantonese black pepper beef, blue swimmer crab dumplings, shaved conch, squab, sil bok choi and poached chicken. Under other circumstances this could have been a feast to savour. But as Korda and Mentha, fellow partners Michael Wachtel, David Winterbottom and James Hatherley (who was dressed in shorts after hurrying in to the office from pre-natal classes with his wife) and senior staffers Damian Templeton and Quentin Law tucked into the range of delicacies, discussion of the forward strategy for Ansett had already begun.

Right now was not the time for blame and recriminations. Korda, in particular, was adamant that no blame would be apportioned. He remained the philosophical voice of reason, as he had been throughout the administration, calming down what could have been a volatile situation after such a stressful and, it appeared, wasted six months. The administrators still had a job to do—and that was to secure the best return possible for creditors. The deal with Fox and Lew was over but there were other deals to be struck. They determined that the administration should continue, that liquidation was not yet an option. There was still a chance of retrieving a return from the judicious sale of assets, despite the flat market for aviation infrastructure.

As they ate, the tension of the day's drama eased and the team began to plan for a future without Fox and Lew. They needed a shut-down strategy for the airline, the final curtain call for Ansett, as well as a strategy for dealing with the 3000 employees Tesna had been scheduled to take on and other key stakeholders. One of those present described the gathering as a bonding in adversity, an attempt to accept the unacceptable, to explain the unexplainable. The meeting went until the early hours of the morning when the exhausted participants withdrew to consider the options of the day ahead.

They were not left in doubt for long, with the front page of that morning's *Herald Sun* newspaper, in an exclusive scoop, trumpeting the end of the deal. The media went into frenzied overdrive and, by 10 a.m., it was clear that a media briefing would have to be convened. It was duly scheduled for 12.15 p.m. Korda and Mentha would once again have to face both their greatest supporters and their harshest critics.

18

THE END OF AN AIRLINE

GREG COMBET WAS understandably embittered by the eleventh-hour back-down by Solomon Lew on a personal promise that he had given to the union leader. Vivid in Combet's memory is a meeting he had with the businessman on 12 February, in which he says Lew told him: 'We are going to complete and 3000 people will be employed.'[1] Present at that meeting in Lew's Collins Street office were Lew, Fox, Combet and various advisers for both parties.

Fox appeared determined to the end to go through with the sale. An Ansett staffer said that was obvious from discussions he witnessed in which Fox had arranged football sponsorships for what was to be the Fox–Lew Tesna-owned Ansett. Lew meanwhile continued, even as late as February, to chisel at the $270 million cash price that he and Fox had earlier agreed to pay from their own funds for Ansett. At one point in his discussions with Korda and Mentha during that period the pair were asked to discount the deal ten per cent, which would have effectively trimmed $27 million from future entitlements dividends to displaced workers. Korda and Mentha held their ground, rejecting the attempt forthrightly.

> Lew told Combet: 'We are going to complete and 3000 people will be employed.'

Combet and the Ansett unions had called for the Fox–Lew talks on 12 February over their alarm that the Tesna syndicate had shifted ground and was no longer prepared to take the 4000 former Ansett staff flagged to transfer to their group in the original sale announcement. During the previous weeks, 4000 had become 3500, then a figure of just 3000 was being touted.

On 12 February, Combet demanded: 'What the fuck is going on? What are the real numbers?' Combet told the pair that they should also be sharing the losses Ansett was then incurring as a result of hold-ups in the transfer of various terminal and aircraft operating leases that had delayed final settlement. Combet pointed out that the creditors, mostly Ansett workers, were left to shoulder losses amounting to $6 million a week that could eventually total some $24 million.

Combet wanted guarantees about staff numbers and the liabilities that Fox–Lew would accept. Combet was sitting directly opposite Lew and eyeballing him when he took his stern line and elicited Lew's now-broken promise. 'I directed my question at him because he was the commercial man,' said Combet.[2] Fox and Lew then briefed Combet on their revised business plan which reaffirmed that the deal was not conditional on finance. Combet's confidence grew three days later when the Tesna syndicate confirmed in a press release that all the commercial issues with the Sydney Airports Corporation (SACL) had been resolved. After Fox and Lew claimed that uncertainty over third party issues linked to the Sydney terminal lease had ended the deal, Combet asserted: 'Fox and Lew knew that had been squared away before they made the decision [to pull out]).'[3]

Bitter as he was at the time, in an interview with the authors three months after the walkout by the tycoons, Combet appeared more conciliatory and reflective.[4]

In the interests of everyone and to achieve closure on what happened, it is important that Solly Lew and Lindsay Fox come out publicly in whatever forum they think appropriate and explain their reasons for pulling out of the sale.

Time has now passed and regardless of what they say were their reasons, there is nothing to prevent them from coming out and saying, 'Look we couldn't pull off the finances, and finance was an issue, or we just couldn't tie up this or that. It was a combination of things and the risk was looking too great, or our business model didn't add up at the end of the day.' They look bad enough now and they won't look any worse in coming out and explaining their position. I think people would appreciate it. What happened messed a

Greg Combet after collapse of Lew–Fox deal.

lot of people's lives around and they deserve an explanation from Fox and Lew. I would strongly encourage them to come out and do it.

Solomon Lew and Lindsay Fox gave every appearance they were totally committed to their Ansett takeover until Max Casen pulled the plug that fateful Tuesday evening. Advertising campaigns were arranged, footy sponsorships were signed, and placards bearing the words 'under new management' had been sign-written and were ready to be placed on prominent view at Ansett headquarters and various airport terminals. Combet's enthusiasm had been sparked by what appeared to have been the successful outcome of months of dogged negotiations that had resulted in a ground-breaking agreement with the Tesna group that would have given the new Ansett staff equity in the revived airline.

According to Combet[5] the unions and Tesna had reached a novel arrangement in which there were common conditions for all of the workforce.

> There were four or five other sections, like appendices, that dealt with pilots, flight crew, maintenance, customer service staff. There was a commitment that five per cent shareholding would be issued to a trust that the ACTU would establish for all the employees, and that five per cent would be funded by a profit share arrangement—that is, it would be equity that would be properly capitalised. The capital would be derived from future profits. There was five per cent up front in a private company which was fully convertible at float, but the financing of it, given the business plan they had, was that the profit sharing was not expected to kick in until after the float. So an arrangement had to be made that would be acceptable and be contained in a prospectus. Effectively Fox and Lew were going to finance the 5 per cent for the staff.

Combet described the arrangement as 'a good and important thing'.

> I had no hesitation in recommending the agreement. It was a good agreement. We had an unusual wages setting arrangement in it. We accepted that there would be a period of time to allow the business plan to be consolidat-

ed. But after two years there would be a pool of money set aside for wages. About $4.2 million was to be in the pool initially and we would decide how that would be divided among the staff.

Combet argues that the unions had done everything they possibly could with the support of the Ansett workers who were offered a job to make the business plan work.

That is the reason there is so much anger and frustration about it. Everyone was into us along the way, saying 'the bloody unions and the workers rorted it'. I can tell you it was a very good agreement in terms of a commercial operation. Dixon [the Qantas CEO] had his eye on it pretty closely. We maintained the rates to a parity with Qantas, but it was a productive flexible agreement with different arrangements in it, and it gave people a bit of equity in the show. It would have worked very well.

> **Tesna continued to send messages that everything was on track for the sale to be completed.**

Combet added that the ACTU and the unions were around a lot of businesses 'and we are not naive commercially. This would have worked and you would have had a very committed staff to make it work.' Everybody— from the administrators to the unions, the employees to the suppliers, the executives appointed to the Tesna group to the person in the street— expected that the deal would be concluded. Everybody, that is, except for News Limited's economics commentator Terry McCrann.

McCrann was adamant from the outset that Fox and Lew would pull out, that they would not risk their own cash in a high-stakes airline venture. He believed they wanted the lucrative high-rent properties that belonged to the Ansett portfolio; flying the airline was secondary. His commentaries, not all of them popular, lent commercial reality to an emotive news story. Nevertheless, Tesna continued to send messages that everything was on track for the sale to be completed. Ansett executives gave up their weekends for weeks helping the Fox–Lew group draft a new frequent flyer strategy. A premier catering outfit provided samples of the food it would serve on the full-service airline. The event became a prime-time television news item. Some Ansett executives remained sceptical and regularly leaked a flow of confidential operating data. An early draft of the proposed frequent flyer scheme that reached the *Herald Sun* prompted an angry outburst from a Lew adviser, who said that publishing it 'could undermine the whole sale process'[6]. The next day the wrong man was suspended and barred for a time from his job at Ansett headquarters.

Fox went on a confidence-building trip across the country, speaking to Ansett workers and telling them that their full-service airline would include in-flight seat-mounted videos and telephones. He stunned and delighted Ansett staff at Melbourne Airport by dropping his pants in response to a question about the follow-up bid that Lang Corporation's Chris Corrigan had made for the airline. Bearing his not-insubstantial buttocks, he proclaimed: 'Corrigan can kiss my arse!' Word of this larrikin antic spread rapidly throughout the company.

It has been revealed[7] that, despite the losses that were racked up, some pluses did emerge from running the administrator's scaled-down airline and were successfully trialled for Fox and Lew. They included a strongly supported rebate offer, with a single aircraft type being proposed by Tesna, and an impeccable on-time performance. This was said to have added up to an attractive product that was well on its way to working effectively and profitably, had the Tesna deal gone ahead. But in the hiatus between the deal being signed and the deal being completed, the extent of the corporate revenue available became a sticking point and a source of dissent for Tesna and the Texas Pacific Group, whom Fox and Lew had purportedly brought in as investors in their bid to restore Ansett's fortunes. TPG, a highly experienced airline operator, sent consultants to Australia to undertake due diligence, a process that had Tesna making initial estimates on revenue projections of $1.1 billion, whereas the consultants could only find $900 million.[8]

The difference became a hotly debated issue in the lead-up to the Tesna walkout and was at least one of the underlying reasons for TPG's withdrawal from the consortium. Insiders believed that both Tesna and

TPG were a little off the mark in their estimates and should have met in the middle at around $1 billion. In getting a share of the corporate spend, both parties agreed that the new Ansett could achieve somewhere between $400 and $450 million, given the greatly reduced network, a trimmed-down thirty aircraft model and its inability[9] to service any of the mining industry accounts, themselves worth $115 million alone.

A key change that occurred during the administration was that of direct leisure distribution. During the early days of administration, when Ansett had only a call centre and a web site, loads on peak leisure flights were very healthy—a clear sign that, on simple point-to-point domestic flights, customers did want to deal direct. With over forty-five per cent of all direct bookings being made over the Internet, it proved a very cheap form of distribution. And with the reopening of the global distribution system (GDS), which dealt with travel agents, it became incremental revenue as the direct booking numbers did not stop. The administrators were making all the right moves in their valiant attempt to resuscitate the Ansett operations. It was not enough.

While the administrators, from long experience, recognised there were risks that the deal could fall over, they were nevertheless confident and had no reason to suspect otherwise. It was the same with the unions, as priority creditors, although Greg Combet added that 'at no point was the union movement naive'.

> We were very mindful of the conditions precedent in the 8 November agreement and the possibility that the sale might not complete. But as things went along we looked at it objectively and, for example, we concluded and certified our enterprise agreement with Tesna before Christmas. Other conditions precedent were gradually being ticked off and all the points seemed to be coming together and we were basing our judgment on that fact.

While the union movement had to take a hard-headed view of the deal struck and the dangers to its completion, it was not until the end of January that Combet and his team recognised danger signs. He said of their concerns:

We could see commercially how an extension was justified but we also saw that we were heading into quite risky territory. At that point we had to take a different view to the administrators because we were not prepared to just provide carte blanche for another 28 or 30 days.

Instead the unions insisted that it be a week-by-week proposition, reviewing the losses, seeing how the conditions precedent were being ticked off, particularly the Sydney Airport terminal leases, and what point the commercial negotiations had reached. 'We were getting into territory where the entitlements of the people we represented were increasingly at risk if the deal failed.' Then Combet was taken aback at the creditors' meeting when it was disclosed that Tesna expected to be going forward with some 3500 employees when he understood the figure to still be at 4000.

That was the first time I had heard that number and I needed to be certain about where the numbers were actually at because of the impact it would have not only on the value of the transaction but on the possible return to creditors.

This surprising development led Combet to front Fox and Lew on a number of occasions over the next fortnight leading up to 12 February, when the 3000 figure emerged. The revised number was not a surprise to Jensen who later said:

The Ansett management team and the Andersen people had certainly discussed 3000 as the correct staff complement for the 29 aircraft model Fox and Lew had proposed on several occasions. After all, the Ansett Mark II strategy was built around the Easyjet model of 105 staff per aircraft. And that multiplied out to 3045 staff. Fox and Lew did their due diligence against this model so I am sure 3000 would have been in their business plan. Mind you, none of the management team ever saw their plan. Staff numbers were always destined to be an issue.[10]

Combet's early fears were further jolted on the day before the deal fell through when Fox stormed out of a meeting with maintenance unions at

ACTU headquarters and had to be coaxed back to the table by his son. It was then that the message became clear to Combet and his colleagues: Fox and Lew were thinking the unthinkable.

In his *Herald Sun* column on 28 February, the day the deal should have been completed, Terry McCrann summed it up in this way:

> The reality was that, as the Ansett business all but evaporated in recent weeks, it became clear it only made sense to buy Ansett if you were going to merge it with Virgin.

McCrann had been running front-page stories highlighting aircraft load factors and revenue streams, heavy stuff that normally would sit in the business pages. Because Ansett was Ansett, and because the outcome of the sale affected the lives of thousands of families, what McCrann was writing had become required breakfast reading in tens of thousands of households. McCrann had a feed of 'confidential' information that caused alarm and consternation for Korda and Mentha and sounded danger for the Fox–Lew camp.

McCrann questioned, on 7 February, the falling employment figures and how they represented significant discounts for the two businessmen. He pointed out that by downsizing job numbers Fox and Lew would also cut their operating risk. With 1000 fewer staff, employee entitlements transferred to Tesna would fall by $61 million, which would have to be met immediately from the administrators' asset pool. McCrann pointed out that the cutback also meant that any new Ansett, if it ever got going, would be smaller and leaner and would, therefore, lose less on its operations. He saw this as a second acquisition discount, with Fox and Lew likely to end up with a very good deal.

The reason Fox and Lew finally withdrew must lie in the personal losses they would have suffered running head-to-head with a formidable opponent in Qantas and Virgin Blue's cut prices. But they had a gift horse in the properties, shelling out just $270 million for a long list of assets, one of which was the retail-rent-rich Sydney Airport terminal valued at $300 million. Coupled with that was a block in the city of Melbourne, bordering Swanston and Franklin streets, including the headquarters building, which would be ideal to convert into apartments or to be used as student accommodation for patrons of Melbourne University or RMIT nearby.

The property jewel was undoubtedly the terminal at Sydney Airport, and it was only late in the sale process that it became patently clear that anyone holding the lease had to be a licensed operator of an airline. Fox and Lew were barred from taking the rents and selling off the Air Operator's Certificate to another airline operator. Perhaps that is why 'legal advice' convinced them that they could not do the deal. The nation and 15 000 displaced and still devastated Ansett staff would like to know the answer.

19
FACING THE MUSIC

AT 12.15 P.M. ON Wednesday, 27 February 2002, the Marks Korda and Mentha faced what could have been their Waterloo. It was at that precise time that they walked through the swinging glass doors of the Ansett first-floor canteen to tell more than a hundred media representa-

Korda and Mentha after the collapse of the Tesna deal.

tives that the deal with Fox and Lew was officially dead. Considering that they had been up for most of the previous night discussing with other Andersen partners and staffers the possible ongoing strategies, they were remarkably composed and determined to proceed normally and professionally. There was a strange air of serenity about Korda that morning, hardly what anyone expected after the dramas of the previous night. Throughout the administration his pragmatism and cool-headedness had been guiding lights for the rest of the team.

In the early days of the administration, heavily attended media briefings were a daily occurrence which Korda and Mentha used to communicate news to Ansett employees. Within Australia and the Asia–Pacific region the Ansett story competed for space with the international 'war on terrorism' arising from the 11 September attacks on the New York World Trade Center and the Pentagon. It remained big news at home and continued to be prominent right up until Korda and Mentha's last media briefing.

Korda had requested that a formal statement be drawn up for him to read out to the media and to serve as the basis for the many questions he anticipated. While there was not much that could be said, he wanted to get it right and he made a number of running changes until he was satisfied that his message was clear and unequivocal. The deal was dead but the administration would continue in the interests of getting the best deal for creditors. Of the hundreds of formal briefings, doorstops, one-on-one interviews and radio talkback chats that had taken place during the administration, this final media briefing was to be the hardest and, at the same time, the most defining moment for both Korda and Mentha. They were to be forced to confirm that morning's News Limited exclusive announcement of the collapse of the deal and the likelihood that Ansett was dead and headed for the graveyard.

> **Korda simply repeated the words 'We were ready, willing and able to complete the deal.'**

The report, published in the second, city edition of the *Herald Sun* in Melbourne and in other major papers interstate, caused a media frenzy unlike any other incident or 'exclusive' throughout the administration. Mark Korda had over ninety unanswered calls on his mobile, Mentha over forty, and media adviser Peter Wilms not many fewer, with thirty-odd inquiries. None of the three could keep up with the incredible level of interest in the development—not surprising, perhaps, given the nature of the administration and what hung in the balance. The deal's death was to prove more interesting, more exciting, than its birth a mere four months earlier.

Early on that Wednesday morning Mentha and Korda had returned to the seventeenth floor, their virtual home-cum-workplace for the previous six months, sleep deprived and physically and mentally exhausted. Clearly they were disappointed and said as much frequently during the briefing. To an observer not aware of what had happened they might have appeared to be two businessmen providing a report on a company restructuring. In fact they were, and remain, bitterly disappointed at the ultimate outcome. No blame was apportioned. Korda simply repeated the words he had used in the press release accompanying the briefing: 'We were ready, willing and able to complete the deal.' It was the sharpest rebuke he made.

In his opening remarks, Korda said that he and his fellow administrator were disappointed to announce that the proposed sale of Ansett to the Tesna consortium would now not occur. In itself this was a curious understatement. In another example of understatement, Korda indicated that he and Mark Mentha thought the development was unexpected. After all, had not Fox and Lew employed twenty new management people and offered jobs to some 3000 former Ansett employees?

'As administrators, we are ready, willing and able to complete the transaction,' he repeated. He did not just say 'we were ready'. It was as if he was offering an olive branch to Fox and Lew, as if the deal might some-how still be completed. He might have been leaving the door ajar for the pair to re-enter. Meanwhile, though, he and Mentha had to be realistic. The airline would cease flying the following Monday night 'and refunds will be arranged for all passengers with bookings after Monday night'. All passenger revenue had been held in a cash-backed trust account. And then he uttered the words he had hoped he would never have to say: 'We'll organise help with people on Qantas and Virgin Blue.' It was as if he had admitted that the vision he and Mentha had formulated so meticulously was now in the hands of others!

Korda then said what everyone knew: 'Mark and I have tried and tried to save Ansett, which is our duty under the *Corporations Act*, but we're not going to get there with Tesna.' Questions followed and Korda was asked: 'Do you believe Mr Fox and Mr Lew were fair dinkum in light of their decision to back away from the deal?' Ever the diplomat, he replied that Tesna had spent tens of millions of dollars on the transaction in legal and advisory fees alone, although this figure has not been confirmed. The administrators believed the two businessmen had been unambiguously committed to the transaction. Still the questions swirled around the issue of why the deal had fallen through, to which Korda replied reasonably that it was a question that should be directed to Fox and Lew; the purported outstanding issues were the assignment of the five intercapital domestic terminal leases and the assignment of the nineteen aircraft.

'I mean, that's what Tesna have said,' he stated enigmatically. He went on to say that the third part of the issue was that they could not see that they could get all those finished and completed by the twenty-eighth. The media knew the Sydney Airport terminal issue had been resolved and that no other issue that might be outstanding was incapable of resolution by the due date. They were also aware that the consortium had had four months in which to complete—an adequate period even for a transaction of its size. Add to that ninety-plus legal minds working on the deal and there seemed no good reason why the airline could not resume full operations on 1 March if the buyers had really wanted it to.

For most of the administration, Mentha, rather than Korda, had been the public face of the rescue attempt. He had key responsibilities for dealing with staff, unions and government. Mentha summed up for the staff who would lose their jobs, saying: 'We are gutted for the employees, even for our team and the legal team and everyone who has supported us in this effort.'

> 'We are gutted for the employees, even for our team and the legal team and everyone who has supported us in this effort.'

He pointed out that Tesna had made letters of offer to more than 2800 people; they had put in place their management team; they had entered into arrangements with Star Alliance; they had entered into arrangements with Airbus to deliver a new fleet; they had entered into maintenance arrangements with the administrators, they had entered into catering contracts with Alpha Catering; they had put in place a Golden Wings program; and they had put in place a frequent flyer program. He let his words hang for a moment before adding, perhaps unnecessarily but certainly poignantly: 'Mark and I are equally perplexed that we find ourselves in this position today.'

The problem now for Korda and Mentha was of course that, unable to sell the airline as a going concern, they would be forced to sell off assets in an environment in which world global aviation assets had depreciated materially. While Mentha acknowledged the difficult selling environment, he was quick to add, 'Now international passenger numbers are coming back, people are starting to fly again and obviously we need to continue to reassess the value of the assets.'

Asked whether they had considered giving an extension, Korda at first said that they had drawn a line in the sand at 28 February, but later added:

> we looked at the possibilities of an extension, in terms of 'is it 24 hours you
> need or 48 hours?', but they continued to indicate that their legal advice was
> that they couldn't complete.

It was clear that they wanted out.

The final question of the briefing concerned what the administrators would be doing for the rest of the day, to which Mentha, the master of the one liner, responded: 'I know if I said business as usual, you'd just laugh.' And then, on a more serious note he said:

> 'We've put grief counselling on in relation to the call centres with employees. Obviously, they've been taken to the top of the mountain and they've fallen off again.'

> We're trying to get to all our employees, through management, through our call centres. We've put grief counselling on in relation to the call centres with employees. Obviously, they've been taken to the top of the mountain and they've fallen off again. You know, this is a tragic day for the Ansett employees. The hopes and aspirations of so many people rode on this deal completing and I think all of those people are gutted. We are getting to the employees. We have empathy for them. Those that stayed on backed us, backed Tesna and it is a grave disappointment that their support is not going to be rewarded.

Mentha had echoed the feelings of every Andersen and Ansett staffer present that lunch time. The questions and answers had gone back and forth for nearly an hour. No attempt had been made to cut short the session or duck the bouncers. The two Marks themselves stayed behind after the meeting and were in no hurry to leave. They acted just as they had done in dealing with the media throughout the administration: they were responsive and ingenuous. They were bitterly disappointed but they had tried to make work a strategy they believed achievable.

Lindsay Fox (centre) and Solomon Lew speak to Ansett Corporate Affairs Chief Heather Jeffrey after their plan collapsed.

But when the briefing stopped and they attempted to farewell the crowd they had come to know, something quite extraordinary happened. Journalists, photographers and camera staff and recordists stood and applauded. Only on rare occasions in the realms of daily journalism does that happen between interviewer and interviewee. The two Marks, who had arrived stony-faced and serious, believing that, in meeting the press as a result of the collapse, they would find themselves in the camp of the enemy, were bewildered but smiled at the peremptory compliment.

> Lew said: 'The fact is that the administrator, who signed with us on 8 November, could not get the parties over the line.'

The media left, wanting answers from the only people who could give them. Till now, Fox and Lew had been saying nothing and appeared to have bunkered down to let the administrators take all the heat. They had indicated on several occasions that they would prefer to keep their own counsel and not make comments until the deal was over the line. They honoured that self-imposed discipline. But four hours after Korda and Mentha hosted their last press conference the pair emerged from the shadows to announce a 4 o'clock press conference on the lawns of the Fitzroy Gardens.

Last Ansett flight on departure screen at Perth Airport.

Asked how he had responded to the offer of an extension of the sale deadline, Lew replied that, if an extension was offered, it was after the administrators were issued with a notice of termination. One journalist asked whether Fox and Lew would consider making a charitable contribution to the workers who were now to be made unemployed. Lew began with the words 'Well, I think that's up to the ...' but before he could finish, Fox interrupted, chipping in: 'Federal Government.' They wanted to sheet home the blame to Canberra.

Lew suggested that some forces appeared to be working against the deal, particularly 'where maybe landlords of certain airports may have had a better outcome by not delivering the airports to Tesna'. Another key issue was the question of funding and whether Fox and Lew were seeking bank financing or whether they would be using their own financial resources. Lew said he and Fox looked after their own finances. Then he turned on the administrators. 'The fact is that the administrator, who signed with us on 8 November, could not get the parties over the line.' His comment conflicted with remarks made earlier by Korda and Mentha that they remained 'ready, willing and able to proceed'.

Lew and Fox walked away with their bank accounts intact. Korda and Mentha had to reflect on what might have been. They still had the problems they had inherited at the start of the administration. The assets still had to be sold, but the job was that much harder in a world still recovering from the tragic events of 11 September 2001.

Ansett staff after last flight

The voice from the Melbourne Airport control tower crackled a sad parting message into the cockpit radio of Ansett VH-HYB on 8 March 2002. 'You're cleared and we're really sorry to see you guys go.'

Captain Geoff Love at the controls of the A320 Airbus acknowledged the message with thanks. It was a poignant, albeit short, eulogy for an aircraft and an airline that had collapsed after a proud 66-year history only four days earlier. Eighteen months before, the A320 Airbus had been the Ansett flagship when the carrier strutted its stuff as the official airline for the 2000 Olympic Games in Sydney.

First Officer Greg Toole, who co-piloted the last Ansett flight into Melbourne on 5 March, had the dubious distinction of helping to ferry out of the country the first of the Ansett planes. It was a sad departure, indeed, leaving under the cloak of darkness for the Mojave Desert airport in California, graveyard to the world's aircraft.

Like Flight Commander Captain Geoff Love, First Officer Toole knew that, as a trunk routes airline, Ansett would never fly again. All that was left was the bitter sweetness of memories and the need to get on with life.

Mark Rindfleish said of his twenty-eight years at Ansett: 'I was part of a family. I worked with a lot of wonderful people, not *for someone.*' Rindfleish had been appointed executive general manager, operations, in the final months of the airline. For a time he held the dual role of chief pilot, Air New Zealand.

Gary Kimberley was an Ansett pilot for twenty-six years and had dreamed since boyhood of being an airline pilot. Not for *any* airline, just Ansett. Privately owned and operated all its life, Ansett had a reputation for being practical and being more efficient than the government-owned airways Trans Australian Airlines, which in its later life became Qantas. Said Kimberley:

When I met Reg Ansett for the first time, it was on a charter flight on a Fokker Friendship, which took him and his family to Narrandera, in New South Wales, for a stay on their stud farm. Meeting Reg was a highlight of my career, because of the very high regard that his employees had for him.

Working for Ansett was so good that virtually nobody ever left. Certainly, amongst the pilot group, we were there to do our absolute best for our airline and to have a good time doing it. Unfortunately, good times don't last forever, and the pilots' dispute of 1989 certainly put an end to it—friendships were shattered forever.

Kimberley, like many of his colleagues, sheeted home to Air New Zealand the blame for the collapse.

They took away a secure future for Ansett by blocking Singapore Airlines. They could not finance the purchase of Ansett, and they were grossly incompetent in running the business.

Gary Kimberley, professional pilot, had a job with Singapore Airlines until Lindsay Fox and Solomon Lew emerged on 8 November 2001 as the white knights who would save Ansett and his passion for the name, the people, the environment returned. He accepted an offer from Tesna and returned to the fold. In hindsight it might have been the worst decision of his life but Gary is philosophical: 'I want to employ all the discipline and good work habits from Ansett and convert it into a successful business of my own. I will succeed. Ansett people will succeed.'

Mark Sullivan was an Ansett Airbus A320 first officer for eleven years. Like his colleagues he regarded Ansett as a 'great employer and airline to work for'.

However, as time progressed, treatment of staff took a back seat as the consuming 'turn the airline around', 'make it profitable', 'return a profit to investors' mentality set in; to the detriment of the heart of the airline—its workers—while money continued to be wasted in other areas.

The final nail in the coffin, Sullivan believes, was when Air New Zealand exercised its option to block the Singapore Airlines bid for a half share in the carrier. He said staff were led to believe that Singapore Airlines would come to the rescue if necessary. Life for Mark, his wife, Margaret and their children, has been turned upside-down. He has suffered what he refers to as a 'double whammy' as far as flying jobs go because of 11 September. The couple had to sell the house and take casual work while Mark applies to overseas airlines who may be recruiting pilots.

Sir Reginald's grand-daughter Sarah Richards remains numb and disbelieving. 'Poppa would be appalled. He was not a quitter. He was determined as all get-out. He would not have stopped fighting for survival.'

Sarah Richards

'Poppa would be appalled. He was not a quitter. He was determined as all get-out. He would not have stopped fighting for survival.'

Sarah worked for eight years as an injury management adviser with Ansett's Workplace Safety and Environment Department. When the planes were first grounded she was stood down. She had been back at work just two and a half weeks when the planes were finally pulled out of the air. It was a traumatic time. 'It did not hit me on the day but I do know that I just could not believe it was happening. Poppa's dream was over.' Sarah is not into blaming anyone. 'There were so many people to blame for what happened. It serves no purpose to single out anyone.'

Sarah recounted flying from Sydney on 17 March, two weeks after the collapse, with her fiancé, Ashley Williams, on a Kendell flight. They were in a holding pattern before landing and above them was a Qantas 767. 'Ashley looked at the Boeing and saw from the registration—BZI—that it was in fact an Ansett B767. It had been leased from Ansett before the collapse and Qantas had not painted the tail. Ansett Australia was written only on the side of the aircraft. I couldn't believe that a BZI flew overhead that day, just as I was coming into land.'

It was the last time Sarah Richards saw an 'Ansett' plane in the air. With her flying career over, Sarah has started her own business, Willards Management Pty Ltd ('Willards' combining the first part of her married name and the last part of her maiden name), specialising in injury management and general human resources.

It may not be the start of a new Ansett dynasty, but they probably said that about Reg in the 1930s.

THE AFTERMATH

THE DAYS FOLLOWING the peremptory walkout of Fox and Lew and the formal close-down of 4 March 2002 were busy but less frenetic than before. The seventeenth floor of the Ansett headquarters had for months been the scene of a busy administration in full swing.

Now, the office phones no longer rang in constant unison, the mobiles had disappeared from the ears of Andersen staffers, the printers had stopped churning out reams of documentation and no longer were Korda and Mentha in and out of boardroom meetings. The world as everyone dealing with the administration had come to know it had changed. Ansett was now just another large insolvency which, given creditor approval, would take years to conclude.

Creditor approval had to be given for a vote either to liquidate the company or to enter a Deed of Company Arrangement (DOCA) that would allow Korda and Mentha to sell off assets in an orderly manner, with the expectation of some return. The DOCA-versus-liquidation scenario became a matter of considerable and aggrieved debate at the meeting, referred to officially as Part 2 of the second creditors' meeting, held on the morning of 27 March 2002 at the Melbourne Exhibition Centre at Southbank, a stone's throw from the salubrious Crown Casino ballroom where, six months earlier, the defining first meeting of creditors had been held. What began as an exciting, once-in-a-lifetime rollercoaster ride for Korda and Mentha and their diligent team of operatives had become mundane by that March morning.

Mentha, more subdued than normal, opened the proceedings with a report covering the period since Part 1 of the second creditors' meeting on 29 January. Then Fox and Lew had sought and obtained a month's extension to complete the deal that collapsed and went unfinished. It had been the beginning of the end and the effervescent Mentha was galled to have to repeat details of the litany of promises, commitments and indicators that led the administrators, their staff, the union movement, creditors and most of the media to believe that Fox and Lew would pursue their improbable dream, that Ansett would once again return to the skies as a viable airline.

He told the audience:

The Tesna sale, if it had been completed, would have kept the Ansett mainline airline in existence and provided a return to all creditors. After taking into account all of the advantages and disadvantages of the Tesna sale, on balance, we recommended to the creditors that the sale be approved with an extended completion date.

He went on to outline some of the *faits accompli* that had led the administrators to deem that the sale would be completed by the extended date of 28 February. These included Tesna's:

- announcement of Heads of Agreement with Airbus for the leasing of $3 billion worth of aircraft
- expenditure of millions of dollars on accounting with KPMG, and on legal services with Clayton Utz
- appointment of a chief executive officer, a chief operating officer, a chief financial officer and twenty other key executives
- offers of employment to 3000 former Ansett staff and announcement of re-badged loyalty programs
- conclusion of enterprise bargaining agreements with various unions and reservation of advertising space for the launch of the new Ansett
- agreement on the provision of engineering services for a minimum of two years, and
- successful negotiation of the timely transfer of airport terminal leases.

Mentha's last observation and the one that hurt most was that 'the principals of Tesna, Mr Fox and Mr Lew, had repeatedly stated that the sale would complete'. It had looked like a watertight deal in the making. What he was saying, in effect, was that the stage had been set for an opening-night blockbuster.

The first of March, the proposed date of the relaunch, would have been a day like no other in the 66-year history of Ansett. The Ansett 'family' would have partied long and hard—not only because their jobs had been saved but also because an Australian icon had had its status preserved. Certainly it would have been a different airline but at least it would still be around. In the three weeks that had passed since the administrators closed the operation, it had become clear not only that Ansett was dead but that there would be little left over in the wash-up of asset sales.

Mentha outlined what had been occurring since the Fox–Lew fiasco of a month earlier. The administrators had tried to keep faith with the travelling public by keeping planes in the air until 4 March instead of grounding them immediately, they had embarked on a cost reduction program to minimise ongoing costs and had retrenched all staff not required for the realisation of assets. While Mentha went through the formalities, he did so in a way that both defied and obfuscated his real feelings. He was shattered that the relationship with Fox and Lew—the deal that should have happened, that showed all the signs of completing—had come down to a decision on whether to liquidate what remained or continue under the DOCA. He may have appeared his normal self but underneath he was hurting.

When Korda took the floor, he went to the core of the matter. What he termed 'the real purpose of this meeting' was for the creditors to decide whether to enter the Deed of Company Arrangement or to liquidate the companies. One of the primary objectives of the deed was to maximise the sale proceeds of the assets, including the domestic terminal leases. Priority creditors could be paid during the DOCA and the administrators would make sure that they kept enough money for the superannuation funds 'in the event that they are determined to be a priority creditor'. Korda outlined both the advantages and disadvantages of the DOCA before opening the meeting to questions, a move that brought out in force critics of the attempt to continue the administration. First came Linda Abernethy, proxy holder and legal counsel for the Sydney Airport Corporation (SACL), whose terminal space remained the single most important asset in the Ansett pool. SACL would be voting No in relation to the DOCA, she said, 'primarily because it unfairly prejudices and seeks to deny fundamental rights of classes of creditors, particularly airport lessors'. She went on to assert that:

> Sydney airport remains of the view that the Deed will merely serve to prolong what has already been an unsatisfactory process ... One of the primary reasons the administrators are asking creditors to vote in favour of the Deed is that they will circumvent airport lessors from terminating the domestic airport lease.

Abernethy said that, contrary to the legal opinion given to the administrators, it was Sydney Airport's view that the fact of entry into the DOCA did give SACL a legal right to re-enter and take possession of the terminal and buy back the terminal facility at fair market value. The administrators were vehemently opposed to such a possibility and wanted to extract the maximum price for their 'jewel in the crown'. If the truth be known it was probably the *only* real jewel in the crown. On this important point, Abernethy noted that:

> in our view the administrators have not satisfied creditors that a better price for the terminals would be obtained in an open market scenario as opposed to a price obtained by having an independent valuer determine the fair market value if Sydney airport exercised a right to buy back the terminal.

Throughout the administration, she said, 'Sydney airport has been supportive … and is disappointed that the Deed has been proposed which seeks to substantially prejudice [its] interest without prior consultation.'

The next speaker, also defiantly opposed to the DOCA, was Jon Caneva, self-styled spokesperson for what he said were 2.7 million frequent flyers and $1.4 billion owed debt. While Caneva expressed his opposition, he was not given much chance to elaborate as Mentha took him to task on procedural issues. And if he thought that the frequent flyers and Global Rewards members were going to get a sympathetic hearing, he was soon to be disappointed. Steve Smith, a 28-year Ansett veteran and spokesperson for Ansett staff throughout the administration, immediately launched a scathing attack.

> I am a bit bigger than he [Caneva] is, both his stature and morals as well, I suspect. I am also a Global Rewards member and am owed over $100,000 in entitlements … I suggest to you people [Global Rewards members] that if most of you are owed something like a couple of hundred thousand Global Rewards points, maybe you should come over this side of the table. If you think that you equate losing those points to losing your house; if you can equate that to having to move all over the countryside to get positions; if you can equate that to marriage breakdowns, suicides, all those sorts of things, well maybe your morals aren't where they should be.

In similarly supporting the DOCA, ACTU secretary and Global Rewards member Greg Combet introduced another issue that was on the minds of most of those attending the meeting, and that was 'whether or not there are any investigations underway into the failure of the sale to Tesna and, if so, what potential course of action may be available'. It is probable that Combet was merely flying a kite on behalf of disgruntled and disillusioned Ansett employees. The administrators had made it clear in the creditors' report that, given the millions and millions of dollars a legal challenge would cost, with no certainty as to the outcome, any action was unlikely. 'Our preliminary advice,' Korda replied, 'and we have lived and breathed this—day in, day out, as our lawyers have—[is that] if there is any action we will look at it, we are looking at it, but we have to say to the creditors and be honest with everybody upfront, it is unlikely.' Fox and Lew had already spilled a possible $30 million or so before they walked away from the deal to buy the airline and they would be standing tall in the face of any legal challenge to the deal's failure to complete. Such a prospect would be long and messy—and very expensive.

As if he had been waiting for the full gamut of views to be presented, one of the most articulate faces of the union movement and secretary of the powerful Australian Workers' Union, Bill Shorten, took hold of the microphone and wasted no time in making his points.

> I could try and just stand and explain to some of the people who are opposing the Deed of Company Arrangement about the livelihoods of the people you're putting on the scrap heap, but unfortunately I'm not sure that you give a stuff. So I'm more interested to really have a look at the coalition of the usual suspects arguing in favour of liquidation. First of all, we've got the Frequent Flyers lobby, the militia of the outraged ordinary citizens who are out there saying that our Global Rewards points are more important than your jobs.

He moved into a delicate but brutal assault on people he saw as the enemy:

You've been very helpful for the last six months, you've been there serving the water on the aeroplanes, you've been there fixing the aeroplanes, you've been there in Golden Wings, you've been handling the ramp staff, you've been doing the baggage when you've got no hope at all, but you still keep plugging away. You've been there for the last six months trying to do your best for the business, so now after six months of fair and honest toil, you've decided enough is enough, time to rest, time to hang up your overalls and put the company into liquidation. So thanks very much for your help.

At this point Shorten moved into top gear.

You don't represent anyone, you only represent people in the class action and I've got no problems with lawyers taking class actions but let's not confuse self-interest, public interest or the interests of creditors as a whole. You want your share and you're going after it. That's fine but let's not pretend that in any shape or form you give a stuff about what happens to the people currently working for Ansett.

Shorten, a man of intellect with a blunt, forceful tongue, then turned his attention to the aircraft lessors and SACL. Like Combet, he laid it on the line—sharp, acerbic and uncompromising. For the aircraft lessors he delivered no less than a threat, not untypical of the union movement but necessary in the circumstances:

I was gobsmacked to hear a representative of the aeroplane lessors saying they want to liquidate. Don't they realise that one of their planes, a Gatex, was prepared [by our engineers] during the administration so that it could be sent overseas?

And didn't they know that an airbus was lying in a hangar stripped down. Now, if the business was to be liquidated, what would happen to that plane?

Shorten was in his element as he turned to SACL, launching a vicious attack. He opened with a light piece of sarcasm—'I'm finally glad to have seen a Sydney Airports Corporation person in the flesh'—then moved in with a frontal assault. 'What nearly knocked me off my chair,' he said, 'was the SACL argument, we're a Government business enterprise.'

> What does that mean? That means we act in the public interest. Goodness me, now I've got some unappointed mandarins of the public sector telling us what the public interest is. I'll tell you something about the public interest, I love that test, I love that test, but I've never heard it twisted in such a convenient and spurious manner. You cannot convince me that it's in the public interest to dump 1300 people. You cannot convince me that it's in the interests of those families that liquidation is better than not liquidating and you certainly can't convince me that it's in the taxpayers' interests.

He concluded his remarks in no less confronting a way: 'Win or lose this deed of company arrangement, I know which side I'd rather be on and it's the side of people as opposed to some of the nonsense and mutton self-interest dressed up as lamb.' While he may have been mixing his metaphors, nobody in the meeting was in any two minds about where Bill Shorten stood.

There was never any doubt—given the position of the union movement—that the DOCA would be approved by the meeting, but it came as a relief to Korda and Mentha to know that, having failed to deliver the airline back to the Australian public via the Fox–Lew Tesna consortium, they would now be given the opportunity to complete the task for which they were both eminently qualified: to carry on with the administration and to get the best value for the sell-off of assets.

In closing the meeting, Korda provided a poignant reminder of the effect of the collapse of Ansett:

> Mark and I have found this at times an enormous administration. It's been very stressful for both of us and our families, but nothing compared to the employees and the loss for the creditors. I have found this a particularly difficult meeting because we are trying to be fair and equitable to everybody …

You have my assurance that Mark and I and the many, many people that we have been working with on this will continue to give 150 per cent to get the best return to all creditors.

With their final remarks, Korda and Mentha, the two Marks, accompanied by their legal bloodhound, Leon Zwier, departed the scene to begin the long and arduous process of laying the corpse of Ansett to rest.

Appendix 1

ANSETT'S MAJOR CREDITORS AT 4 MARCH 2002

Creditor (or liability)	Australian dollars
Golden Wings members, trade suppliers, frequent flyer points holders and coupon creditors	1.1 b
Employee entitlements (at 12/9/01)	730 m
Non-union employees	69,000
Credit Lyonnais	420.9 m
Transport Workers' Union	140 m
National Australia Bank	90 m
Flight Attendants Association of Australia	74.5 m
Telstra	15.87 m
Australian Workers' Union	12.5 m
Caltex Australia Ltd	12 m
Qantas Airways	9.9 m
Mobil Oil Australia Pty Ltd	4.1 m
BP Australia	3.46 m
Avis Australia	1.48 m
Transport Industries Insurance	1.42 m
Airservices Australia	1.24 m
Futura Brand FMA	764 291
Australia Post	450 000
Bureau of Meteorology	346 765
Commonwealth Dept of Transport & Regional Service	70 003
Canberra International Airport	35 962

Appendix 2

Gary Toomey
President & CEO

19 March 2001

Rt Hon Helen Clark
Prime Minister of New Zealand
Executive Wing
Parliament Buildings
WELLINGTON

STRICTLY CONFIDENTIAL

Dear Prime Minister,

Thank you for granting us some of your valuable time when I visited you today with Air New Zealand Limited's Chairman, Sir Selwyn Cushing, and Deputy Chairman, James Farmer QC. This note provides a summary of the main points raised about the circumstances of the Air NZ – Ansett Group and its need for access to substantial investment capital to fund future growth and regional competitiveness:

1. In order to survive and develop internationally, the Air NZ – Ansett Group requires access to a larger home base than this country alone can offer. While Australia has always been the obvious extension, and a Single Aviation Market with that country was negotiated in the early 1990s, Australia effectively blocked access to its market unless Air New Zealand purchased that country's second carrier Ansett. The purchase was completed last year at a total price of over $1.3 billion.

2. The aviation market in the region is dominated by Qantas Airways. Apart from being 50% larger than the Air NZ – Ansett Group, thereby enjoying material scale advantages that are crucial to an airline, Qantas also has the benefit of a much lower gearing ratio (48.4% v. our 76.5%). It is fundamental to our Group's future competitiveness that we reduce these disadvantages through rapid expansion and balance sheet restoration. This will require the Group to attract very large sums of additional investment capital – estimated at upwards of $9 billion over the next seven years. Of that amount, some $2.5 to $4.0 billion will need to be in the form of equity and – under present day constraints – $1.3 to $2.0 billion in the form of equity from the New Zealand market alone. Such levels of equity are simply not available for airline investment in this country.

3. Bilateral regulation of international air traffic rights since 1944 has dictated that a nation's carrier(s) be "substantially owned and effectively controlled" by its own nationals. That archaic and increasingly anti-competitive requirement is gradually breaking down. New Zealand, meanwhile, promotes a modern public policy of open skies. It recognises carriers designated by countries in which they (a) are incorporated, (b) have their principal place of business, and (c) are controlled.

4. Air NZ's foreign shareholding remains capped formally at 49% by virtue of Kiwi Share constraints in its Constitution. Yet the home capital market is only about 10% of the size of the capital market of Australia which itself has proved too small for Qantas's comparable equity needs.

5. Locking airlines from small countries like New Zealand into local capital markets for 50% or more of their equity creates artificial competitive advantages for carriers from larger markets. As governments

STAR ALLIANCE MEMBERS

Quay Tower, 29 Customs Street West, Private Bag 92007, Auckland 1020, New Zealand
Telephone 64-9-336 2900 Facsimile 64-9-336 2922

Air New Zealand Limited, registered in Auckland, New Zealand, AKL °04799, ABN 70 000 312 485 incorporating Ansett Holdings Limited, ABN 58 065 117 535

(1) Letter from Gary Toomey, Air NZ–Ansett, to Helen Clark, New Zealand Prime Minister, 19 March 2001.

progressively loosen constraints on access to air routes, it is logical that they should also dismantle outdated ownership restrictions in order to promote airline competitiveness.

6. Air NZ seeks Government's agreement to disbanding the company's ownership and equity constraints while retaining control of the Group in this country. This would be fully consistent with New Zealand's liberal aviation policy of the last 15 years. There may be minor bilateral risks in doing so, but we consider that the risks today are minimal and manageable – provided that the Government is prepared to defend the need for reform in the national interest and to promote competition.

7. There are a number of practical steps that New Zealand can take (via Kiwi Shareholder consents) to achieve deregulation of airline ownership constraints while maintaining control of Air NZ in this country:
    □   Merger of Air NZ's "A" and "B" shares into a single class of ordinary shares freely tradable on the Stock Exchange, those ordinary shares to constitute 49% of the shares on issue.
    □   Division of the existing non-economic Kiwi Share into some 780 million Kiwi Shares representing 51% of all shares on issue. Existing voting rights attached to Kiwi Shares (control over place of incorporation, principal place of business, nationalities of Directors, foreign airline ownership of shares, etc) would support a form of "ownership" compatible with protecting the national interest.
    □   Retention of effective control of Air NZ in local hands through existing constitutional requirements for a New Zealand citizen Chairman and a majority of New Zealanders as Directors.
    □   Maintenance of public policy provisions, enforced through Air NZ's Constitution, limiting foreign airline ownership of ordinary shares to the level determined by Government from time to time.

8. Air NZ has no alternative to achieving access to significant additional equity. The "do nothing" scenario involves the rapid and inexorable decline of a major New Zealand strategic asset. With adequate investment capital, however, a healthy Air NZ - Ansett Group offers New Zealand many benefits:
    □   A reliable, locally-supervised carrier with a full range of services and genuine growth potential;
    □   A locally-based carrier committed to the kinds of passenger and cargo carriage that are a critical component of New Zealand's national infrastructure;
    □   Ongoing international promotion of inbound tourism flows (leading to significant export earnings, net of aircraft costs), in good and not-so-good times for tourism;
    □   Major ancillary export earnings from engineering services – using local skills and other inputs;
    □   Local aviation industry support of Government's aviation policy;
    □   Maintenance and expansion of significant New Zealand employment (including crew basing, major engineering bases, advanced international technical skills);
    □   Upstream operational and professional supply contracts and employment;
    □   Capital inflows; and
    □   Promotion of New Zealand's products, attitudes and culture to the world.

We would welcome an opportunity for two of our senior executives to discuss the detail of our proposals with one or more senior officials of your nomination. Our representatives for discussions would be Adam Moroney (Chief Financial Officer and Senior Vice President – Finance) and Laurie Doolan (Senior Vice President – Corporate, Government & International). Because of the extreme market price sensitivity of our proposals, we request that the circle of those involved be restricted to a very small number.

Thank you for your interest in our Group, Prime Minister.

Yours sincerely,

G K TOOMEY

MEMORANDUM OF UNDERSTANDING

The following sets out the principles whereby Singapore Airlines Limited (SIA) will inject additional capital into Air New Zealand Limited (Air NZ).

1 SIA will subscribe for additional shares in Air NZ to raise its stake to 49% of the enlarged equity such shares to be issued at NZ$1.31.

2. SIA will underwrite and take up its full entitlement under a rights issue on a 1 for 3 basis at a price of $1.00 or such other ratio or price as may be mutually agreed.

3. The provision of the additional capital from SIA as above is subject to the following:
(a) Approval of the New Zealand Government to allow SIA to increase its shareholding in the Company to 49%.
(b) Approval of the New Zealand Government to the Company merging the A and B classes of shares.
(c) Agreement as to the terms of a governance agreement between SIA and Air NZ.
(d) Approval of the Board of Directors of SIA.
(e) Approval of the shareholders of Air NZ in respect of matters requiring such approval

4. SIA will use its best endeavours to assist Air NZ to purchase Virgin Blue expeditiously.

5 The parties will use their best endeavours to conclude a commercial agreement under the terms of the existing and authorised Alliance Agreement.

6. The parties undertake with each other that they will keep the terms of this Memorandum of Understanding confidential and will not disclose its terms to any other person apart from relevant Ministers and Officials of the New Zealand Government and the parties' respective professional advisers and senior management teams such disclosure to be in all cases subject to confidentiality.

7. The parties agree that this Memorandum shall not have and is not intended to have any legal effect except for paragraph 6.

Dated: Tuesday, 19 June 200

....

For and on Behalf of Singapore Airlines   For and on Behalf of Air New Zealand

This is the document marked JAF 1 referred
to in the annexed affidavit of James
Alfred Farmer sworn at Auckland this
9th day of October 200 before me

A Solicitor of the High Court of New Zealand

**Jon Page
Solicitor
Auckland**

(2) Memorandum of Understanding, Singapore Airlines and Air NZ, 19 June 2001.

No.019

3 August 2001

CONFIDENTIAL

Hon Dr Michael Cullen
Treasurer & Minister of Finance
Executive Wing
Parliament Buildings
WELLINGTON

This is the document marked *JAF2* referred
to in the annexed affidavit of *James Alfred*
Farmer   sworn at Auckland this
9th day of *October* 2001 before me

A Solicitor of the High Court of New Zealand

By fax to (04) 495 8442

Dear Minister

Jon Page
Solicitor
Auckland

Air New Zealand Ownership Issues – Effect of Government Announcement 1 August

I write to you in your capacity as Chairperson of the ad hoc Cabinet Committee appointed to consider Air New Zealand's re-capitalisation and related proposals that are before Government.

At a meeting of Air New Zealand's Committee of Independent Directors held yesterday afternoon, I was asked to communicate to Government the independent directors' grave concern about the situation now faced by this company and its directors. The present circumstances arise against the following background:

1. On 20 June 2001, Air New Zealand put to Government a formal request (unanimously supported by its Board) seeking Government policy modifications to facilitate:
   • merger of the company's A and B classes of ordinary shares; and
   • an increase to 49% in Singapore Airlines' permitted maximum shareholding.

2. Our early meetings with Ministers and senior officials from nominated Ministries and Departments confirmed that our request would be fully evaluated in a timely fashion, having regard to the company's need to address publicly on 4 September its substantial losses for FY2001 and its strategy for the future. In many meetings and discussions, Air New Zealand's representatives have emphasised the need to have the policy situation resolved in principle some weeks before the company's early September announcement.

3. Over the intervening six weeks, Air New Zealand has communicated frankly, expeditiously and constructively with Government's cross-functional team of officials, together with local and international consultant advisers retained to advise Government. Detailed submissions and large volumes of data have been provided. Officials and advisers have done an enormous amount of work on the Air New Zealand matter throughout the period, and we are grateful to them and to Government for that consideration.

STAR ALLIANCE MEMBERS

Air New Zealand Limited, registered in Auckland, New Zealand, AKL 104799, ABN 70 000 312 685, Incorporating Ansett Holdings Limited, ABN 56 065 117 535

(3) Letter from Jim Farmer, Air NZ–Ansett, to Michael Cullen, NZ Minister of Finance.

4. At all times we have believed that Government was moving through an assessment of information and submissions that would result in our being advised of Government policy decisions – either accepting our proposals (with or without modification) or rejecting them.

To date, no acceptance or rejection of our request has been communicated to Air New Zealand. Instead, on 1 August the New Zealand and Australian Governments announced jointly a significant change in the process that had been in train. This involved:

a) the formation of an Australia – New Zealand officials working party to consider the Australasian aviation market; the terms of reference of this group are not clear to us; and

b) the appointment of a negotiating group to enter into "discussions with Air New Zealand and associated parties, including Qantas and Singapore Airlines, to flesh out the detail of the various proposals and to report back to the New Zealand Government."

While I have publicly affirmed that Air New Zealand will co-operate fully with Government's wishes, it is important that you know that Government's announcement has created a new air of uncertainty and instability for Air New Zealand. Inevitably that affects the stability of the Group's customer base, the morale of its staff, and the confidence of suppliers and creditors.

The Board had proposed a commercial course of action which it was confident (subject to Government policy endorsement) would underpin a robust strategy of development, competitiveness and ultimate profitability. In addition, the company's representatives have indicated to officials its readiness to comply with detailed governance provisions to safeguard New Zealand control, and to discuss how other national interest matters of a commercial character can be addressed to Government's and the company's satisfaction.

Government's latest initiative in conjunction with Australia appears to have jettisoned prospects of the Board's course of action being implemented. You are aware that the Air New Zealand Board was advised by SIA that it was not willing to sell its shares to Qantas. Unless the decision by the New Zealand Government to cause the Qantas proposal to be investigated reflects an understanding that SIA may be willing to change its position, it would seem that the Government has embarked on a high-risk and speculative course that has the danger of putting the Air New Zealand Group at risk.

The independent directors of Air New Zealand are therefore left in an invidious and potentially compromising position. With no reasonable clarity as to either outcome or timeline, they must review urgently how they can properly acquit their duties as directors, given the unstable situation that now exists.

As the position has become serious, it is necessary for all directors of the company to take advice on and consider their fiduciary duties. Accordingly I have instructed that a special meeting of the full Board be called for next Wednesday, 8 August. This will discuss the company's situation, including how we can best co-operate with Government's agents. I must emphasise again that time is of the essence as we move forward, more so now given the new directions taken by Government and the uncertainty thereby created. The complexities of an outcome based on the Qantas proposal (including major competition regulatory hurdles) and SIA's position are such that certainty by the end of August is most unlikely.

There seems to be a view in Government that an outcome in principle reached by the end of August will suffice. However, the company's representatives have repeatedly advised officials that resolution is necessary some weeks before that time. In the meantime, if the company is compelled to write down the value of its investment in Ansett, thereby creating a material adverse event under the company's borrowing covenants, that would trigger a requirement for the Group's unsecured facilities to be repaid forthwith.

I would be failing in my duty if I did not bring to your attention the seriousness of this situation and the grave financial risk faced by Air New Zealand Limited as a result of the current uncertainties.

Yours sincerely

Dr J A Farmer, QC
Acting Chairman
Chairman of the Committee of Independent Directors

AIR NEW ZEALAND

ANSETT AUSTRALIA

8 August 2001

To: THE DIRECTORS

Ansett Holdings Limited (ABN 065 117 535)
Ansett International Limited (ABN 060 622 460)
Ansett Australia Limited (ABN 004 209 410) (the "Companies")

Dear Sirs,

Letter of Comfort

In its capacity as the ultimate parent company and sole beneficial shareholder of the Companies, Air New Zealand Limited ("ANZ") hereby confirms to you that it is its current policy to take such steps from time to time as are necessary to ensure that its wholly owned subsidiaries (including the Companies) are able to meet their debts as they fall due.

We will advise you promptly in the event of any change in this policy.

The previous paragraphs set out our bona fide intention in respect of the matters mentioned, but shall not create any contract between us and any of you, nor a guarantee nor indemnity in respect of our obligations hereunder, enforceable at law or in equity.

Notwithstanding the previous paragraph, we will make available to you on request in writing from time to time advances for the sole purpose of enabling you to pay working capital liabilities incurred by you in respect of property or services purchased or sold in the ordinary course of your business, subject to the following conditions:

a) the maximum aggregate amount of all such advances (whether or not they remain outstanding at any particular time) shall not exceed the equivalent of A$400 m;

b) such advances will continue to be available to you until withdrawn and such withdrawal has been notified in writing to you by Air New Zealand (provided that such withdrawal shall not take effect earlier than 4 weeks after the date that notification is given); and

c) in making a request for an advance you will be deemed to represent, warrant and undertake to us that the advance is required, and will be applied, to pay working capital liabilities of yourself incurred in respect of property or services purchased or sold in the ordinary course of your business.

This Letter of Comfort is governed by New Zealand law

Yours faithfully

For and on behalf of
Air New Zealand Limited STAR ALLIANCE MEMBERS

Quay Tower, 29 Customs Street West, Private Bag 92007, Auckland 1020, New Zealand
Telephone 64-9-336 2400 Facsimile 64-9-336 2764 or 64-9-309 4134

(4) Letter of Comfort from Jim Farmer, Air NZ–Ansett, to the Directors, Ansett, 8 August 2001. Air NZ Board Report, 8 August 2001 (facing page and overleaf).

8 August 2001 : Special Board Meeting

ITEM FOR INFORMATION

Ownership & Funding Issues

This is the document marked JAF 4 referred to in the annexed affidavit of James Alfred Farmer sworn at Auckland this 9th day of October 2001 before me

A Solicitor of the High Court of New Zealand

Joh Page
Solicitor
Auckland

BACKGROUND

On 20 June 2001 the company sought New Zealand Government approval for:

- The A and B share classes to be merged; and

- Singapore Airlines to increase its shareholding to 49% through a placement of new shares,

both actions being subject to shareholder approvals. These actions would be followed by a rights issue. In aggregate equity of around NZ$850 million would be raised with prospects of a further $150 – $250 million from a subsequent capital notes issue. An integral element of the proposed re-capitalisation and business plan was the proposed acquisition of Virgin Blue.

Since that time independent directors and management, assisted by Salomon Smith Barney, have made extensive submissions to Government. While most of those submissions have been to a cross-functional group of Wellington officials and their consultant advisers (Cameron & Co, Wellington, and PA Consulting, USA), meetings have also occurred with senior Ministers (Helen Clark, Jim Anderton, Michael Cullen and Mark Gosche).

SIA has had an executive present for a number of the important meetings, has made its own direct written submissions (with input from Air New Zealand), has provided input into Air New Zealand's submissions and has held separate meetings in Wellington with Ministers and relevant officials.

By around now, the company had anticipated that the New Zealand Government would be reaching a decision on the proposals put before it in June. Management believes that earlier scepticism about the seriousness of the situation and the strategic importance of an Australasian network had been largely overcome through corroboration of the company's views by Cameron & Co and PA Consulting. The principal sticking points appeared to be political reaction to the proposed 49% cap for SIA's shareholding, and some residual but manageable concern about risks to New Zealand's bilateral aviation rights.

On 1 August, Australian Deputy Prime Minister and Minister of Transport, John Anderson, met New Zealand Treasurer Michael Cullen and Minister of Transport Mark Gosche. Out of that meeting came a joint release announcing the formation of:

- a trans-Tasman officials working party to examine aviation and regulatory issues in both countries relating to the propositions being considered by Government; and

- a New Zealand negotiating team, headed by Rob Cameron of Cameron & Co, to discuss with Air New Zealand, Qantas, SIA and others the implications for New Zealand's national interests of both "the Singapore proposal" and "the Qantas proposal".

Initial contact has been made by Rob Cameron with the Acting Chairman, but at this stage no substantive discussions have occurred.

ISSUES

1. Statements made publicly by Prime Minister Clark and Treasurer Cullen have asserted that Government would have difficulty in accepting a 49% shareholding for an overseas shareholding.

2. Deputy Prime Minister Anderson of Australia has raised publicly concerns about a Singapore-Air New Zealand-Ansett "behemoth" dominating Australasian aviation unduly in 10 to 15 years time, and that outcome not being in Australia's national interest.

3. Treasurer Cullen has commented publicly on allegedly divergent views within the Air New Zealand Board on the SIA proposal, and the possibility that there may be some preference for the Qantas proposal. In fact, there have been several confirmations to Government that the Board is unanimous in its support of the Memorandum of Understanding with SIA and the related public policy issues.

4. The new process introduced on 1 August by the New Zealand Government, with input from Canberra, raises significant issues of timing leading up to the 4 September FY2001 financial results announcement. Government's timeframe appears to be focused on the end of August. The seriousness of these timing issues had been made clear to senior Ministers over recent days, but the Board now needs to consider the position of the company in the circumstances created by this extended period of uncertainty.

5. These issues form a backdrop to the imponderables of the process to be adopted by the Cameron negotiating team, together with its likely outcomes.

6. The acquisition of Virgin Blue remains a cornerstone of the viability of the MOU and of the continued viability of Ansett. Negotiations with Virgin Blue have reached a point where a decision is able to be made to proceed with an acquisition.

CONCLUSION

The company has vigorously pursued with the New Zealand Government the proposals that arise from the Air New Zealand / SIA Memorandum of Understanding agreed on 18/19 June.

The elements of that MOU remain intact pending the work of the Cameron negotiating team and any changes of approach that may emerge from its discussions with SIA, Qantas, Brierley Investments, Government(s) and regulatory authorities.

Dr J A Farmer QC
Acting Chairman

13 August 2001

CONFIDENTIAL

Hon Dr Michael Cullen
Treasurer & Minister of Finance
Executive Wing
Parliament Buildings
WELLINGTON

By fax to (04) 495 8442

This is the document marked JAF 5 *referred to in the annexed affidavit of* James Alfred Farmer *sworn at Auckland this* 9th *day of* October 20c\before me

A Solicitor of the High Court of New Zealand

Jon Page
Solicitor
Auckland

Dear Minister

Air New Zealand Ownership Issues

My Board was disappointed to receive the message in the 7 August letter from your office. The directors recognise and acknowledge your duty of ensuring an outcome in the best interests of New Zealand. The company's interest and wishes are fully compatible with that objective. In addition, however, the directors have obligations the burden of which has been made greater by Government's sudden change of direction on 1 August following your meeting with Deputy Prime Minister John Anderson of Australia.

My 3 August letter drew your attention to the new pressures of uncertainty and timing created by Government's actions last week. My Board's concerns at these developments are serious and considered. I urge you to accept that, while Air New Zealand will work constructively and expeditiously with your newly-introduced process, Government must also do its part by placing a realistic limit on the duration of this process.

There are other issues that my Board feels have been overlooked or disregarded by Government. To eliminate any doubt about the Board's position on these points, I set them out again briefly:

1. The Board unanimously supports the proposal which the company and Singapore Airlines (SIA) have put to Government for the re-capitalisation of Air New Zealand.

2. Modifications of that proposal which entail lower levels of new equity than proposed to be sourced from SIA (prior to a general rights issue) will not result in adequate re-capitalisation of Air New Zealand to ensure its viability and competitiveness.

3. A forced sale of Ansett is not a realistic alternative to re-capitalisation because:

   (a) the proceeds of sale will not be adequate to strengthen Air New Zealand's balance sheet, given that the sale price will be significantly less than acquisition cost;

STAR ALLIANCE MEMBERS

Quay Tower, 29 Customs Street West, Private Bag 92007, Auckland 1020, New Zealand
Telephone 64-9-336 2400 Facsimile 64-9-336 2754 or 64-9-309 4134

Air New Zealand Limited, registered in Auckland: New Zealand. AKL 104799. ABN 70 000 312 685. Incorporating Ansett Holdings Limited. ABN 58 065 117 535

(5) Letter of concern from Jim Farmer countersigned by Air NZ Directors, Air NZ–Ansett, to Michael Cullen, NZ Minister of Finance, 13 August 2001.

(b) the future of Air New Zealand will be seriously compromised, and thereby New Zealand's national interests as well, by the prospect ultimately of competition across the Tasman and internationally between three Australasian carriers.

4. A larger SIA equity investment in Air New Zealand will not lead to competitive imbalances in the region to the unfair disadvantage of Qantas. That carrier's dominant position in Australasian aviation and its long-term partnership with major shareholder British Airways (endorsed by competition regulators) reinforce its long-term competitive strengths.

I am taking the liberty of copying this letter, counter-signed by other Air New Zealand directors, for the information of Mr Rob Cameron as Government's representative in the current process.

Yours sincerely

Dr J A Farmer, QC
Acting Chairman

Sir Selwyn Cushing

Hon Philip R Burdon

Sir Ronald Carter

Elizabeth M Coutts

Dr C K Cheong

Charles B Goode

Ralph J Norris

Prof John Rose

Michael J N Tan

John S Curtis

Gregory J Terry

William M Wilson QC

cc Rt Hon Helen Clark, Prime Minister of New Zealand   Fax (04) 473 3579
    Hon Mark Gosche, Minister of Transport   Fax (04) 495 8468
    Mr Rob Cameron, Cameron & Company Limited   Fax (040 499-6651

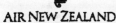

14 August 2001

The Hon John Howard MP
Prime Minister of Australia
Parliament House
CANBERRA ACT 2601
AUSTRALIA

COMMERCIAL IN CONFIDENCE

Dear Prime Minister,

I am writing to inform you and the Australian Government of the extremely serious situation faced by the Air New Zealand Group and, more particularly, Ansett Australia in the current aviation market situation.

I am sure you are aware that Ansett has more than 15,500 employees in Australia, around half of them in Victoria. Ansett is also the largest provider of regional air services in Australia through Flight West in Western Australia; Kendell and Hazleton in NSW and southern Australia; and the recent rescue of Flight West in Queensland.

In previous meetings with you, Mr John Anderson and various Ministerial advisers, we have provided early access to the Group's financial results to be announced to the markets in three weeks' time, including very serious losses of Ansett which are being sustained only with the support of the wider Group. Ansett's regional subsidiaries too are suffering deep losses.

This situation has emerged in part due to additional competition in the Australian market, and in part due to a lack of sufficient attention in the past to costs and investment within Ansett's operations. Both factors are facts of life. However, the Air NZ Board and both Governments are now linked together in dealing with the resulting situation.

This linkage arises from the position adopted by the Australian Government in support of a proposal from Qantas aimed squarely at removing Singapore Airlines (SIA) as an investor in this Group. Whatever its merits in other contexts, Qantas's proposal appears to be unworkable in the commercial sphere where the Group's Directors must operate according to Corporations law.

The reason for this is that the Qantas proposal requires SIA to sell out of Air NZ, but SIA is not a willing seller. The Group has no ability to force divestment by a legitimate owner of shares, any more than Governments have an ability to achieve such an outcome. SIA has the agreement of the Australian and New Zealand Governments to its current ownership level. Moreover, in present circumstances, SIA is a prime force sustaining the Group in the market as Air NZ and Ansett struggle to survive the coming crisis. This crisis may well see the failure of one or more parts of the Group. Removing SIA (somehow) and replacing it with an investment by Qantas would at best be complicated, and in any event would be delayed beyond a workable time frame by competition policy considerations on both sides of the Tasman.

STAR ALLIANCE MEMBERS

Quay Tower, 29 Customs Street West, Private Bag 92007, Auckland 1020, New Zealand
Telephone 64-9-336 2400 Facsimile 64-9-336 2764 or 64-9-309 4134

Air New Zealand Limited, registered in Auckland, New Zealand, ARL 104799, ABN 70 000 312 685, incorporating Ansett Holdings Limited, ABN 58 065 117 535

(6) Letter from Jim Farmer, Air NZ–Ansett, to John Howard, PM of Australia, 14 August 2001.

I particularly wish to advise you that my Board has considered, and will consider again before the results are announced on 4 September, whether the Group's liquidity position is sufficient to enable it to meet its obligations as they fall due. While we are naturally investigating and pursuing all potential avenues for maintaining the Group's short- and medium-term viability, we remain deeply concerned that, without early resolution of the equity situation and re-capitalisation of the Group, there may be breaches of loan covenants triggering a right for lenders to demand immediate repayment of loans. There is no grace period or cure opportunity in such an event. The Directors have formal advice of this risk which is a reflection of commercial reality. In terms of Corporations law, the significance of the risk is not something that can be taken lightly by the Directors. If repayment demands emerge from lenders, the Group will not be able to repay loans without major disruption to the business. This situation is likely to be played out not over months but over the three weeks leading up to 4 September.

Sale of Ansett to any other party is not the simple step that may have been advised to you.

Inextricably, the fortunes of Air NZ and Ansett are tied together by the debt levels entered into to acquire the Ansett business. These debts are secured substantially through covenants in the manner described above. If Ansett were able to be sold (by no means a certainty), Air NZ would need to write down the value of the asset to the level of the price achieved. The likely outcome, equally impossible to sustain, would again be irretrievable breaches of Air NZ's loan covenants.

There is a further factor which is not being given serious consideration in the current context – that the Air NZ and Ansett businesses are now deeply enmeshed. You will recall, for example, the grounding of Ansett's 767s earlier this year. Long term solutions to the problems behind that grounding lie in the application of safety systems which Air NZ has available, and which Ansett does not. There can be no early, simple or inexpensive removal of Air NZ's vital engineering support for Ansett. The investment required for Ansett to operate on its own, and the time and leadership essential to address CASA's concerns, mean that no practical separation can occur. SIA does not have the ability to simply replace Air NZ in this matter.

Similar but slightly less crucial separation problems arise in other areas of the integrated Group.

I ask that the Australian Government urgently considers the significance of this advice. The Group will continue to work actively with the processes of the New Zealand and Australian Governments. However, an early re-capitalisation of the Group with assistance from SIA remains the preferred position adopted unanimously by the Group's Directors.

Yours sincerely

Dr J A Farmer, QC
Acting Chairman

Copy: The Hon John Anderson MP, Deputy Prime Minister of Australia and Minister of
         Transport & Regional Services

12 September 2001

Mr John Anderson
Deputy Prime Minister
AUSTRALIA

Via facsimile: +612 6273-4126

This is the document marked JAF 6 referred
to in the annexed affidavit of James
Alfred Farmer sworn at Auckland this
9th day of October 2001 before me

A Solicitor of the High Court of New Zealand

Jon Page
Solicitor
Auckland

Dear Minister

As you will know, Air NZ has just been advised by Qantas that it does not wish to
proceed with a purchase of Ansett. This will force the hand of the Air NZ Directors to
move forward to a liquidation as advised to you earlier.

However, I am writing to you to see if some co-operative solution can be found to the
present Ansett difficulty that would enable Ansett, at least in a restructured form, to
survive and to participate in an airline market in Australia having a greater degree of
rationalisation than at present.

The concept that I would like to put to you for urgent consideration is that:

1.   Air New Zealand continues to operate Ansett for an agreed period on a basis
      of a full underwrite from the Australian Government while an attempt is made
      to restructure the airline and also to lay the foundation blocks for a
      restructured and more rational market in which competition operates
      constructively for benefit of consumers and not, as at present, destructively.

2.   The concept of the restructured airline and rational market that I think should
      be considered is, in broad outline, as follows:

      (i)   Air New Zealand would form a new airline (Ansett 2) which would, in its
             initial form, seek to be a value based airline with a similar cost base to
             Virgin Blue but undertaking a much broader coverage, nationally and
             regionally.

      (ii)   Existing staff at Ansett, to the extent required, would be offered
             employment with the new company under a new industrial award

STAR ALLIANCE MEMBERS

*(7) Letter from Jim Farmer, Air NZ–Ansett, to John Anderson Deputy PM of Australia,
12 September 2001.*

provided that they agree not to seek redundancy or other severance payments from Ansett. Staff who do not take up that employment would no doubt make redundancy claims. These would be dealt with in the ordinary way on the basis that the Australian Government would meet them but in return for an agreed equity interest in the new company coupled with an agreement for that equity to be redeemed (or sold or the subject of an IPO) in 5 years time at the Government's option in accordance with an agreed formula.

(iii)   Assets, routes, terminals, etc, not required by Ansett 2 would be offered for sale to Qantas and Virgin Blue.

(iv)   Ansett 1 would at that point be put into liquidation with every effort being made to negotiate creditors' claims remaining. To the extent that there were such claims, the Australian Government would meet them on the same basis as stated above in relation to redundancy claims.

Air New Zealand has, as you know, experience at running a low cost, value based, airline (Freedom Air) and believes that, freed of the crippling cost structure that it inherited when it bought Ansett, it could make this venture a success and provide real competition to Qantas and Virgin Blue which, otherwise, are likely to carve up the Australian market between them.

There may be other variants of this proposal and there are also other options that appear to be emerging that could see interest in an acquisition of Ansett if it was still a going concern and if a business case could be put together. I would respectfully suggest that this provides a real opportunity for the Australian Government to assume a leadership role not only in saving many jobs and the Ansett brand but also to provide the foundation for a re-invigorated competitive market based on sound principles.

It would also serve to divert attention away from the pointless exercises that all parties are currently going through in blaming others for the present situation and channel all of our efforts into a constructive outcome.

I will call you shortly to discuss this concept further.

Yours sincerely

Jim Farmer
Acting Chairman

John
For. info. Peter

TESNA HOLDINGS PTY LTD
ACN 090 531 187
Level 53, 101 Collins Street
Melbourne Vic 3000
Telephone (61 3) 9650 0500 Facsimile (61 3) 9654 6665

fwd
to Peter
Langbroeke

(Ctr
office).

13 November, 2001

> OFFICE OF THE PRIME MINISTER
> RECEIVED IN CANBERRA
> .1 4 NOV 2001
> Referred to: AS

The Hon. John Howard MP
Prime Minster
Commonwealth of Australia
Parliament House
Canberra ACT 2601

Dear Prime Minister,

Firstly our sincere congratulations on your magnificent third term victory.

As you know there has been some contact between David Crawford and our advisers, KPMG, in relation to support we are seeking from the Commonwealth for Ansett.

We are highly conscious of the $600 million figure which is being cited in the media and do not understand how this figure has achieved any legitimacy.

We would appreciate a meeting to provide you with a first hand briefing of our agreement with the Administrators, our plans for Ansett and the support we are seeking from the Commonwealth. The attached document details the specific support requested.

We would, of course, be available to meet at any time or location suitable to you.

Yours sincerely,

SOLOMON LEW

LINDSAY FOX

(8) *Letter from Tesna Holdings to John Howard, 13 November 2001.*

COMMONWEALTH GOVERNMENT

- Exemption of non-mainline airports (ie Essendon / Avalon) from airport-airline cross ownership restrictions by 31 December, 2001.

- Support for speedy procurement of AOC by Tesna.

- Support for speedy ratification of Tesna fleet (A319, A320, A321) as airworthy for Australia by CASA.

- Support for allocation to Tesna of international air-slots previously allocated by IASC to Ansett.

- Insurance – identical support as provided to Qantas.

- Extension of Sydney Terminal ground lease and other rental and lease amendments at Sydney to bring into line with privatised airports.

- Provision of powers to ACCC, specifically but not limited to, amendment to Section 46 of the TPA to provide for an 'effects test' and the power to issue 'cease and desist' notices.

- Relief from withholding tax on aircraft lease payments for five year period.

- Accelerated depreciation allowances.

- Guarantee of entitlements to transferring employees for five year period.

- Underwrite 65% load factor for twelve month period or alternative start-up 'insurance' arrangements.

NOTES

Chapter 1

1 Moses, J., 'Courage the key to Sir Reginald', the *Australian*, 17 February 1986.
2 Monks, J., the *Australian*, 24 December 1981.
3 ibid.
4 Trengove, A., the *Sun*, 25 January 1969.
5 Percival, J., *Sydney Morning Herald*, 5 November 1961.

Chapter 2

1 Day, D. (1999), *John Curtin: A Life*, Harper Collins, Pymble, Sydney.
2 Brogden, S., the *Australian*, 17 February 1986.
3 Menzies, Sir R. (1967), *Afternoon Light*, Cassell, Australia.
4 Ansett advertising feature, the *Sun*, 15 February 1986.
5 Frith, B., the *Australian*, 15 April 1972.
6 *Australian Encyclopaedia*, vol. 1.
7 *Herald*, 15 February 1982.

Chapter 3

1 The leading Australian film and stage actor of the 1940s and 1950s.
2 The *Sun News–Pictorial*, 25 January 1969.
3 Australia, House of Representatives, *Debates*, April 1963.
4 National Archives of Australia; Department of the Prime Minister and Cabinet; A5619, Cabinet Files; C3 Part 2, The Australian domestic airline policy.
5 ibid.
6 Trengove, A., the *Sun News–Pictorial*, 25 January 1969.
7 McCrann, T., the *Age*, 17 October 1979.
8 Blazey, P. (1972), *Bolte, a political biography*, Jacaranda Press, Sydney.

Chapter 4

1 Hewat, T. and Peter T., the *Australian*, 31 March 1979.
2 ibid.
3 McCrann, T., the *Age*, 17 October 1979.
4 McCrann, T., the *Age*, 29 September 1979.
5 Chubb, P., the *Age*, 29 September 1980.

Chapter 5

1 Anonymous former Ansett director, interviewed by authors March 2002.
2 The *Australian*, 1981.
3 ibid.
4 Interview with the authors, Melbourne, 21 March 2002.
5 Franklin, R. (1980), the *Sun Herald*, 20 January 1980.

6   Derryn Hinch, Radio 3AW, 30 April 1980.
7   Commonwealth Department of Aviation figures for year ending 31 March 1983.
8   The *Australian*, 28 April 1982.

Chapter 6
1   Lawson, V. and Cunningham, J., 'Migrant lad who moved Australia', the *Age*, 26 June 1999.
2   Brown, T., the *Herald Sun*, 26 June 1999.
3   McCrann, T., the *Age*, 29 September 1979.
4   Anonymous, March 2002.
5   Trevor Jensen, February 2002.
6   McMahon, March 2002.
7   ibid.

Chapter 7
1   McMahon, interview with authors, February 2002.
2   Department of Transport and Communications figures.
3   McMahon, March 2002.
4   ibid.
5   Bureau of Air Safety Investigation report into incident at Sydney airport involving VH INH, 19 October 1994.
6   ibid.
7   Information from a highly confidential source who cannot be identified.
8   Interview with authors, late March 2002.
9   Annual report of Ansett Transport Holdings, 1999.
10 Notes of anonymous Ansett executive, interviewed March 2002.

Chapter 8
1   T2001/1184 New Zealand Treasury document: Air New Zealand—Assessment of Growth Strategy and Shareholding Policy Issues.
2   Affidavit Anthony John Waller, 9 October 2001, Federal Court of Australia.
3   T2000/975: Air New Zealand; Assessment of problems and options, page 11.
4   Interview with Peter Wilms, late March 2002.
5   McMahon referred to the incident in an interview with the authors. He subsequently recounted in his eulogy for Frank Pascoe, a report of which was published on 18 January 2001 by the *Age* newspaper.
6   Interview with Peter Wilms, March 2002.

Chapter 9
1   *Networknews* (staff newsletter), February 2001.
2   Gary Toomey, reply at press conference for release of Air NZ annual results 13 September 2001, recorded by authors.
3   Anonymous, interviewed by the authors, March 2002.
4   NZ Treasury Air NZ document collection, released www.treasury.govt.nz\releases\airnz.co, 11 April 2002.
5   Letter from Qantas CEO Geoff Dixon to New Zealand Finance Minister, 25 June 2001.

6   Australia, House of Representatives, *Debates*, 18 September 2001.
7   Text of speech provided by Air NZ public relations.
8   NZ Treasury papers released April 2002 under Official Information Act, on
    www.treasury.govt.nz\releases\airnz.co
9   Letter from Rob Cameron, Cameron and Company, to New Zealand Finance
    Minister, 29 August 2001.
10 NZ Treasury Air NZ document collection, released
    www.treasury.govt.nz\releases\airnz.co, 11 April 2002.
11 Jason Koutsoukis, *Australian Financial Review*, 29 September 2001.
12 www.treasury.govt.nz\releases\airnz.co
13 Former top Ansett executive, interviewed by authors March 2002.
14 Selwyn Cushing stood down because his involvement with Brierley Investments at
    the time might have been perceived as a conflict of interest in the process of recapi-
    talising the airline.
15 Affidavit of James Alfred Farmer, Australian Federal Court, 9 October 2001.
16 This and following quotations from Peter Macourt: press release issued by News
    Limited, 13 September 2001.

Chapter 10
1   McMahon, interviewed by authors, March 2002.
2   Department of Transport and Communications figures, June quarter 1993.
3   McMahon, interviewed by authors, March 2002.
4   McMahon, the *Australian*, September 1993.
5   Affidavit to the Australian Federal Court, 9 October 2001.
6   Gary Toomey at Air NZ results press conference on 13 September 2001.

Chapter 11
1   Zwier, interview with the authors, April 2002.
2   In an interview with the authors at ACTU headquarters, Melbourne, 20 March 2002.
3   All quotations from Greg Combet in this chapter are from an interview with the
    authors in March 2002.
4   Authors' interview with Mark Mentha, 12 October 2001.
5   ibid.

Chapter 12
1   Zwier, interview with the authors, April 2002.
2   Interview with Geoff Easdown, 5 October 2001.
3   The *Herald Sun*, Melbourne, 5 October 2001.
4   Press conference given after the first creditors' meeting, 18 September 2001.
5   Administrators' report to creditors, 16 January 2002.
6   Affidavit sworn by Delma Lynne Thompson on 28 September 2001 and tabled in the
    Australian Federal Court, Melbourne, 1 October 2001.
7   Affidavit of Leon Zwier, solicitor for Mark Korda and Mark Mentha, and partner of
    Arnold Bloch Leibler, of Collins Street, Melbourne; tabled in the Federal Court of
    Australia, 27 December 2001.
8   Geoff Easdown and Peter Wilms, 31 October 2001.
9   Korda, interview with the authors, 4 October 2001.
10 This and remaining Mentha/Korda quotations in this chapter are from interviews
    with the authors on 4, 5 and 8 October 2001.

Chapter 13

1. Reproduced courtesy of Sony/ATV Music Publishing. Writer/Composer: Donald Alan Schlitz, jnr.
2. The *Herald Sun*, Melbourne, 5 October 2001.
3. The *Justinian*, electronic newsletter: www.justinian.com.au, 26 September 2001.
4. In discussion with the authors, 5 October, 2001.

Chapter 14

1. Mentha, M., interview with the authors, 5 October 2001.
2. Korda, M., interview with the authors, 4 October 2001.
3. ibid.
4. Mentha, M., interview with Geoff Easdown, 28 May 2002.
5. ibid.
6. This and subsequent Mentha quotations in the chapter from an interview with the authors, 5 and 8 October 2001.
7. Interview with the authors, 5 October 2001.
8. Mentha, M., interview with the authors, 8 October 2001.
9. Niesche, C., The *Weekend Australian*, 15–16 September 2001.
10. Bloomberg Financial Wire Service, 4 October 2001.
11. Fox, Andrea, 'Ansett never got reforms it needed, says Matthew', the *Dominion*, 26 September 2001.

Chapter 16

1. Zwier, L., interviewed by Peter Wilms, May 2002.
2. ibid.
3. Anonymous former Ansett executive, who provided a copy of the material to Geoff Easdown, April 2002.
4. Greg Combet, interview with authors, ACTU Headquarters, 20 March 2002.
5. See letter from Tesna Holdings Pty Ltd to John Howard, Prime Minister of Australia, dated 13 November 2001, Appendix, page 279–280.
6. Trevor Jensen, interview with the authors, 12 April 2002.
7. ibid.

Chapter 17

1. Zwier, L. in discussion with Peter Wilms, June 11, 2002.

Chapter 18

1. Greg Combet, interview with authors, 20 March 2002.
2. ibid.
3. ibid.
4. Author interview with Greg Combet at ACTU Headquarters, 24 May 2002.
5. ibid.
6. Late-night heated telephone conversation with Geoff Easdown, February 2002.
7. By a corporate insider who cannot be identified.
8. Anonymous former Ansett executive, who provided a copy of the material to Geoff Easdown, April 2002.
9. According to the same corporate insider as in Note 8.
10. Trevor Jensen, discussion with the authors, 12 April 2002.

INDEX